FRED

The Authorised Biography of Fred Winter

ALAN LEE

PELHAM BOOKS

Dedication

The writing of this book has depended upon the friendly co-operation and long memories of very many people, members of Fred Winter's family and his friends and colleagues over a lifetime in racing. It could not have been contemplated without their patient help and although they are too numerous to name here, my thanks go to them all. This is their book as well as mine. Above all, of course, it is Fred's, and I only hope he feels it does him justice.

ALAN LEE,
November 1990

PELHAM BOOKS

Published by the Penguin Group
Penguin Books Ltd, 27 Wrights Lane, London w8 5tz, England
Viking Penguin, a division of Penguin Books USA Inc,
375 Hudson Street, New York, New York 10014, USA
Penguin Books Australia Ltd, Ringwood, Victoria, Australia
Penguin Books Canada Ltd, 2801 John Street, Markham, Ontario, Canada l3r 1b4
Penguin Books (NZ) Ltd, 182–190 Wairau Road, Auckland 10, New Zealand

Penguin Books Ltd, Registered Offices: Harmondsworth, Middlesex, England

First Published 1991
1 3 5 7 9 10 8 6 4 2

Printed in England by Clays Ltd, St Ives plc
Text set in 11/13 pt Garamond

A CIP catalogue record for this book is available from the British Library.

ISBN 0 7207 1941 0

Photo acknowledgements

Mrs Diana Winter (1, 3, 7, 9, 13, 14, 15, 16, 21, 27); Planet News Ltd (2); Keystone Press Agency (4, 11, 25); Mrs Price (5, 6, 8, 28); Portman Press Bureau Ltd (10); Fred Meads (12); Gerry Cranham (17, 18, 19, 20, 24, 29, 30, 31, 32); Columbia Newspapers (22); Provincial Press Agency (23); RH Wright (26); LPA International Photo Services Ltd (33).

Contents

Foreword by *Diana Winter*   *v*

1 The making of a hero   *1*
2 Lifelong friends   *8*
3 The Captain and Miss Paget   *16*
4 Good breaks and bad   *24*
5 Celebrity status   *32*
6 Winning was all that mattered   *40*
7 Mandarin in France   *52*
8 Seeing the red light   *65*
9 A new life at Uplands   *77*
10 The improbable dream   *87*
11 Jay Trump's National   *99*
12 For the second time, and the last . . .   *109*
13 The class of the 1960s   *118*
14 Lanzarote and his lad   *130*
15 Francome, faith and loyalty   *140*
16 Second in command   *149*
17 Winding down   *162*
18 The cruellest fall   *173*

Index   *183*

Foreword

by Diana Winter

It is not possible to spend twenty-five years in the same home, while involved in such a business as racing, without forming many attachments, and as I write, shortly before Fred and I move from Uplands, I am aware that this is the end of a chapter, though not the end of the story.

Many people have been exceptionally good friends to us over the years and, more particularly, in the time since Fred's accident. We are grateful to them all. We also appreciate and admire the way in which Charlie Brooks has taken on the training role at Uplands, with the staunch support of men such as Brian Delaney, and would like to wish him every success in the future, a future both of us will observe with interest and enthusiasm.

Lambourn
November 1990

I

The making of a hero

Heroes are seldom what they seem. All too often, closer inspection reveals the feet of clay which destroy the illusions of idolatry. With Fred Winter, a hero to two generations of racing folk, there is no myth. He is precisely the promised product, 'money back if not totally satisfied'. But beneath the unblemished record of a man who created standards to which others still aspire lie two baffling contradictions. He had more than 4,000 rides in his first career, yet freely admitted that he had no love of steeplechase riding; he was champion trainer eight times in his second career, yet he had never even wanted to train.

There is more to this reluctance than misplaced modesty. The inhibitions were serious and they played upon his mind. He would never have 'resorted to' training, with such stunning results, if the Jockey Club had not made the happiest howler of its hierachical existence and refused him a job as a starter. He would never have ridden over fences at all but for a combination of war years and weight worries which cut short a promising career on the flat; and he confesses he was close to giving up when he broke his back having only his eleventh ride over jumps.

All of this can be explained quite simply. Fred Winter is a winner. He was good at whatever he chose to do because he could tolerate nothing less. He was, in the carefully selected description of his brother, John, 'a perfectionist'. John, who insisted on prefacing his thoughts with the warning that Fred was a hero to him too, went on: 'I know how hard it was for him to become a champion, and that is why I admire him so much. Riding over obstacles did not come naturally to him. I don't think he ever was in love with jump racing.

To him it was a job, but he would never accept second best, so there has to have been a ruthless streak within him.'

Perhaps, looking back to that autumn of 1948, it was more a case of wounded pride than ruthlessness which convinced Winter that nothing so trivial as a broken back would persuade him to seek a saner, safer, day job. 'I honestly don't know why I didn't turn it in,' he recalled, much later, 'but maybe I had to prove to myself that I had the guts to go on. It certainly wasn't for love of steeplechasing. I had had two falls in very few rides – one resulted in a dislocated shoulder which hurt, and the other a broken back, which hurt like hell. I loved winning races, and always have done since, but the actual jumping side of it never really appealed to me the way it seems it does to some people . . . At the time of that fall I had won only three races and, quite honestly, I was not all that enamoured of the sport.'

It happened, as many of the worst jump-racing falls seem to do, in utterly unprepossessing circumstances. Fred had taken a spare ride in a modest novice hurdle on the modest and since extinct course at Wye in Kent. That the horse concerned was equally modest can be gauged from career details. Tugboat Minnie, an eleven-year-old mare, had never been so much as placed in a race and she did not intend to start now. The first hurdle proved her undoing, and Fred's. Stretchered back to the ambulance room, the jockey was diagnosed to be suffering from broken ribs – painful but not serious – and told to go home and rest.

John Winter, who had driven his brother to Wye, takes up the story: 'Freddy saw our local doctor, who went along with the broken ribs theory, but although he walked around for a few days he was in terrible pain and we finally called in a London physician called Dr Aiden Redmond, an old family friend.

'He got Fred to lie on his stomach, felt carefully down his spine and then announced that he had damaged vertebrae. He sent him to London for an X-ray, which confirmed two fractures. Dr Redmond told him that he must lie on his back for three months and that he could not even think of riding again during that season. For a young man setting out on a career this was a terrible thing to be told – a year virtually written off – but Fred's determination, which was to serve him so well, came to the surface and he worked incredibly hard to get fit again.'

If one of his driving forces, during the long months of convalescence, was the fundamental worry of what on earth he could do if he had to give up riding, Fred was also unarguably helped by his environment. He still lived at home in the Kent town of Southfleet, where his father trained privately for a farmer named Percy Bartholomew. Every day there were horses around him. Every day there was talk of racing. It had been that way for much of his life. Racing was Fred's inheritance and he regarded it as precious.

Fred Winter Senior, father to Fred and Johnny, had been a teenage prodigy as a jockey, prior to the First World War. He began his apprenticeship in Newmarket in 1908, aged thirteen, and three years later won the Oaks during a season which brought him seventy-six winners and the title of Champion Apprentice. His Oaks win came on a filly called Cherimoya, and it was the only win of her career. Fifteen years on, Fred Junior came into the world in a bungalow named after the horse, the family home in Andover, Hampshire. It was 20 September 1926 and Fred Senior was seeing out the closing seasons of a career savagely shortened by the war years.

Most people who have lived through it recall exactly where they were the day war broke out. Fred Winter Senior had no trouble remembering because he was actually in Germany, where he had taken a job riding for the Royal Estates. He was riding out for the Kaiser himself in 1914, and achieving an enviable reputation for his skills, when hostilities commenced. He failed to get out of the country in time and spent the next four years in the Ruhleben prisoner-of-war camp, near Berlin. Quite apart from any other indignities he may have suffered, his four years of captivity cost him heavily in racing terms, for his weight increased by 50 per cent; when he emerged he tipped the scales at 11 stone and faced a long fight to restore credibility as a flat-race jockey. The fact that he managed it speaks of that familiar Winter determination. He rode until 1929, first for Frank Hartigan and then, in Newmarket, where Johnny was born, for the Joel family.

In those days one had to apply for a particular licence to train in Newmarket. Fred failed to obtain one and settled instead for Epsom, where restrictions were not so tight. The family moved south in 1929, when little Fred was three years old, and they set up home, with a medium-sized yard, near the railway station on Epsom Downs.

Fred Senior and his wife Ann had four children altogether, the two boys and their older sisters, Sheila and Pat. All were keen on horses, as was only natural, but none was as fanatical as young Fred. By the age of four and a half he was riding out each morning with his father's string, mounted on a pony named Snowball which, indirectly, forged a lifelong friendship. Snowball had been passed on to Fred by a boy two years older. His name was Dave Dick.

Through his childhood, his youth and then his dedicated bachelor-hood, Fred counted Dave Dick as his closest friend. From schoolpals in Ewell they became inseparable as carousers on the London social scene, an exercise they contrived to blend successfully with being, in Fred's case, the best jockey, and in Dave's the bravest jockey of their era.

Snowball was just the first of many links in their two lives, but it was not an insignificant one. Fred learned the basics of horsemanship aboard the pony, quite apart from winning a variety of showjumping prizes. He also, evidently, acquired a confidence which plainly did not desert him on the day he finally went public. Fred was thirteen years old and weighed only 5 stone 7 lb when his father decreed that he was ready for his first race-ride. A day off from Ewell College for his son was requested by Mr Winter and granted by the headmaster who was by now doubtless well aware that the quest for academic excellence came a tailed-off second to the quest for equine experience in the priorities of this particular pupil.

The meeting chosen for young Winter's debut was Newbury and the race – appropriately, considering what was to follow some years later – the Lambourn Nursery Handicap. Twenty-eight years after winning the Oaks, Fred Winter Senior found himself surging with parental pride, while his wife, Ann, shivered with parental fear, as their son was given a leg-up in the Newbury paddock. Young Fred was to ride a horse called Tam O'Shanter, one of a dwindling number in the Winter's Epsom yard, and as a curious gallery of pressmen looked on, eager as ever for the human interest in this family saga, there was not a sign of nerves from this boy who had scarcely entered his teens. Those who were there report that he was chewing gum and looked to have 'the confidence of an old hand'. It is also reported that he was cheered back to the unsaddling enclosure, which is quite something as he finished only ninth of twenty-one!

A certain amount of tabloid hyperbole followed this ride, including a confident prediction by at least one newspaper columnist that he had seen a future champion jockey at work. How he divined this from such skimpy evidence would be interesting to hear, but if the writer was still around thirteen years later, when Fred won the first of his jump jockeys' championships, he might have felt entitled to a pay rise.

At this infant stage of his riding career, however, it is doubtful if Fred wasted a single second on the option of National Hunt racing. His mind was cluttered with the speed, competitiveness and challenge that flat racing presented him. But for war, which had already damaged one Winter's career and was now about to stall the progress of the next generation, he might well have pursued flat-race riding indefinitely, to the infinite detriment of all those who ever watched him ride over obstacles.

If the acclaim he received for his Newbury debut seemed premature, he did not have to wait long for something more tangible to celebrate. He rode a winner at the eighth time of asking, and even the humble £100 stakes for the Wilton Maiden Seller at Salisbury could not detract from the moment. Fred staggered from winner's enclosure to scales, humping almost 3 stone of lead in his weight-cloth, after partnering Tam O'Shanter to victory. It was an appropriate first winner, not only because this mare had been his first ride but also because he did her at home each day and had struck up the first of innumerable jockey–horse rapports he was to enjoy during his career. All this occurred on Friday, 15 May 1940, and when, a fortnight later, he won an apprentice race, again on Tam O'Shanter, a decision was taken. Fred would leave Ewell College at the end of the summer term and head for Newmarket, where his indentures would be taken over by a trainer named Henry Jelliss, who had ridden with Fred's father and now had a large enough stable to support an apprentice properly.

Fred Winter Senior was plainly seeking to maximise his son's opportunities, for his own yard was not going well. In fact he was about to cease operations, albeit temporarily. John Winter recalls: 'Father had only a few small owners and he could no longer make it pay. So, with Fred off to Newmarket, he gave up training and went to work on the night shift in a factory on the Kingston by-pass. It was a disaster. After a lifetime with horses, life on the shop floor nearly killed him. He was rescued by Percy Bartholomew, who asked him to move to Kent and train his private string of horses. It was then that the family settled at Southfleet.'

On the face of it, young Fred's move to Newmarket made sound sense. After all, if he was to make the grade as a flat-race jockey, Newmarket was the place to do it, for its entire existence revolved around the sport as it still does today. Any young jockey with ability would rapidly attract the attention of the Newmarket grapevine, thus earning himself a regular supply of rides and, with luck, winners. For some unexplained reason, however, this was a phase of Fred Winter's career that he would unhesitatingly put down as a failure.

He had moved into lodgings in Nat Flatman Street, a slightly haphazard jumble of solid, old houses just behind the High Street and a haven for racing's nomads for many years. His name was already known to many trainers, as the son of an accomplished former rider, and he did not go short of work, both on the gallops and the racecourse. Yet of eighty race-rides during the summer of 1941 he achieved only two wins, one at Haydock Park and one at Newmarket itself. It was the sole winner he was destined to ride at headquarters, because by the start of the following season he was encountering problems with his weight, which had shot up to 8 stone 7 lb, and his motivation, which, compared with the obsessional will to win for which he became known, was unaccountably low.

At least part of the reason could have been that the war was raging in Europe and Fred felt he should be part of it. Whatever the cause, he had not settled in Newmarket and had begun to accept that flat racing held no future for him. He packed his bags and rejoined the family in Southfleet, where he began working for his father as nothing more glamorous than a stable-lad. With few horses in the yard, however, his attention soon returned to the war and, as he approached the services' minimum age, he determined to join the RAF.

A brief spell in a factory in west London, helping to repair damaged aircraft, and another nine months as a stable-lad in Epsom brought Fred up to his eighteenth birthday. He still hankered after the Air Force but, with the war drawing to a close and flying action rapidly on the decrease, he was persuaded to join the Army instead. He qualified as a parachutist, obtained a commission in the West Kents and, eventually, served nine months in Palestine. Brother John recalls: 'Mentally Fred was not satisfied to be in the ranks. He wanted to be an officer and, as is his way, he became one – though, by his own admission, not a very good one!'

Fred served four years. His demob came in 1948, by which time he was twenty-two years old with no prospects of returning to flat-race riding and no qualifications or ambitions elsewhere. The story goes that he had never considered National Hunt until, sitting in the officers' mess in Palestine one day, reading a magazine, he chanced upon a photograph of a jump race. He decided to give it a go and mailed off a letter home, asking his father if he had any jumpers he might ride.

So it was that Fred, on demobilisation leave in December of 1947, went home to Southfleet and rode some schooling work on a horse who knew far more about the job than his rider. The horse's name was Carton and he provides yet another link with Dave Dick.

2
Lifelong friends

Carton simply loved to race. His first win was in a humble two-year-old seller in 1938, and his last came in a handicap chase thirteen years later. Miserable in his eventual retirement, he was put down when eighteen, but kept a place in the hearts of at least two of his successful riders.

Dave Dick is remembered in racing as long, lanky and invariably laughing. His contemporaries in jump racing recall him as the maddest, bravest and very nearly biggest of them all, so it demands something of a mental adjustment to absorb the fact that he weighed just 6 stone 5 lb when Carton gave him his initial winner of an inevitably brief flat-race career.

Eight years later the horse was still owned by Percy Bartholomew and trained by Fred Winter Senior when he, the horse, taught Fred Junior the rudiments of riding over obstacles. Paddock routines can never be authentic preparation for the demands of a race, however, and when Fred made his public jumping debut, at Kempton Park's 1947 Boxing Day meeting, tactics were plainly still a mystery to him. Riding a four-year-old-named Bambino II for a family friend, Brian Garrood, Fred made the running at a pace more suitable for a mile race on the flat than 2 miles over hurdles. The horse understandably failed to see out the trip and finished, exhausted, in fifth place. For Fred it was a lesson learned, and when he rode Carton in the 2-mile chase the following day, he followed his father's instructions to the letter, holding up the old horse in midfield, delaying his challenge until the final fence and then drawing away on the flat to win by six lengths.

Lieutenant Winter of the 6th Airbourne Division, as he was introduced in the day's racecard, had thus scored the first of 923 winners he was to partner in the ensuing seventeen seasons. His second success was also on Carton, back at Kempton the following month, and after his eventual demobilisation he won twice more on the game, old horse who, to the end, retained such a turn of foot that if he was upsides the leaders at the last he was virtually sure to win.

More than forty years on, Dave Dick nodded that great head of his as he sat in the lounge of his Oxfordshire home. 'Yes,' he said, 'Carton winning for both of us like that was a coincidence, but then Fred and I had so many links and ties over the years that I don't suppose we thought about it much.

'It certainly all began with Fred having my first pony, Snowball, and by the time we both started going to school we were already mates. I was two years older than Fred but he was brighter than me, so we were in the same class – in fact, we sat at the same desk. We both rode out, first lot, and we had special permission to arrive at eleven o'clock so long as we stayed on to do an extra hour's work in the afternoons.

'To be honest, that didn't always happen. Cycling to school together in the mornings, we would dream up all kinds of dodges. Some would say we spent more time playing truant than we did at school, but all either of us wanted to do was ride horses.'

This might sound familiar. The majority of boys, especially those of an outdoor persuasion, would rather do almost anything than go to school. But Fred and Dave were more single-minded than most, and as they dreamed together of the winners they would soon ride, academic studies did not figure very high in their thoughts. 'Neither of us was very bright,' admitted Dave, 'but I was worse. They threw me out when I was twelve!'

By then Fred and Dave had formed an attachment which was to last all of their riding lives. They not only spent schooldays together, they also shared holidays, usually at Bognor, where Dave's father had a house. When they did have to do some school work there was often a tame, educated friend to help out ... when they did not, there was tennis to play and, most important of all, horses to ride. The war separated them, as it separated so many, yet by another odd quirk they both ended up serving in Palestine with the Army, though not simultaneously. By the time Fred returned to civvy street, Dave had been back riding for some two years. The old friends had some catching up to do, and Carton helped bring them together again at Kempton.

It was later in that same Christmas meeting, when Fred was on leave, that he was initiated into the painful unpredictability of the jumping game. His first fall was from Carton's half-brother, Bright Boy, and it frightened him. Some time later, he candidly confessed: 'It was the first real pain I had ever had in my life. We fell at the last but one when I was lying second, and the thought of the three horses behind coming over the fence and landing on top of me absolutely terrified me. I got up, dived for the rails and rolled underneath them before the others arrived.'

For those of us who have always regarded Fred as indestructible, this admission takes the breath away. Terrified? Surely not. But as one delves deeper into the rationale by which he pursued his life in the saddle, it seems less far-fetched. The words of Fred's brother, John, explain so much: 'He wasn't a natural steeplechase jockey. In fact he found it very hard. It was a job to him, a job he was determined to conquer because he had no wish to go into anything else.'

And what he plainly had to conquer, more urgently than anything else, was the fear which made him dive under the Kempton rails, the fear which accompanied him on his painful rehabilitation after breaking his back at Wye, the fear which was bluntly advising him that the jumping game was only for the brave and the foolish. There was ample incentive, during his twelve months' convalescence, to take the decision, to put it all down as one of life's misadventures and to find a proper job instead. For one thing, Fred had next to no money. He had bought a car, a Ford 8 with upwards of 100,000 miles already logged, and he had come out of the Army with a suit of clothes. Other than that he possessed virtually nothing and, faced with a year of enforced idleness, his prospects were not immediately bright. He stayed at home with the family in Southfleet and wondered if it was all worthwhile.

His luckiest break, during this period, was a chance reunion with a boyhood friend, George Archibald. Fred was staying in Newmarket with his sister Pat, who by now had married the flat jockey Doug Smith. During a weekend dance at the Bedford Lodge Hotel, Fred met up with Archibald, a trainer who concentrated on the flat but retained a few jumpers for the winter. He asked when Fred would be fit to resume riding and offered him the chance of some race-rides.

This was the motivation Fred had required. He was on the way back, though at first still racked by apprehension. Every time he went to watch racing he studied the fallers, waiting for the jockeys to rise unharmed as, more often than not, they did. He had never yet had a 'soft' fall and, fear having no logic, he wondered if he ever would. Seeking to give himself an easy reintroduction only made things worse. He returned to the saddle early in September of 1949 and was to ride Carton at the Winters' local track, Folkestone. An old friend of a horse, and a very safe jumper, Carton could have been hand-picked for Fred's comeback ride. The bookmakers agreed and made him favourite, but the partnership trailed in last of five finishers without ever threatening to get closer. Fred returned to some boos and jeers from racegoers who may well have been reacting to a lost investment but, nevertheless, had some justification on their side. Fred had arguably been more intent on getting round safely than on winning.

Gradually Fred shamed his nerves into submission. Gradually, too, he began to bring himself to wider attention. Ryan Price, then living in a caravan in Findon and struggling to make his way as a small-time trainer, gave him a ride at Taunton on a horse called Smoke Piece. Winter was beaten a neck and, walking the horse back to unsaddle, silently gave thanks for the fact that the Captain had not travelled. He did not expect to be asked again; he was hopelessly wrong.

At Plumpton, a few days later, he had his first ride for George Archibald on a hurdler called Dick the Gee. He won comfortably. For Fred this was of far-reaching significance. Not only did the winner rescue and revive his battered confidence, but the ride he gave the horse was observed and approved by Ryan Price. By the end of a season which had begun, for Fred, in such a despair of doubts, he had been enlisted by Captain Price as his stable-jockey. It was a partnership which was to endure sixteen seasons.

The first of them, 1950–51, was the season in which Fred graduated from being a youngster of promise to a jockey accepted by the seniors as one of their own. This was swift elevation and, after all the agonising he had been through, remarkably straightforward. He was attracting good rides for good trainers, and winning on plenty of them. He had thirty-eight winners from 221 rides; he also had eighteen falls and, although he suffered one broken finger, they were all of the 'soft' variety which had begun to obsess him the previous year.

This was also the year in which Winter began his association with the race which was to enchant him, both as a jockey and trainer. His

first Grand National ride was Glen Fire, for Warwickshire trainer Syd
Mercer, and, as is the way of things in the weighing-room, much
good-natured banter preceded the event. Glen Fire's regular pilot had
been Tim Molony, champion jockey that year and a man on whose
knowledge Fred had drawn deeply, as they both rode for George
Archibald. 'He taught me a lot,' Fred was to relate. 'He was terribly
brave and always kicking, kicking, going into a fence to try and get
his horse to stand back and really jump. I think he was one of the
bravest people I ever saw – certainly one of the toughest.' At Aintree,
however, Tim Molony's mind was on mischief and he bet Fred that
he would get no farther than the sixth fence, which is Bechers, aboard
Glen Fire. Fred won the bet, surviving a pile-up at the first which
accounted for no fewer than eleven of the runners, negotiating
Bechers safely but then coming to grief two fences further on.
Although he won money, this was not the most distinguished of
starts in the world's most famous race, but better – much better – was
to come.

Winter's name figured in fifth place in the jockeys' championship
that year; when it was over he left, well satisfied, for the sort of
holiday which was to fill in every summer until he married. It was a
holiday which involved sunshine, water-skiing, women and, inevitably, Dave Dick. They were holidays which appealed to a variety
of racing folk – some years Fulke Walwyn, for whom Dave rode and
who would later become Fred's Lambourn neighbour, accompanied
the bachelor boys. As the fame of F. T. Winter began to grow and
'Freddy' became the one jockey's name instantly recognisable to the
most indifferent racing observer, the holidays also appealed to the
new style of gossip reporting in daily newspapers. William Hickey
had begun his column in the *Daily Express* and the exploits of Messrs
Winter and Dick were regular entries.

'I can't remember how it all started,' says Dick. 'It just became a
routine. We'd go as soon as the season ended, sometimes even
missing the last day if neither of us had anything worth staying
around for. I had a big Allard two-seater in those days and it was
perfect for holidaying in the sun – the girls loved it!

'We always headed for Juan les Pins and stayed in a pension called
La Marjelane. We'd have a go at anything but we both enjoyed the
skiing. In those days, water-skis were just like boards, but Fred got
really good at it because, in his usual way, he wouldn't be beaten by
anything.'

The days passed idyllically, on the beaches and in the surf. The evenings were spent socialising. The two friends patronised the coastal bars, Dave drinking whisky and Fred the gin and tonic he favoured throughout his racing life. Neither of them worried about over-indulging and, when it came to the time for returning home to a new season, only Dave had any weight problems. 'Fred never had to waste in his life,' he says with a touch of friendly envy. 'He enjoyed his food and could eat exactly what he wanted, even in mid-season. Sundays were always great social days. We'd have a big lunch and plenty to drink. I would usually have to end up in the Turkish baths all night, but not Fred.'

At the start of August 1951, Fred drove Dave down to Devon for the opening meetings of the new season. As usual they planned to stay down, the programme for the first few weeks being concentrated on the three Devon tracks at Haldon, Newton Abbot and the now extinct Buckfastleigh. Although there were horses to ride and races to be won, jockeys of the time regarded August as a working holiday and the hotels of Torquay housed any number of lively racing parties.

Long before the revolution inspired by Martin Pipe, the leading stables tended to ignore August, and usually September, waiting for the better ground to arrive before loosing off their expensive inmates. Their jockeys, consequently, were under no great pressure early on, and with the meetings generally spaced out at the rate of three per week there was ample scope for rest and relaxation.

As Fred nosed his new Jaguar, the first perk of his success, down towards the south-west, both he and Dave were looking forward to the ritual. This year, however, it was to be short-lived. Dave Dick won the first race on the opening-day card at Newton Abbot; Fred then looked to have the second at his mercy. But at the last flight of hurdles his mount fell and Fred broke a collarbone. It was a nuisance, but nothing more. Within a month Winter was back with a treble at Plumpton, the first of his career. Two of the winners were in chases and the irony is that he was soon to take an unusual decision and make it known that any trainers seeking a jockey to ride over the Plumpton fences must eliminate F. T. Winter from their short-list. Certain jockeys of more recent times have expressed a dislike for the hilly Plumpton steeplechase course, John Francome and Peter Scudamore among them, but none has gone to the extent of refusing to ride there. For Fred, though, this was not a sign of failing nerve but much more of calculating the risk factor and concluding that it was best eliminated. The formbooks show that he failed to finish eleven times in twelve starts on the Plumpton chase course, so his decision was not without good grounds.

In later life he was to make a revealing admission about his shortcomings over fences in the early stages of his career. 'I was far from natural,' he said. 'In fact I had a distressing tendency to fall off whenever my horse hit a fence.'

Dave Dick, reflecting on his old pal's achievements, bluntly agreed with this assessment. 'Fred got good results, but in his early years he wasn't a very good chase jockey . . . he used to be lucky to get round once a week over fences.'

It was hereabouts in the story that Dave gave Fred some advice which was to benefit his riding to an incalculable degree. He simply suggested that Fred would be better, over fences, if he dropped his irons a couple of notches and rode longer. Fred was still inclined towards the flat-race perch position and, whereas Dick rode very long indeed, by settling on a happy medium Fred discovered that his balance was much improved.

As that 1951–52 season drew to its climax, such balance was to be put to the test. Now aged twenty-five, Freddy was receiving ever-increasing attention from the racing press. *The Racehorse* commented flatteringly: 'He has a ready word and smile for everyone,' while in the *Evening Standard* Richard Baerlein, more recently the doyen of the racing press box, preferred to concentrate on his riding. 'He swears he was the world's worst flat-race jockey,' he wrote. 'Practically unknown to the public two years ago, but probable champion National Hunt jockey within two years, Winter is the man to break Molony's run.'

He had earned such a tribute by riding fifty winners before January was out. Baerlein's prediction, indeed, began to seem dated as Winter launched a challenge to Molony's title in only his third full season. It was to prove beyond him, due in part to an arm injury suffered late in March and discounting him from Aintree, but at the Cheltenham Festival any who still doubted his horsemanship were put firmly in their place. In one of the most competitive Gold Cups for many years Winter was slated to ride a grey horse called Shaef for Jack Gosden. Crossing the water for the first time, Shaef collided with another runner and the impact dislodged his bridle, leaving it hanging limply round his mouth. This approximates to driving a car round a corner and having the steering wheel come away in your hands: drastic measures are required. The bridle was held in place by a tight nose band but Fred had to keep hold of the horse's head for the remaining 3 miles or pull up. The latter option probably never occurred to him; this was, after all, the Cheltenham Gold Cup. And so Fred sat tight, holding on to Shaef's head and pushing for all he was worth. The grey responded gamely and finished second, ten lengths adrift of Mont Tremblant.

The winning jockey was Dave Dick, the winning trainer Fulke Walwyn and the winning owner Dorothy Paget. As Fred joined the celebrations, toasting the first Gold Cup triumph of his best friend, he can have had no notion that he was to come into direct and successful contact with the two other connections within the year, thanks to the misfortune of Dave Dick. For it was back at Cheltenham, in November of 1952, that Dave was seriously injured. Partnering Prince of Denmark, again for Miss Paget, he was forced into the running rail, agonisingly trapping his ankle and scraping it along the paintwork. This was not the rounded, plastic railing used on racecourses these days, but sharper and metallic. Dave was ruled out for the rest of the season and sued the Cheltenham course for damages. He was awarded £5,000, but his predicament left the redoubtable Miss Paget seeking a replacement rider for her string of horses. Fred was to get the call and, in their own singular ways, Dorothy Paget and Ryan Price were to contribute fully to the season in which Fred not only became champion jockey for the first time, but also set a new record number of winners.

3
The Captain and Miss Paget

Fred's season of 1952–53 was the most successful any National Hunt jockey had ever enjoyed – and by a considerable margin. Until 1953, the 100-winner mark was virtually uncharted territory, its elusiveness fitting testimony to the risks and rigours of the jumping game. Fred Winter broke down the barrier in spectacular style and his figure of 121 winners was to stand for fourteen years.

The essential factors in Fred's momentous season were fine weather, freedom from injuries and a constant supply of high-quality rides. Many of these came from Ryan Price, who himself set a training record with seventy-one winners. A further healthy proportion were provided by Dorothy Paget.

It is a cliche to categorise racing's successful women as 'formidable'. Mercy Rimell has suffered from the label; so, too, has Jenny Pitman. Beneath a veneer of calculated steel, both are actually sensitive and emotional people. Whether the same is true of Miss Paget I am unable to say, but there seems no doubt that she was among the more eccentric owners of either sex. Intensely superstitious, detached and aloof, she never appeared on a racecourse without an entourage of secretaries who would accompany her into the parade ring. She communicated little with her jockeys before a race but, according to Dave Dick, was unusually generous in victory. 'She was a very kind and misunderstood woman,' he explained. 'I enjoyed riding for her and always felt confident she would treat me well. She did live in style, though. When she arrived at a hotel, half of Fortnums would arrive with her!'

There was undeniably a ruthless streak in Miss Paget. For some years her retained jockey was Bryan Marshall, a stylist of a jockey rated by Fred Winter as 'out on his own as an all-rounder'. But when, during the 1951–52 season, he was beaten half a length in a novice hurdle at Sandown, Dorothy Paget informed Marshall that he was out of a job. Dave Dick was appointed, and won her the Gold Cup on Mont Tremblant. His subsequent injury created the vacancy and Miss Paget sent word that she would like Fred to ride her horses.

By one of those baffling coincidences, Winter's first ride for the leading lady was on Lanveoc Poulmic, half-brother to Mont Tremblant and the horse whose defeat at Sandown had cost Marshall the position. It was back at Sandown, this time for a novice chase, and Fred took him to the front three fences from home to win comfortably from a horse called Approval, ridden, no doubt disapprovingly, by Bryan Marshall. Fred won five times on Lanveoc Poulmic that season and was beaten on him only once. The defeat, in this instance, was far harder to forget than any of the victories. It came at the Kempton Park Boxing Day meeting; the horse went off at 6–1 on for the final event of the day and looked like landing the odds until meeting the last fence all wrong and unseating his jockey. But instead of being thrown clear, Fred was suspended upside down by a foot which remained caught in the iron.

'The horse started getting back into his stride again and I thought: "This is it, this is the worst thing that can happen,"' he recalled. 'I remember staying terribly cool and reaching up to grab hold of the bridle, then heaving with all my strength and pulling his head round so that all he could do was go round in tight circles.'

This was an example of the Winter strength in self-preservation, but having averted the immediate danger by halting the horse, he was still strung up in uncomfortable and undignified fashion until a spectator ran out on to the course to help disentangle him.

It was an alarming end to an otherwise triumphant day. The King George VI Chase, traditional mid-season highlight of the chasing calendar, had given Winter the biggest win of his career to date – although the prize money, £2,158.10 shillings, would today be the equivalent of what is on offer for the lowliest of novice chases. His winning mount was Halloween, who had been a champion point-to-pointer and hunter chaser until bought by the prosperous Contessa di Sant' Elia for £8,000. In the course of the next five years he was to recoup that outlay and more, winning a total of seventeen races and being placed three times in the Cheltenham Gold Cup. Yet when Fred was first asked to ride him he had deposited two competent professional jockeys on the deck and had seemed inclined to run, and jump, only for his former owner, Captain Dick Smalley. Fred was never above seeking advice and now he went to Captain Smalley in an effort to find the secret of riding Halloween. He was told that the horse resented being organised, so he simply sat quietly on him and allowed him to do the work. The discreet tactics worked and Fred struck up a relationship with Halloween which was to bring him much success and considerable kudos, as this was a horse whose following was in a league exceeded, in recent times, only by the likes of Arkle and Desert Orchid.

Fred's first King George also had its poignant side as the runner-up was Dorothy Paget's Mont Tremblant. Halloween, sent off at 7–4 favourite, came to challenge the Gold Cup winner at the last and outpaced him on the run-in, justifying Fred's decision to take a first retainer, worth £500 a year, from the Contessa, simply to ride this one horse. Halloween was second in the Gold Cup that year. Again he started favourite, for his swelling band of followers ensured that nothing else was possible, but he found one too good, a fate which was to become sadly familiar for him at the Festival meeting, and Vincent O'Brien trained the winner for the fourth time in six years.

By Cheltenham time Fred had his first jockeys' championship in the bag. The magic century of winners still awaited, however, and when he rode his ninety-eighth of the year on the Saturday following the Festival, winning the Triumph Hurdle at Hurst Park on Clair Soleil, the sporting nation was in a rare state of anticipation. Number ninety-nine came later the same day, in a humble selling hurdle, but then Fred experienced the frustration of a batsman who becomes rooted on ninety-nine in a Test Match: the hundredth winner simply refused to come, during a week of seconds, thirds and also-rans. Doubtless this was destiny doing its stuff, for the moment was saved for an important meeting in illustrious company.

It was Imperial Cup day at Sandown Park and Fred was to ride the favourite Nuage Dore. Still his luck obstinately refused to change and he finished unplaced. Half an hour later, however, the maiden century was recorded in dramatic style. Winter, riding Air Wedding in a 3-mile handicap chase, landed in front over the last but was headed on the run-in and needed all his redoubtable power and determination to force his horse up again to win by a short head. If he could not ride the hundredth at Cheltenham, this was a very acceptable substitute, for among the enormous crowd were the Queen and the Queen

Mother. They sent word for the champion-elect to join them in the royal box but, on hearing that he still had to ride in the next event, they joined the throng in the winners' enclosure to pass on their personal congratulations. Fred understandably considered this, at the time, as the proudest day of his career. There were many more to come.

Fred's first winner in this record-breaking season was Sea Bird, at Newton Abbot on 15 August. His last was Gribun, at Fontwell Park on 25 May. These bookends to ten months of rewarding slog around the byways of Britain in his overworked Jaguar were both trained by Ryan Price. Nothing could have been more appropriate, for Price was very much more than just another source of winners to Winter. He was the biggest single reason for his rise to pre-eminence in the field of jump jockeys. He had become an exceptionally gifted trainer but, more important in the long term, he had become one of Fred's closest friends, someone he trusted and with whom he felt comfortable.

The Captain, forthright, flamboyant and irascible, cannot always have been the easiest of employers but Fred believed him scrupulously fair. 'I think I had three rockets from Ryan the whole time I was riding for him,' he said, 'and really it was the most marvellous association between a trainer and a jockey that they could wish for. Apart from the times when you had obviously done something wrong, and he let you know in no uncertain terms, he never blamed you for being beaten. He enjoyed winning a race at Devon and Exeter just as much as winning a big one at Cheltenham.'

Fred Winter was to win three Champion Hurdles and a Grand National for Ryan Price before, on retiring from riding, his job passed to Josh Gifford. The links are endless. Gifford was to break Winter's record for winners in a season, largely through riding for Price; eventually he was to take over the Findon yard from the Captain and make an enormous success of training jumpers. He was to become a serious rival in the training field to F. T. Winter, and yet they were to develop such a close friendship that they began to take annual mid-season holidays together. Few can be better placed than Gifford to assess the peculiar yet productive partnership between two masters of their art. 'I was a generation apart and seeing them both in an impressionable way,' he admits. 'Fred was always God to me, and still is. A great man, great jockey, great trainer. He was fair and helpful off the course but tough in a race. You could not ask for more. As for Ryan, he could be a very intimidating man. My generation was very frightened of him. Under it all, I think Fred was too, at least to some extent. Both of us learned good and bad from Ryan. He didn't do everything right but there is no doubt he had an enormous influence on our lives. Ryan and Fred seldom saw each other away from racing, yet they remained extremely close, strikingly so.'

John Winter recalls how the pairing was forged and how it grew stronger. 'Ryan was really a friend of our parents. He was a bit wild when he was young but became a commander in the Army before going into racing. He started off in a very small way, living in a caravan in Findon with just a few horses to train, but as Fred was turning into a top jockey, so Ryan was becoming an exceptional trainer.

'They had a wonderful relationship, possibly because Fred would never allow anything to be turbulent. Ryan was an exuberant, enthusiastic man who exaggerated everything and put himself into positions where he should never have been. He did things his own way, just like Fred, and I believe they were very good for each other.'

In the early, piecemeal days of his training career, the caravan era, Ryan's horses were generally led up by his wife, Dorothy. Since Price's death, Dorothy has continued to live in Findon and her memories remain vivid.

'Fred and Ryan hit it off from the start because, in general, they saw things the same way. They were friends, and I don't recall them ever rowing at all,' she says. 'Fred always told the owners what he thought was the truth about their horses, rather than what he thought they wanted to hear. It didn't always go down very well but it was totally honest and Ryan approved wholeheartedly.

'Ryan was always very lucky with the people he had riding for him, even when he switched to training on the flat. I like to think it had something to do with the way he chose them. I don't think he ever became as friendly with a jockey as he did with Fred. They really were very close. They spoke on the phone most evenings and, although Fred's telephone manner has always been businesslike and abrupt, they understood each other perfectly. If he had had a bad day, Fred would always be looking for reasons, rather than excuses, for why he was beaten. He would never write it off as just another race.'

One of the repeating themes of Fred Winter's career as a jockey is his ineptitude at schooling horses. He neither liked it as an exercise nor remotely mastered the art of it. Dave Dick, who both enjoyed and excelled at schooling, recalls: 'It got to the point where he hardly ever bothered because no one would ask him. I think he schooled once for Fulke Walwyn and that was the end of it – Fulke would get somebody else.'

Dorothy Price confirms that this was the champion's Achilles heel. 'He did come down to school the horses at first, but they all either stopped or ran out. It was hopeless. It reached the stage where Ryan neither wanted nor expected him to come down on schooling mornings.'

What Fred did do, as an annual routine, was spend two or three weeks at Findon just before each season began. He would look at the new horses and, at least in the early years, he would pop them gently over some obstacles on the schooling grounds. He later admitted how he felt about this part of the job: 'It was obviously very essential but I just didn't enjoy it. I thought it rather a waste of time. I was far happier for someone else to produce the finished article for me to ride on the course, even if I had never seen the horse before. Certainly there was seldom anything to complain about regarding the way Ryan's horses jumped on the course.'

In his spare time during this annual trip to Sussex, Winter would potter around in the Price's garden. Later in his life this was to become his abiding hobby, a release from the strains of training, but in those youthful days he was not very discriminatory. 'Mostly he would dig up Ryan's favourite hydrangeas,' recalls Dorothy Price.

One year, as trainer showed jockey the yard's new inmates for the season ahead, Winter peered at one utterly unprepossessing animal and scoffed: 'What on earth is that?' The Captain, unabashed, replied: 'Something I bought for Dorothy.' Fred, who had clearly taken against the horse, was in the process of voicing a fervent hope that Dorothy did not expect him to ride her acquisition when a voice behind him said coolly: 'No Mr Pompous Winter, she doesn't.'

Unnoticed by either of the men, Mrs Price had strolled out to join them and overheard the scathing remarks about her new horse. He was called Charlie Worcester and, true to her word, she never did ask Fred to ride him. Josh Gifford, young and very new to the game, was given the ride instead. 'I won four times on Charlie Worcester,' he recalls. 'He was the horse who got me started, and it was thanks to Fred!'

Charlie Worcester was expertly placed to win his share of races but he remained one of the small fry in Price's increasingly accomplished yard. Clair Soleil was the horse who was to establish him in the very front rank of jumping trainers, as we shall hear, but the winners were coming at an agreeable rate and, because Ryan Price was such an ebullient character and so very clever at his job, there were inevitably those who were ready to cry 'foul'. It has happened time after time down the years in racing. Every trainer who achieves more success than the pundits deem to be reasonable can expect to find himself the subject of many muttered discussions about shady deals and sinister behaviour. Martin Pipe suffered this phenomenon when he revolutionised jump training in the late 1980s; thirty years earlier it was happening to Ryan Price.

In the spring of 1964, shortly before Fred's retirement from the saddle, Price lost his licence over the running of a horse called Rosyth, an incident which is described in more detail in Chapter 8. Rosyth's regular jockey was Josh Gifford but Fred felt as affected as anyone by this slur on the stable, an immense setback to his friend and trainer. There were many whispers, years prior to the Rosyth case, but Fred Winter was never implicated. Nor has time soured the memory of those who were close enough to know the man's honesty. 'Snowy' Davis, who was travelling head lad for the Price yard, volunteered the comment: 'Freddy hated riding non-triers. He was always scared someone would spot it, so he rode the horses on their merits as a matter of routine.' John Winter adds: 'I don't believe that Ryan and Fred ever laid out a horse with prep races in which he simply did not do his best. I don't think it was in Fred to do so. If you want to win as much as he did, what is the point of stopping one?'

In 1953, when the Price–Winter roadshow was beginning to rake in the profits, another character reference came from Peter O'Sulleven, then writing in the *Racing Review*. 'Ask one of the "boys" who are inclined to view a race darkly, through the recesses of their pockets, what they think of Winter and you'll hear: "With Freddy, you are sure to get a run." When even these demolishers of reputations admit to the possibility of integrity, a blow has been struck on behalf of the riding fraternity.'

None of this, however, should persuade anyone to believe that the crooked element which existed in racing then, as it does now, simply ignored the new champion. They did not. What they found, however, was an unco-operative man who had learned his lesson some years earlier. Fred had not been riding long over obstacles when an owner booked him to ride a horse on one of the Devon courses and added the proviso that he was under no circumstances to win. This was the first time Fred had been instructed to lose a race but, as rides were scarce and his future uncertain, he agreed. He managed to get left at the start and, steadily making up ground without trying as hard as he made it appear, he finished fifth. It may have been a masterpiece of its kind but Fred hated every minute of it. He was simply not of the peculiar persuasion for whom one improbable *coup* is worth any number of risky defeats. Fred went straight.

Two further such incidents, within the next year or so, indicated that Winter's resolve on this score was strong. He was offered £200, not to be sneezed at in those days, to stop a horse winning a selling chase at Nottingham. He refused and told the owner he must get another jockey if he wished to pursue that idea. The upshot was that Fred kept the ride, won the race and ended up with approximately £50, but a clear conscience. At Plumpton, where he still rode over hurdles though never over fences, Fred was asked one day to give a well-fancied novice an easy race. He refused, won the race in a driving finish and faced the predictable wrath of an owner who had confidently not placed a bet. This particular owner, however, was well known to Fred Winter Senior, who happened to be at the meeting, and a quiet threat to report his behaviour to the stewards of the Jockey Club was enough to subdue him. Fred Junior recalled: 'I was asked to give horses easy races after that but they did not have much chance when they started. If at any time through a race I found that the horse was within striking distance and had a chance of winning then I would go and do my best to win.'

Integrity and religion do not always go hand in hand but in Fred Winter's case it appears that they did. His mother, Ann, was an Irish Catholic and the entire family was brought up in the Catholic church. Fred took his religion seriously and each Sunday he would take round the collection plate at early mass at the Oratory of St Francis de Sales, a thatched church in the Kentish village of Hartley.

'I would not describe myself as a deeply religious person,' he explained, 'but I seldom miss going to church and it has been a great help to me. I think it would be fair to say that I was living with fear the whole time and it helped to be able to get down and pray for courage, which I did quite often.'

Seldom in his illustrious career did Winter need the power of prayer quite so much as in the season immediately following his record-breaking first championship.

4
Good breaks and bad

'Snowy' Davis drove Ryan Price's horse box upwards of 30,000 miles a year. The son of a coastguard, he had been working as a milkman when, in 1951, he heard that Captain Price was moving to Findon and needed a travelling head lad. He got the job and stayed thirty-one years, first with Price and later, when the jumping licence changed hands, with Josh Gifford. He has an abiding respect for Ryan Price, especially for his loyalty, and an unbending admiration for the man he knows as 'Freddy'. He loved his job, as anyone with such demanding hours needs to, and he liked nothing better than the early-season trips to the west country and his favourite of all racecourses, Newton Abbot.

'We had a lot of luck there, a lot of winners,' recalls Snowy. 'And there was a special atmosphere about the place at the start of the season – like a reunion of old friends. I always enjoyed racing there . . . except the day when Freddy had his accident.'

The accident occurred, with a cruel contrariness, in the first race of the 1953–54 season. Winter had no time to savour being champion. The first race of his title defence took the crown away.

On his final riding day of the previous season, Fred's 'double' at Fontwell Park had included winning the selling hurdle on a horse called Cent Francs. He was trained by Syd Warren, but Ryan Price, watching from the stands, saw enough potential in the animal to bid for him successfully at the subsequent auction. A fast-ground horse, ideal for the early weeks of the season, he was schooled over fences (though not by Fred) during the summer and entered for the novice chase which launched the new term at Newton Abbot.

Fred, as usual, had spent a few idyllic weeks in Juan les Pins, water-skiing and womanising with Dave Dick, before going to Findon to look over the new horses. He would have nodded recognition at Cent Francs and, knowing Ryan Price as he did, would have had no qualms about the horse's ability to jump fences. If Ryan said he could jump, that was good enough for Fred.

Trainer and jockey travelled down to Devon together for the first meeting. As was their custom, they were booked into the Moorland Hotel at Haytor, one of several hotels peopled by racing folk at this time of year. The Prices later established a social tradition: they hosted a party at Findon on the Thursday of Goodwood week and then, the following morning, headed for Devon and the jumping. One of Price's foibles was that his horses should travel to and from the racecourse on the same day. 'Sometimes,' says Snowy Davis, 'we would get back from a meeting at one in the morning and have to set off again at six. There were no motorways and it was hard driving, but I never got lost.' That August morning Cent Francs was loaded up at dawn in west Sussex for the long haul to Devon. Snowy was in good spirits. Not only was he going to his favourite course, but he also expected the horse to win and, as usual, a winner would mean generosity from Fred Winter. 'He was like that,' says Snowy. 'Our wages were poor – I took home £13 a week – and Freddy knew it, so he would quietly ask me how many lads I had with me and then give me some money to take them out to dinner.'

There was to be no celebratory dinner that night, just a long and unhappy drive home. Fred did not get home at all and nor was he to do so for the next month. His left leg was broken messily in several places by an early fall – his introduction to a year which was to see him confront and ultimately conquer some of the most taxing personal crises of his life.

The first thing he had to do was to come to terms with the fact that he was not going to be around to defend his title because of a fall which at first he had thought harmless. He later recalled: 'I had absolutely no pain whatever as I sat on the grass and began to get up. Then I could feel the bone grating and I knew I had broken my leg. It still wasn't hurting – just this grating sensation in my boot. So there I was, one moment starting off the season full of confidence, the next being carted off to hospital. I think this really is a wonderful aspect of this game. No matter how successful you are you can come to earth again very, very quickly. Any fellow who starts getting big-headed is asking for trouble, because along comes something which slaps him down in very smart time.'

After one night in the Torquay hosital which has habitually acted as a clearing station for the casualties of the Devon meetings, Fred was transferred to a London clinic in a special ambulance which, he was to muse, resembled nothing more closely than a hearse. If such an observation indicates that his sense of humour remained intact then, it was to undergo a severe test in the coming months as a succession of complications impeded his recovery. At first Fred had estimated that he would be riding again by December. Even when he revised this hope to a more realistic January, he was confident of being back for all the major meetings at the season's climax. In fact, he was destined to miss them all.

When the initial plaster was removed from Fred's leg, the extent of the damage was laid before that noted friend of injured sportsmen, the orthopaedic surgeon Bill Tucker. He was required to perform three separate bone grafts before he was satisfied – and even then flakes of bone were regularly emitted from the wound for many months afterwards. Fred was allowed to return to the family home in Southfleet after a month of hospital care and, in December, he even attempted gentle riding-out on one of his father's horses. All this achieved was to teach him just how far from real fitness he was.

Frustration was obviously intense and Fred, hating the prolonged and enforced idleness, did what many others might have done in similar circumstances and concentrated on his social life. He began to spend more and more time in London, and the nightly carousing took its inevitable effect. Fred's brother John, still living at Southfleet at the time, recalls how this difficult phase developed: 'I don't doubt that Fred was spending too much time in London and falling into the wrong company. Hangers-on began to do him down and this, combined with his hard living in the nightspots, began to upset father. He eventually told Fred he must either leave home or pull himself together. It was a family crisis of a sort and Fred could have told him to mind his own business. Thankfully, he saw sense. In the year that followed I do not think he found it easy to resume race-riding. In fact there was a stage when I felt he *nearly* lost his nerve. It was very much a make-or-break season and a lesser character would not have survived. Freddy not only pulled through but was champion jockey three times more afterwards!'

For a jockey to miss an entire season through injury could, in those days, involve considerable hardship. The weekly payment from the Injured Jockeys' Fund was 8 guineas, roughly the equivalent of one riding fee. The married men, the breadwinners in a family, were bound to suffer. Fred was not so badly affected, being a bachelor, though this was a status he was soon anxious to discard. Girlfriends had flitted in and out of his life up to now, but he had seldom given thought to establishing a serious and long-lasting relationship. All this was to end on the morning of Grand National day in April 1954, when an elegant young lady strolled into the breakfast room at Liverpool's Adelphi Hotel and irrevocably changed Fred Winter's life.

Seated at the table opposite Fred was Dave Dick, who had long since tired of commiserating with his friend over his broken leg and had doubtless been responsible for some energetic lifting of the spirits (literally and metaphorically) the previous evening. In the 1950s and 1960s the Adelphi was the central point of the social life which surrounds Grand National week, and Dave Dick was seldom far from the action. He was still an enthusiastic bachelor and it is mischievously said that he once booked two rooms in the hotel to avoid complications if he should get lucky; on another occasion, so racing legend goes, he was in the process of being booked by a female traffic warden in the city when he asked her to the National party at the Adelphi. She tore up the ticket and turned up at the party.

We are not privy to the scale of merrymaking on the Friday of the 1954 meeting, Dave's memory being sketchy on the subject. We do know that he was slated to partner Legal Joy for the redoubtable Dorothy Paget in the afternoon's big event. It can be surmised that the two great pals were discussing Legal Joy's prospects, if they were not detained in debate on social matters or sporting disasters, such as the fact that Fred had been obliged, by his injury, to decline an invitation to represent Great Britain in the World Water-skiing Championships in Austria. Whatever their conversation, it ceased the moment Diana Pearson accompanied her mother into the dining-room. What then ensued was undoubtedly comical, though Fred would not have seen it that way at the time.

The story is best told by Diana herself: 'Mummy was very keen on racing and had asked me to go to Liverpool with her. The Adelphi was the natural place to stay in those days and, on the morning of the National, we went out to Aintree to walk the course. Only after that did we go in for breakfast and see Freddy and Dave. By the end of the day Dave had asked me out to lunch and Freddy to dinner. I told them both the same thing. I was bad news – a very reluctant escort.'

Fred was not inclined to take 'no' for an answer. Later in the day, Royal Tan having won the National, he made it his business to discover all he could about this vision with whom, he was already convinced, he was devotedly in love. What he did find out was the gloomy news that she was soon to embark on the sort of world tour which girls of a certain class were apt to undertake at the time. Many men would have been put off by such a setback but Fred never has been one to lose anything without a fight. Having received a predictably cool response to his rather intoxicated suggestion on National night that he should tour the world with her, he tried subtler but no less persistent tactics, finally winning a lunch date and an invitation to Diana's farewell party at the Dorchester in London.

If this was a sign of progress in the relationship, it was one of strictly limited joy for Fred, who sank into a deep depression as, along with various other friends and family members, he stood on the platform of Victoria station the following morning, waving Diana off as the boat train pulled away. He admits, melodramatically but candidly, that he felt like throwing himself off the train which ferried him back to Kent. He had gone straight from Victoria to the morning service at Westminster Cathedral (another indication of his faith in religion) and remembers: 'I didn't go as far as tears, but I felt very bad indeed. I was so depressed, what with the leg being so painful and taking so long to mend, and the girl I had fallen in love with going away.'

Dave Dick could not credit what had happened to his friend. Probably he did not want to, for their carefree bachelor existence would never be the same again. Dave was a social animal, Fred's long-time companion on holidays and on jaunts around the racing fraternity's favourite London attractions, such as Jules' Bar, the Berkeley Hotel and the Savoy Baths, where many a jockey could be found steaming off the effects of a vigorous evening. Fred, it seemed, was preparing to turn his back on all this for the pursuit of a single woman.

Still working at the wasted muscles of his mending leg, Fred went to stay with his sister Sheila in Morocco for a while, then joined Dave in the south of France for what was to be their last water-skiing holiday as bachelors. Not that either of them knew this at the time; indeed, Fred's depression over his abruptly interrupted love affair allowed him little scope for hope that his feelings would ever be returned with interest. In the next few months he received just a couple of impersonal postcards from Diana and it was only when news reached him that she had fallen ill in India that he made any serious attempt to re-establish personal contact.

Dave Dick recalls: 'He got a phone call through to Di in New Delhi – on my phone. He was forever being cut off and reconnected, and heaven knows what it cost, but it certainly seemed to cheer him up.'

The story is taken up by Diana herself. 'I had to have my appendix out in India and it was quite touching to get a phone call. I invited Freddy to my homecoming party in the April, and within a fortnight we were engaged, which I think took both of us by surprise.'

Surprise or not, this seemed to be the spur that Fred might just have needed in his professional life at the time. His comeback season had been difficult, though not lacking in success; by the time he was married, late the following season, he had recaptured his jockeys' championship.

In 1954–55 Fred was only narrowly beaten for the title by the one man who had a greater number of rides, Tim Molony. His compensations were considerable, however; after a battle with himself, and with the public expectation that he would return from a year off riding better than ever, his confidence and strength returned in full. He won the King George VI Chase at Kempton's Christmas meeting on Halloween and went to Cheltenham buoyed by news of Diana's imminent return and encouraged to believe that this horse could win him his first Gold Cup. Halloween was again the bridesmaid, starting at 7–2 second favourite and beating all his market rivals, only to fall foul of the 33–1 long shot, Gay Donald. Runner-up for the third time, Fred did mark this Cheltenham with his first of three Champion Hurdles, aboard Ryan Price's brilliant but moody Clair Soleil.

Now this was a horse with a real kink in his character. Fred said of him: 'When he was 90 per cent fit he was a great horse and when he was 100 per cent he was a little bit mad. He used literally to go down and eat the ground.' It was presumably on one such occasion that his infuriated trainer tried to kick the errant horse on the nose, only to find his swinging boot gleefully snapped up by Clair Soleil's mouth. Ryan Price's reaction to being thrown in the air by this animal would unquestionably be censored, but it could be described as reflecting the fact that Clair Soleil had missed the previous season after being reduced from a colt to a gelding.

Among Clair Soleil's greatest fans, however, was Snowy Davis who, as travelling head lad, had to handle him in some of his frothier moods. 'I think he is the best horse we ever had,' says Snowy. 'Funny temperatment, I know, but a really good horse.' And so, as he moved into his digs on a cold and frosty Cheltenham eve, Davis was quietly confident that his yard, which had never to date sent out even a placed horse in the 'Champion', would have plenty to celebrate the following night.

Snowy was right, although anyone witnessing the first conversation between Messrs Price and Winter after the race could be forgiven for thinking otherwise. This was what Fred describes as one of only three occasions on which they argued – and at the conclusion of their first great triumph together. Anyone not privy to the riding instructions Price had issued would probably have decided that Winter had ridden a difficult horse incomparably well. Sulking early on in the slipstream of a very hot pace, Clair Soleil was left in front a mile from home by the leader's blunder. He cheered up, racing with more enthusiasm, but Winter had to be at his strongest to win. Stroller, a high-class Irish hurdler trained by Vincent O'Brien, had just headed Clair Soleil on the uphill haul from the final flight to the line, but Winter refused to be beaten and found a resolute response from a horse who, despite his quirky temper, was undoubtedly brave in a battle.

At the line, the winning margin was only a head. Fred walked the horse back to find that his trainer was not exactly intoxicated by the joy of the moment. One might have thought, in fact, that his horse had been beaten, such was his hostile reception in the winner's enclosure. Price had explicitly told Fred to hold up the horse for a late challenge, believing that he could win the championship through turn of foot. Fred had always doubted this, being more of the opinion that Clair Soleil was a stayer lacking acceleration, but when challenged to explain why he had disobeyed orders, he replied: 'I had to go on when I did – anyway, I won the race, didn't I?'

Soon, too, Fred was to win the lady in his life, so that all the pain and frustration of the preceding months seemed suddenly remote and irrelevant.

He was initiated in the lifestyle of the Pearson family, but apparently not without certain indignities. Diana relates: 'We were a hunting family, which in later years never did us any harm, because one makes so many useful contacts. I used to hunt a lot and I made Freddy go a few times, but he absolutely hated it. The first thing he hated was "dressing up". He has always been naturally smart and tidy but he took against what he saw as a hunting uniform. One day when he had agreed to come, we parted at the start and I said I hoped to see him later. I had a wonderful time and got back to find poor Fred swearing unhappily about the bloody horse which had buried him in a hedge!

'I think the reason he didn't like hunting or fishing, which was another favourite sport of mine, is that they are basically not competitive. Fred simply had to win at whatever he did and could see little point in devoting an entire day to something if nobody came out winning. There was an extension of this when he began training because he had no interest in seeing a race unless he had a runner in it. He would never watch other people's horses, could never see the point.'

Diana came to learn about the religious devotions of the man she was to marry, who, like the rest of his family, went to church every Sunday and, like his friend Dave Dick, always wore a St Christopher for luck. She came to learn something of the motivations behind the man who was in the process of establishing his name as the greatest in the history of National Hunt racing. And, in the blissful year of their engagement, neither had cause to regret the comically corny way they first met in the breakfast room at the Adelphi.

5
Celebrity status

In the year of his thirtieth birthday Fred Winter was married and regained his title as champion jump jockey. True to form, the business came before the pleasure. The wedding was scheduled for the first week of June 1956 – two days after the end of the National Hunt season. It achieved considerably more newspaper inches than his recapture of the jockeys' title for, by this time, Fred's eminence in his field of sport was being taken for granted. He was becoming that rarity in jump racing, a household name, and his marriage was perceived to be public domain. In this, as in so much else, Fred was a reluctant pioneer. By dint of act of God, personal choice and pedantic disciplines, he had neither the physique, extrovert personality nor roistering lifestyle of, shall we say, Ian Botham, and yet the attention the media were now beginning to devote to his private life, as well as to his riding, was a foretaste, though thankfully a harmless one, of the unceasing and often unkind scrutiny directed upon Botham's generation of sporting superstars.

As Dave Dick, Fred's great pal, explained: 'Newspapers were changing at that time. Diary pages, like William Hickey's in the *Daily Express,* were being started and they were all looking for something to write about. Jump racing was more of a social scene than it is nowadays and jockeys and trainers were obvious subjects. None come any bigger than Fred, so he was always in the papers.'

Had the diary columnists of today chosen to shadow Fred and Dave during their bachelor bashes in Mayfair and the south of France, some salacious copy might easily have resulted, but in fastening on to Fred Winter, husband and father-to-be, they were portraying a reformed man. From being one who seldom missed an opportunity for a night out in London, Fred rapidly became a man who needed to be prised away from the family home. Dave Dick found it remarkable.

For both Fred and Dave, however, the 1955–56 season was one to remember with enduring pleasure. As Fred won back the title which, arguably, he had lost only through injury, Dave was victorious in perhaps the most sensational Grand National of all time. In vain pursuit of the leader on that merciless Aintree run-in, Dave had settled for being a gallant runner-up aboard ESB when Devon Loch, owned by the Queen Mother and ridden by Dick Francis, jumped an imaginary fence 30 yards from the post and landed in an undignified heap, legs splayed and the race dramatically conceded. To this day the '56 National is readily recalled as Devon Loch's race, one which confirmed the Queen Mother as one of the unluckier royal owners and, just perhaps, prompted Dick Francis on his subsequent course as a peerless and prolific writer of racing thrillers. Few remember it for Dave Dick's victory, which may sadly sum up his under-rated career; even fewer will remember that F. T. Winter's one distinction in the race was to be the year's only casualty at Bechers. Fred, however, will doubtless have enjoyed his friend's victory party at the Adelphi and, or course, he had much to console him. Confident in his work, content in his personal life, the frustrations and doubts which hounded him after his broken leg seemed but a dark and distant memory as, in the final weeks of that season, he closed in on Tim Molony's long-held lead in the jockeys' championship, creeping ahead in the first week of May and extending his lead to four by the final day. Molony, the vanquished champion, was philosophical. 'Call it my wedding present to Fred,' he is quoted as saying while, like everyone else in the Winter racing circle, heading for London's St James's and one of the weddings of the year.

The ceremony took place at a Catholic church in Spanish Place, with Fred's brother John as best man and a bridesmaid and page boy from the offspring of Fred's sister Pat, now married to Doug Smith, the flat-race jockey. Smith was in hectic pursuit of the flat championship at the time and after a few glasses of champagne at the reception in Stanhope Gate he had to leave for the evening meeting at the now defunct Alexandra Park course. As the revelries continued back in Mayfair, Smith was adding three winners to his score.

Among those present at the reception were a parade of Fred's weighing-room colleagues, including Tim Molony, Dave Dick, Michael

Scudamore and Bryan Marshall. These are men who know how to enjoy themselves and, as Diana recalled, it was neither a genteel nor an inhibited gathering: 'I remember going into Freddy's room when I was dressed ready to leave and spotting him stark naked in a corner surrounded by people christening him with champagne. It was that sort of wedding, that sort of party. I think we received a £100 bill for some damage to a Rolls-Royce, so it is fair to say that spirits were high.'

Fred and Diana had agreed that they would spend their honeymoon in Juan les Pins, with Fred's usual holiday companions the Walwyns and Dave Dick in close proximity. Before that, however, their plan was to enjoy their wedding night at a hotel in Folkestone, convenient for the morning ferry. This, according to Diana, was a comical disaster, the hotel providing the newly-weds with a room containing two single beds. There followed a few idyllic weeks in the south of France, during which Fred resumed his love affair with water-skiing without managing to convert his wife. 'He taught a lot of people but I was his one failure,' said Diana. 'I thought it was a frightfully over-rated sport which seemed to involve spending an awful lot of time at the bottom of the sea.' The Winters returned to take possession of their first married home – Kitsbury Orchard, a cotswold stone house in the village of Oddington, near Stow-on-the-Wold. It had been found for them by their great friend, racecourse steward and racehorse owner Brigadier Roscoe Harvey, and it was all either of them could have wished for, with a large garden, initially resembling a jungle but pretty soon knocked into shape, and some loose boxes and paddocks on site. One of their first moves was to Ascot sales ring, where a couple of hunters were purchased for Diana's use. Fred, by this time, had decided that he had taken against the sport.

Soon it was time to begin the defence of his championship once more, and on this occasion the defence was neither so short-lived nor so painful. It was, in fact, a total success and Fred, now in the halcyon days of his riding career, was to retain the title for two further seasons.

His closest opponent during 1956–57 was Michael Scudamore, whose son Peter was to become Fred's stable jockey thirty years later. 'Freddy Boy', as his ardent betting-shop supporters had come to know him, won the title by a distance that year, his total of eighty winners leaving him twenty-two clear of Scudamore and the field, but the focuses of his season were two horses with whom he had become acquainted the previous season, Sundew and Galloway Braes. Their fortunes could scarcely have been more at odds – Fred won his first Grand National on Sundew, but on Galloway Braes, in the King George VI Chase, he suffered a dreadful fall which left the jockey unconscious and the horse dead.

Fred had taken the ride on Galloway Braes for the same race twelve months earlier only when his expected mount, Halloween, suffered a slight strain. Not that this was a poor substitute: Galloway Braes had won the King George in 1953 and was runner-up to Halloween the following year. He was tremendously fast, though not the safest of conveyances. Now and again, without reason or warning, he would 'miss out' a fence completely, simply foregoing the hassle of taking off. The first time Fred partnered him, however, Galloway Braes was on his very best behaviour, and would have won the great Christmas feature race but for a rare and self-confessed misjudgement by his jockey.

'We led all the way and jumped the last clear,' Fred later recounted, 'and then I made the unforgivable mistake of looking round. Not only did I do that, but I also looked the wrong side. While I was looking to the left, Jimmy Power was coming up on the other side on Limber Hill. All I had to do was to keep my horse going and he would have won but, by the time I realised what was happening, Limber Hill had headed me and it was too late.'

Being the perfectionist he was, such an error would have bugged Fred, and he was doubtless grateful to have the opportunity to atone, back at Kempton, on Boxing Day 1956. It did not work out as he had hoped, however, for on a misty, bleak day, Galloway Braes decided to ignore the last open ditch. It was a crashing fall and, although Fred was little the worse for the experience once he had come round, the horse broke a leg and had to be destroyed.

It was probably just as well that the new Mrs Winter was not among the crowd at Kempton that day. Instead, as she was now expecting their first child, she had decided it would be wiser to avoid the jostling throng which traditionally descends upon this meeting and to watch the race at home on television. Diana was not a wife who lived in fear of her husband falling, probably because she herself rode regularly and capably on the hunting field. What did concern her was the hidden effect that a bad fall, and a knock on the head, could have. 'He had a fall at Leicester once and passed out when he got home. He could so easily have done it while he was driving. Jockeys had to drive in some of the worst conditions and I felt it was one of the toughest aspects of the job. National Hunt jockeys did not have chauffeurs, and still don't today.

'Wives used to go racing far more then than they do today, but in most cases it was not for the social side. We used to try and help by doing some of the driving, though Tim Molony's wife, Stella, took it all a stage further as she regularly walked from the weighing-room to the paddock with him. Freddy used to encourage me to come, and sometimes I would drive him, but in those days badges for jockey's wives were hard to come by. At Wincanton one day they wouldn't give Freddy one for me, but instead of having a row about it, he simply said that he would not take me there again. He was very proud in such matters and he did not care for the way in which jockeys were often looked down upon.'

Diana had no greater worries about the Grand National than any other race, for the simple reason that Fred told her that the worst falls a jump jockey could expect would occur, invariably, in hurdle races or 2-mile chases run at breakneck speed. The National, despite its intimidating obstacles, is run at a conservative pace and many of its casualties are relatively 'soft' falls. It is all very well knowing such comforting probabilities, but the realities of confronting Aintree's 4-mile course in a field of forty defy the most phlegmatic of temperaments. The jockeys' weighing-room, prior to the annual spectacular, is a den of pinched nerves and poor attempts at humour. The strain is as much about the means of losing as the distant possibility of winning the one race which can change a jockey's life.

Fred had an enduring belief in the ability of Sundew and it was unimpaired by the horse's failure to complete in two previous Nationals. He had been bought for the relative pittance of £3,000 after winning three races in Ireland and represented the third attempt of the Kohn family to own a National winner. An enormous horse who might have been bred with Aintree in mind, Sundew was trained in the Warwickshire town of Henley-in-Arden by Frank Hudson, but for his first National, in 1955, his regular Irish jockey, Paddy Doyle, kept the ride. Sundew was still in touch when coming down at the twenty-sixth fence. Three weeks later Fred was engaged to ride Sundew in the Welsh Grand National at Chepstow but, as is often the case with a horse who has had a hard race at Aintree, the effects were plain to see. Sundew was 'over the top' and, in the circumstances, ran gallantly to finish second to Monaleen.

Winter was impressed enough to accept gladly a retainer to ride

Sundew in all his races the following year. He was aware that this would include the National if the horse was fit and well, and he would not have swapped his ride for anything. A third-fence fall at Newbury was followed by two wins, the second of them in the National Trial at Haydock, in which he beat the previous season's Aintree winner, Quare Times. Stable confidence for the National was now reaching a peak and it was far from dampened by a defeat in heavy ground on the old Manchester course, where the winner, ESB, was receiving 6 lb. ESB, of course, was also bound for Aintree with his regular pilot, Dave Dick, and it was to be their year, not that of Fred and Sundew. It might have been different, however.

Sundew had been allowed to bowl along with the leaders throughout the first circuit and plainly enjoyed himself. 'He was the sort of horse you had to leave alone and let him run his own race,' explained Fred. Which is exactly how he rode him until one of the great imponderables of Aintree, a loose horse, persuaded him to change tactics. Along the railway bank on the second circuit Sundew was going well enough to fill Fred with confidence that they would win. Then the riderless Mariner's Log, an early casualty, began to interfere. Bechers was looming and, against his instincts and his knowledge of Sundew, Fred elected to drive his horse into the fence. 'Although he was tremendously large, he couldn't stand back at a fence,' recalled Winter ruefully. Sundew hit Bechers halfway up, and there is no surviving that.

Fred's admissions of fallibility, aboard both Galloway Braes and Sundew during this period, emphasised the constant pursuit of perfection on which the jockey was engaged. He would be more likely to spend time analysing the reasons for a defeat, or a fall, than enjoying the merits of a winner. But whereas there was no coming back for Galloway Braes after his Christmas tragedy at Kempton, Sundew returned for a third assault on Aintree in the spring of 1957.

It was actually his fourth race on the course, for in those days Aintree also staged a November fixture (as so many believe it should still do now) and Sundew had run in the Grand Sefton Chase, a shorter version of the National course. He jumped appallingly and this, combined with his two previous falls in the big race itself, probably accounted for the fact that this high-quality chaser, despite a recent and impressive win at Sandown Park, was sent off at 20–1 when finally he fulfilled a great deal of hopes and expectations.

The Grand National had dominated Fred Winter's thoughts for

some weeks – certainly since Cheltenham, which was unquestionably the low point of his season. He went to the festival with an enviable book of rides but emerged without a single winner. Clair Soleil, apparently in brilliant form, started favourite to win a second Champion Hurdle but finished down the field, and the hope of consolation on Ryan Price's promising novice, Cortego, was dashed when he could finish only second in the Gloucestershire Hurdle, forerunner of the Supreme Novices Hurdle which annually begins the modern-day Cheltenham week.

Cortego's reversal failed to persuade his ebullient trainer from the belief that he was potentially a special talent and he was declared to run in the Coronation Hurdle, the first race on Aintree's National day card. Price's confidence was clearly infectious, as Cortego went off the 9–4 favourite. Stable money had plainly been expended.

This, by all accounts, was not one of F. T. Winter's finest hours. Ryan Price's instructions were to keep Cortego up with the pace, as Aintree's hurdles course is a far cry from the National course, sharp enough to suit front-runners and to make it very difficult to concede much early ground and still win. Fred conceded a lot of ground, right at the start, and had no realistic chance thereafter. Cortego finished faster than anything but it earned him no more than third place and, far from sparing the jockey an ear-bashing, possibly served only to heighten the trainer's anger.

For all the warmth and longevity of their relationship, Price and Winter remained men who believed in expressing their opinions bluntly, not least to each other. Fred's National day had got off to a poor start and as he returned to unsaddle in the third-place enclosure, the withering blast from his trainer can have come as no surprise. Dorothy Price recalls the moment with amusement, for it did have a swift sequel: 'Ryan told Fred it was the worst race he had ever ridden. He was very angry. Fred did not say anything much, just went back to prepare for the National, which of course he went out and won. When Fred passed the post on Sundew, Ryan was so excited for him that he ran down from the stands and was virtually the first to reach the horse. He was greeted by a two-fingered salute from Fred!'

Fred was a year older but very much the wiser for his experience on Sundew in the previous year's race and, this time, he was determined neither to pull the horse about nor to push him into an obstacle. Everything was to be done at Sundew's pace, for it was the only way he would consent to jump round – and, if he did that, Fred was quietly hopeful that he could win. From the fourth fence onwards, Sundew pretty much made all the running. He survived a mistake at Becher's on the second circuit, the fence which had finished him a year earlier, and looked in danger only when ESB, ridden again by Dave Dick, cruised up to his flanks as the reduced field came back on to the racecourse proper. 'Dave seemed to be going much too well,' Fred relates. 'In fact he was grinning all over his face and shouted that I would have to get a move on if I was going to win.' But ESB tired the quicker and Sundew jumped the last in command. Still his jockey was not convinced that the prize was theirs: 'I shall never forget looking at that long run-in. I was thinking, "Oh my God, we will be in the first three but we certainly can't win, he's so tired." He literally felt as though he was going up and down on the same spot . . . miraculously, nothing got to us.'

The Kohn family, their ambition achieved, threw a party – not at the Adelphi in Liverpool but at the Prince of Wales Hotel in Southport. Two days later the celebrations moved on to Henley-in-Arden, with the customary parade through the streets. Sundew was a household name for the week, yet he was destined never to win another race. In November of the same year he broke a shoulder when blundering at the water jump in a 3-mile chase at Haydock Park. His own vet drove north from the midlands and, some hours later, decided that the horse must be put down. Ironically Fred had not been available to ride Sundew that day; Ryan Price claimed him for the Windsor meeting. His sadness, on being told, needs no expansion.

6

Winning was all that mattered

Looking back from a distance of more than thirty years, it is easy to imagine that these halcyon days of Fred Winter's riding career were one long round of triumph, glamour and idolatry, the days of a champion in clover. The reality, of course, was quite different. Fred was the best, the most successful and the most popular jockey of his time, three qualities which are rarely found together in a sportsman. But he did not command any special privileges in a game which was harsh by the nature of its public and private routines and could still be primitive in terms of comfort and facilities.

In those days there were no motorways to shorten the long hours spent behind the wheel of a car. Jockeys' agents, taking the burden of booking rides and communicating with trainers, had not been thought of. As for the racecourses, many were spartan, uncivilised places in which the jockeys were fortunate to have a wash-basin. In the late 1950s jockeys may occasionally have become celebrities in the public eye, but to those responsible for running horseracing they remained of lowly status, addressed by their surnames and expected to behave in a suitably subservient manner.

The racing itself was also different from the jumping of the 1990s. Rougher, less regimented and altogether more open to the rogues, it survived on the character, finesse and integrity of most of its leading lights rather than being able to call upon the technology which, nowadays, records in slo-mo, technicolour detail any minor transgression of the moral or physical rules of racing, whether committed a mile from home on the farthest corner of the course or directly in front of the stands and the stewards' noses. The game has been cleaned up, sanitised even, and there are those not wholly convinced it is any the better for it.

While the equivalent of the law of the jungle prevailed in jump racing, the rules were made, and justice administered, by the jungle chiefs, or senior jockeys. It was a system which, by and large, worked effectively, though its dependence on pecking order was little help when the protagonists were both jockeys of eminence and experience. This happened often enough and, despite his deserved reputation for being fair and honest, Fred Winter did not claim immunity from involvement. Dave Dick recalls one occasion at Wye, in Kent, when even he fell foul of his friend's unshakeable desire to win. 'Fred was not a rough or dirty rider, but nobody achieved his sort of success by being soft either. He would do you if he thought he was entitled to, and in this race at Wye I was on the inner in a hurdle race and he buried me into the wing of the obstacle. I was a bit shaken but otherwise surprisingly OK, and as I wandered back to the weighing-room I remembered that Fred and I were due to travel to Perth together that night on the sleeper. When I saw him I just said: "You're bloody lucky to have anyone going with you after that." Nothing more was said. It was part of the game, and it did not matter how friendly we were away from racing, on the course winning was all that mattered.'

Further evidence of this came from Josh Gifford, Winter's successor as stable jockey to Ryan Price, when he said with meaning: 'Fred was very tough and uncompromising once a race was under way. It did not matter whether you were his greatest friend or some youngster he had never seen before – you would never get up his inner.'

Gifford had only recently joined the ranks of National Hunt jockeys in the late 1950s and remained pretty much in awe of his peers. He remembers with gratitude, however, the learning process in that democratic privacy that is the jockeys' weighing-room. A tradition which has never altered is that the senior jockey occupies the prime seat in each weighing-room around the country, and that his near neighbours will be the same so long as they are at that meeting. In more recent times John Francome, Steve Smith Eccles and Peter Scudamore have claimed the number one peg; in those days it belonged to Fred by unarguable right. Dave Dick was usually next to him, and third in line was Johnny Gilbert, who once rode ten consecutive jumping winners, a record which stood for many years.

'I was in the far corner at first,' relates Gifford, 'which is how it should be. Fred was always very businesslike. When he walked into the weighing-room before a meeting, you sensed he was just like a

business executive walking into his office. The tasks of the meeting
ahead took priority over all else but that did not make him aloof or
unsociable; it is just that he would enjoy a joke rather than tell you
one.

'The most striking thing about him, to a kid like me, was that he
was full of good, friendly advice. If he saw a boy struggling with his
cap, he would never laugh at him or do him down – he would help
him do the thing up. He was forever telling the kids they must look
like jockeys if they hoped to get anywhere in the game. I have always
remembered that, and it is as true today as it was then.'

John Winter, who still occasionally drove his brother to the races
even after Fred and Diana had married, picks up on this theme. 'He
uplifted the standard of National Hunt jockeys, though he would be
surprised if you told him so., He was a leader without wanting to be
one, an example not only because he always did his best, meaning that
no one could ever point a finger at him, but also because he never did
as well as he wanted to do. He might ride three winners on the
bounce and then get caught on the line in the last race. He would be
more livid about that, on the way home, than happy about his
winners. It is the perfectionist streak, and while few can come even as
close as he did, it is a good thing to aspire to. That is why he was
such a good influence during those years.'

Jumping, however, has never been all about Ascot and Sandown
and Cheltenham. It is about Plumpton and Bangor and Sedgefield; in
Fred's day it was also about Wye and Buckfastleigh and Birmingham.
It is a bewildering merry-go-round which, even now, has its stark and
unwelcoming venues. Thirty years and more ago, the luxurious ones
were much easier to count. The valets, those unseen and indomitable
backroom men, had a still more thankless job than they do today in
trying to compensate for lack of facilities on a foul and muddy day.
Each valet will, on an average day, have eight or ten jockeys to look
after. Fred's valet, almost throughout his career, was the late Dave
Stalker, fondly remembered by Dave Dick for his simplistic method
of giving his 'boys' a shower where non existed. 'He just used to tip a
bucket of water over us.'

In 1957 so much was happening in Fred's life that a less stoical
character might have needed a few buckets of cold water over his
head – before believing it was all true. There was the jockeys'
championship again, the Grand National on Sundew and even a
winner for his brother John. This came at Sandown Park aboard a

horse called Gads Hill, which was only Johnny's second runner since he had taken out a licence to train jumpers for Percy Bartholomew. It was not to be a long career, John soon deciding to concentrate on training flat horses in Newmarket, but it was an understandably exciting day for the Winters, even if Fred himself maintained reservations about such family matters, later explaining: 'I have never particularly liked riding for the family. So much seems to depend on the result that it gets one in a state of nerves before the start. It is much easier if you don't really know the connections, because then it doesn't matter to you *personally* whether he gets beat or not. You just ride the race dispassionately and as best you can.'

Family matters remained much to the fore, however, as Fred became a father; Diana gave birth to twins in February of that year. Named Denise and Joanna, they completed the lifestyle of contentment to which Fred had become accustomed in the Cotswolds. He and Diana lived well, and the newspaper diary columns were soon to draw attention to just how well. 'Dapper Freddy is seeking a cook' ran the headline in one paper, later in 1957. The Winters also engaged a nanny to look after the twins and, in due course, a third daughter, Philippa. Fred never did have a son but, if he regretted the end of the riding dynasty, he never said as much. On being asked whether he would wish any son of his to be a jockey, Fred was quoted as replying: 'I would allow it, but I would prefer him not to be. I've been through the mill and hurt myself a lot. I would not want my son to go through that.'

What Fred did not do, at any stage of his career in racing, was to bring the worries of the job home at night. Diana says: 'We seldom discussed it. We would talk about anything but racing, both when he was riding and training. I certainly had no wish to become deeply involved and I knew that Fred never approved of women in racing. I had my hunting, which I kept up, and I took the view that racing was Freddy's job and I should leave him to it.' This doubtless helped create a home routine which was settled, predictable and greatly enjoyed by them both for being so.

Fred's love of his home curtailed his hours on racecourses. Rather than mingle with other jockeys and trainers in the bars after a day's racing, he invariably changed and drove straight back to Oddington. It was a pattern to which he adhered throughout his riding and training life as a married man. And once home, he stayed home. 'He was not particularly introverted,' says his brother John, 'but then neither was he especially sociable. Race-riding was his job, to which he was totally dedicated, and his home gave him everything else he wanted out of life.'

Diana adds: 'Fred never has been a pub man, and he always hated cocktail parties because he considered that people talked such bilge at them. It has never been in Freddy to gossip. He didn't talk about other people – in fact, he did not enjoy talking at all, simply for the sake of it.'

What Fred did enjoy, even during his race-riding years, was eating and drinking. He was one of the great fortunates of his sport in having a body which obeyed orders and never betrayed him on the scales. Because his weight problems were virtually non-existent, he could eat pretty much what he liked, and this usually involved doing himself very nicely at dinner time. He was also able to eschew the regimented restrictions many modern jockeys place upon themselves with regard to alcohol. A single glass of white wine before dinner is the maximum most will permit themselves without rushing in panic towards the bathroom scales. There are, of course, exceptions, but in Fred's day the exceptions tended to be those who counted the calories through their glass; there was no such thing as the breathalyser and jump jockeys were, on the whole, a more gregarious bunch than their modern-day successors.

The difference in lifestyle is aptly described by Michael Scudamore who, in 1957, finished second to Fred Winter in the jockeys' championship and, thirty years on, was proudly watching his son, Peter, win the title while riding as retained jockey to Fred's stable. 'We used to live for today,' he explains. 'Bugger tomorrow – that could take care of itself. The social side was part of the pleasure of the job to us. On a Saturday night, with no racing the following day, we would probably make several stops on the way home and not clock in until pretty late, with a good few drinks inside us.' Nor, for some, was Sunday a quietly recuperative day, as Dave Dick explains: 'That was always a big day, with a proper Sunday lunch and plenty to drink, even if we had to go to the baths that night to sweat it off.'

Scudamore and Dick, in common with most riders of their generation, liked to drink whisky. Fred Winter did not. 'Never touched the stuff,' confirms Dave emphatically. 'Don't think he liked the taste. No, Fred would always drink gin and tonic, and still did right through his training life too.'

Fred was an organised man who liked routine and orderliness, possibly a throwback to his Army days. Each evening he would drink two gin and tonics before dinner, followed by a large glass of sherry. After eating, if the jump season was in progress, he would go to bed early. Interestingly, he would definitely not have spent the evening discussing his day's rides, or even racing in general. Other than his regular call to Ryan Price, in which performances and prospects would be assimilated without frills or verbosity, he would not telephone any trainers either. His week was thoroughly planned each Sunday, the calls to his usual trainers made and the rides entered in his office diary. Things have a habit of altering in jump racing, a horse's health being as unpredictable as the weather, but wherever possible Fred liked to stick to the plan without prevarication. If he had worries, and every jockey does at times, he was careful never to transmit them to his wife. He succeeded at all times of year except one. 'Freddy would always get tense, just before Cheltenham,' explains Diana. 'It was the only time he did show any anxiety and I think it was because the Gold Cup eluded him for such a long time. It began to niggle at him, because it was something he had not been able to conquer.'

This, of course, was characteristic of the Winter mentality, which could never quite accept the concept of defeat at anything and baulked furiously at failure in the most prestigious championship race jumping can offer. And, considering the wealth of success he was annually achieving, the Gold Cup had begun to assume the identity of a jinx. His frustrations were epitomised by his relationship with Halloween, a splendid yet unlucky horse who, in the mid-1950s, was placed in four consecutive Gold Cups, three times ridden by Winter, without winning one. The sequence was to continue until the end of the decade, by which time Fred had been either second or third six times in the race. Small wonder then that, as March came around, a touch of tension began to affect the Winter household.

The 1958 Festival not only failed to cure the Gold Cup irritation, it also provided Winter with a disappointment in the Champion Hurdle, in which Ryan Price's Fare Time fell at the first flight. This, indeed, was a contradictory season, as Fred failed to win any of the major races and yet took the jockeys' title again by a wide margin of twenty-three winners and established himself more firmly than ever as the rider to whom all others looked up. He rode his 500th winner at Ludlow in October, but possibly the winner which gained him the greatest acclaim, from those whose opinion he would respect, was in a long-distance hurdle race at Sandown Park in mid-season.

Fred was riding Pouding, a tough horse but giving weight away all round after two hard-fought victories in quick succession. Every aspect of jockeyship was demanded, as the horse survived errors and then seemed sure to be swamped by his weight and his justifiable fatigue. Fred, typically, was having none of it, and his strength, peerlessly applied, won the day by a short head. Pouding's trainer was Fulke Walwyn, and he expressed himself unreservedly in the winners' enclosure, telling anyone who cared to listen that Fred was the greatest jockey he had ever seen. Walwyn's wife, Cath, who now trains their horses in Upper Lambourn, confirms that this was no idly offered comment in a moment of triumph. 'Fulke has always thought that about Fred,' she said. 'No one else could have won some of the races he did.'

Walwyn and Winter were to have greater moments together, building even higher the trainer's opinion of a jockey who had also long been his friend . . . but that is another story. It was enough, back in 1958, that a sufficient number of people agreed with Walwyn's sentiments to supply Fred with all the ammunition he needed to win the championship for the third year in succession. It was the fourth time, in all, that he was champion jockey. It was also to be the last, although his most memorable feats in the saddle were still to come.

The tributes continued to accumulate. The man now known to millions of television viewers as 'my noble lord', John Oaksey, was then riding as an amateur as plain John Lawrence. He was not without his share of success either, but it seems he knew his place in life, for he said of Fred: 'I decided early on that this was the man to follow and I know no safer place to be in a race than a length behind Fred Winter. The only drawback is that, when it comes to the finish, behind him is where one is apt to remain.'

If the vast majority of racegoers and betting-shop punters loved their 'Freddy boy', however, there were always some waiting, in that unattractive English way, to knock and mock at every sign that the maestro was not infallible. The Boxing Day meeting at Kempton Park was a case in point. Each year this valuable card attracts an enormous crowd, many among them avid and regular racing people but some once-a-year spectators, glad to get out of the house and the festering which follows the festivities. A minority, and an unwelcome one, will know nothing about racing and care nothing about horses or jockeys. They are the type who will openly cheer when a horse falls at the last fence to allow their own fancy to win. This particular year a number of this type had plainly exhausted the remnants of their Christmas money on a horse called Jim, ridden by F. T. Winter, in the Mistletoe Chase. They did not get much of a run for their money and it did not please them. Approaching the first fence, Jim tried to refuse. He simply dug in his toes at the intended point of take-off and, when a horse does that, there is little that even the greatest of jockeys can do. Fred was ejected forcibly, fired into the air in a fashion that must have been spectacular for those in the stands but alarming for the man himself. Reunited with his reluctant partner, surprisingly intact, Fred returned to a hostile reception which must have shocked him. Reporting in the *Daily Mail* the following day, John Rickman wrote: 'I have never heard such unsporting behaviour or such unmerited criticism . . . a disgusting example of through-the-pocket booing.'

It was another salutory reminder for Fred that you cannot please everyone all the time, but something rather touching did come out of the scene. Most newspapers had used a photograph of Fred after he had been launched like a skyrocket; some days later, he received a letter from the Queen Mother asking for a copy of the picture. Fred was suitably flattered, obtained the relevant photograph and set about writing a reply. Like many of us might have been, however, he was stumped for the proper form of respectful language. He settled for: 'In humble duty . . .'

Fred might well have retained his title in 1959 despite giving the latest pretender, Tim Brookshaw, a start of twenty-two winners in what, for the champion, was a singularly unproductive start to the season. By April, Winter was back at the head of the winners' table and, on being asked about a fourth successive title, would doubtless have ventured the jockeys' traditionally superstitious: 'If I can stay in one piece'. Fred did not. Riding a novice chaser at Leicester, he suffered the sort of head-first fall which every jockey dreads. The consequent concussion alone would have had him signed off for a compulsory few days but an X-ray confirmed that he had fractured his skull, ending his season and presenting the championship to the persistent Brookshaw.

It was, however, a season in which only the end was disappointing. No season can be said to have fallen below expectations when it includes five winners at the Cheltenham Festival, three of them on the opening day.

Flame Gun was the first of the five. This was one of the horses Fred was now retained to ride for Ivor Herbert, today a writer on racing and travel matters but then private trainer to Michael Sobell in the Cotswolds. Flame Gun was good too, so good that Fred jumped off after the Cotswold Chase and called him 'the best 2-mile chaser I have ever ridden'.

Fare Time was probably not the best 2-mile hurdler Fred ever rode; neither was he the safest jumper nor the soundest horse, for he suffered a career punctuated by leg injuries. But if all this conspired against pretensions to greatness, he was still quietly fancied by Ryan Price and his stable for the Champion Hurdle in which, twelve months earlier, he had failed to survive the first obstacle. This time, things were different. There was mayhem all right, but Fred and Fare Time avoided it. The favourite, Tokoroa, fell at the downhill hurdle, two from home, and brought down the fancied Merry Deal, the winner two years earlier. Fred steered his mount safely past and drove him hard up the inside rail to win by four lengths.

Fare Time was not fit to defend his title the following spring; indeed, it was three years before he ran in another Champion Hurdle and then he finished in the pack. He never quite achieved the affection in Findon hearts accorded to the brilliant yet malevolent Clair Soleil, who was forgiven all his spite and stubbornness because of his moments of magic. He had not taken to jumping fences, perhaps unsurprisingly for one of his temperament, but flourished when put back to the smaller obstacles. Because he was now ten, conditions had to be in his favour, but he relished the severest tests of stamina and Price's decision to run him at the Festival in the Spa Hurdle, over 3 miles, was richly vindicated. Winter led from start to finish on Clair Soleil, a masterful example of the art of waiting in front.

As for the Gold Cup, Fred would be the first to acknowledge that he did not deserve to win this particular running – but he might well have done with just a shade more luck. Pas Seul, whom Fred was later to rank the best chaser he ever rode on the brief, backwaters evidence of one winning ride in a 2-mile race at Stratford, appeared to have the Gold Cup at his mercy approaching the final fence but, as was sometimes his wont, he made one calamitous error and fell. Fred was lying second at the time, on the 1957 winner Linwell, and could so easily have been given the race. Instead, Pas Seul came down virtually in Linwell's stride-path and it was all Fred could do to snatch him up, negotiate the danger and settle for the runner-up spot yet again, behind the Irish challenger, Roddy Owen. Somehow this summed up the Gold Cup in the 1950s for Fred Winter. The 1960s were destined to be gloriously different.

It was in 1961 that Fred finally broke the hoodoo and won the Gold Cup. He also won his third Champion Hurdle, thus becoming the eighth man to achieve the most coveted double in the sport. In the thirty years since Winter's achievement, no one has joined the elite band; indeed, greats of their generation, such as Jeff King and Peter Scudamore, failed even to win the Gold Cup, which puts Fred's long wait in a kinder perspective.

The year prior to this triumph ended curiously. It had been another solidly successful season for Fred and, for much of its course, he had again looked destined for the championship. On 2 May he was six winners clear of his closest challenger, the fast-emerging Stan Mellor, a man who made up in strength, determination and rapport what he lacked in artistic impression. Through the final weeks Mellor stealthily cut back Fred's lead until, with two racing days remaining, the score was a precarious 67–66. Each rode a single winner on the penultimate day, whereupon Fred did something which, nowadays, would seem intensely bizarre. With the title at stake, and the tangible reward for ten months' hard work in the balance, he did not ride on the last day of the season. He had made a prior arrangement to miss racing and take the night train from Paddington down to Cornwall, where he would join Diana and the girls on holiday. It took a special sort of man to keep to that plan in such circumstances, a man for whom other things in life were even more important than the job of race-riding.

The worst happened, so far as Fred was concerned, for Mellor rode two winners at Uttoxeter and secured the first of his three consecutive titles. Fred, typically sporting even at such a time, had wired him a good-luck message before boarding his train. If there were those who assumed, however, that the Winter appetite for success was sated, they misjudged him. Perhaps, after four championships, the jockeys' title did not mean quite as much to him as it once had, but there were other ambitions driving him on, the priority among them being the Gold Cup.

He had already made the acquaintance of the horse who was to fulfil this ambition. He had ridden Saffron Tartan for the first time at Cheltenham's April meeting in 1960, and he had won comfortably.

His jumping had been faultless and Fred was delighted to accept a retainer, from trainer Don Butchers, to ride the horse in all his races the next season.

Not everything went to plan. Butchers ran Saffron Tartan in the Mackeson Gold Cup over an inadequate 2 miles, and after one untypical mistake Fred accepted his fate and the partnership trailed in as also-rans. Some believed Winter should have made greater efforts to get back in the race, but he had taken a view about this horse's strengths and he was proved unarguably right when he quickened impressively to win a competitive King George VI Chase on Boxing Day. Now, at last, the much-vaunted potential of this horse had been proved in public, and although another setback followed when he came to grief in the Gainsborough Chase at Sandown Park, a regular landing stage even today for prospective Gold Cup horses, Fred went to Cheltenham as hopeful as he had ever been.

By the time the Gold Cup came to be run, Fred and Ryan Price had teamed up to take the Champion Hurdle on the third occasion in seven years. Not for the first time Fred's love of the inside rail paid handsome dividends, as he and Eborneezer received an untroubled run past an almighty pile-up at the second-last hurdle which accounted for four horses, the long-time leader among them.

The Gold Cup was the following day and it was a high-quality field. The race developed, however, into a duel between Pas Seul, ridden by Dave Dick, and Saffron Tartan. This was the confrontation the punters had come hoping to see; it was box-office, in the way that so many great jumping head-to-heads have been over the years, and it was only decided after a titanic struggle. It had looked all over between the last two fences as Saffron Tartan drew clear of the hard-ridden Pas Seul. But the Cheltenham hill has not for nothing earned its formidable reputation and, as the last fence loomed, Fred realised he was in trouble. They met the fence perfectly and this may have decided the race, for Pas Seul's advance was stalled by a mistake, but the inimitable Winter finish was essential as the renewed challenge of his old friend was held off by a length and a half.

'Fifty yards from the last fence my horse almost collapsed with tiredness,' reported the relieved jockey. 'I thought the winning post would never come. The truth is that he never really stayed $3\frac{1}{4}$ miles, and a stride after passing the winning post he was down to a walk. I, too, was completely exhausted.'

A spontaneous ceremony ensued. As Fred returned, limp and tired, to weigh in, the weighing-room emptied and his colleagues applauded him in. It was, as John Oaksey reported in the following day's *Daily Telegraph*, 'a memorable demonstration of how, unlike so many champions, he has achieved complete supremacy without exciting the slightest envy in the hearts of those among whom he is supreme'.

7
Mandarin in France

Every great career has a focal point on which, many years on, people will continue to reflect with awe and admiration. Fred Winter's came in 1962, but it is not his second consecutive Gold Cup which endures in the memory, nor his triumph aboard Kilmore in the Grand National. Famous double though this was, it pales almost to the commonplace against Fred's staggering – and the word is used advisedly – victory in France's most celebrated steeplechase.

The story-line is far-fetched. Put before a publisher of fiction it would probably raise a mirthless laugh and a recommendation to try it on a boys' comic. Put before any sober and self-respecting racing man, it would doubtless bring a pitying shake of the head and the verdict that no race over the demanding fences at Auteuil, in Paris, could be won under such circumstances. After all, we are talking here of an acutely sick jockey with no means of steering his horse who, just to add to the insurmountable odds, broke down before jumping the last fence, yet still held on to win by a head. It is inconceivable, and yet it came about, this immortal victory combining the courage of horse and jockey. No one who saw it will ever forget, and many who did not see it now believe they did, such is the vivid nature of the story.

Mandarin's glory never was usurped, in the minds of Winter or of the trainer, Fulke Walwyn, as the highlight of their respective careers. 'I think,' said Fred's wife Diana, 'that he has always considered it his greatest day and that, even if he didn't, others would think it for him. It sticks in people's minds and he will be remembered for it just as, for less happy reasons, Dick Francis and Devon Loch are inseparable.'

It was Mandarin, bred in France and owned by the Hennessy family for whom Walwyn continued to train for a great many years, who also gave Winter his second Gold Cup, an atonement, perhaps, for all the years of frustrated waiting. And yet, even amidst the almost unprecedented sequence of major wins now coming his way, Fred was the subject of speculation about his future. Perhaps it was inevitable. He was thirty-five years old and, following his Cheltenham double of the previous spring, had apparently conquered every available mountain. He had not been champion jockey since 1958 and, the media being traditionally preoccupied with the premature obituaries of exceptional men in every field of entertainment, they began to question his desire to go on in this singularly punishing field.

To every inquiry regarding his plans, Fred gave the same answer – he did not intend to stop riding for two years or more. He also, significantly, had no clear notion of what he might do when the moment arrived. Of only one thing was he certain: he was not going to train. A day or so after his first Gold Cup win, on Saffron Tartan, he was quoted as saying: 'I never intend to become a trainer when I retire from race-riding. It is too precarious. Frankly, I do not believe I know enough about horses to make a success of training and, for the sake of my family and my future, I don't intend to risk everything I've worked for in this kind of gamble.'

At the time these comments came from the heart. So too, I suspect, did his protestations on the retirement issue. Some of those who were close to him, however, evidently detected subtle changes in his approach to riding and put the understandable construction upon them. Dick Francis, himself retired from the saddle and starting out upon his lucrative new life as a writer, was then contributing to a Sunday newspaper, and he summed up the issue like this: 'The human body reaches a saturation point from continual battering. At the same time, the constant travelling to meetings becomes a bore. This stage, more or less, has come for Fred and he confesses that he now looks upon steeplechasing as a job of work and no longer as fun.'

What nobody questioned, either now or later, was that Fred still retained an indomitable will to win. Second best remained anathema to him, and one can only wonder how he coped when, in November of 1961, as Scobie Breasley and Lester Piggott were fighting out the finish of one of the tensest flat-race championships, their counterpart in excellence over jumps was enduring the longest losing sequence of his career. In a dire period of twelve days, Fred rode thirty-two consecutive losers; then, when the nightmare ended in a double at Sandown Park, he hardly had time to feel relieved before breaking his collarbone the following day.

Jump jockeys live with the constant possibility of this injury; many have broken their collarbone upwards of half a dozen times. It is an accepted hazard of the job, and by no means the most serious. But for Fred it was three weeks of enforced inactivity just when he had begun to emerge from the doldrums. What made it worse was that his lay-off coincided with the Hennessy Gold Cup, in which the sponsoring family were to run Mandarin.

Fred's relationship with the horse went back some years. He rode him at Sandown Park in the 1955–56 season, a 3-mile hurdle race which did little to alter his trainer's opinion of him. 'He was hopeless over hurdles,' said Fulke Walwyn. 'I nearly sent him back to France. He won some races but it was nearly always crash, bang. I did not think he would jump fences at all but in fact he really took to them once he had learned that you cannot go straight through them.'

Walwyn, as has already been stated, had an unshakeable belief in the genius of Winter the jockey but, although they had teamed up for any number of winners over the years, it was not until the 1961–62 season that any formal arrangement existed between them. Fred accepted a second retainer to ride the Walwyn horses on the under-standing that his commitments to Ryan Price, and his association with the Gold Cup winner Saffron Tartan, must take precedence. He feared that there would be regular clashes of interest and took the contract only because Fulke was so insistent. The last thing he wanted was to fall out with a man who had been far more than a productive employer; over the years he had been one of Fred's closest friends, often holidaying with him and Dave Dick in the south of France. Ten years earlier, when Fulke and Cath Walwyn were married, it was to the familiar coastal retreat in France that they chose to go for their honeymoon. Fred, who was already installed there and busily engaged in the usual social activities, volunteered to collect the newly-weds from the airport and drive them to the pension. As Cath recalls, however, things did not quite go to plan.

'Fred was a romantic at heart and had arrived at the airport with flowers for me and champagne for us to drink on the journey. But unfortunately our plane was so delayed that it was two o'clock in the morning by the time we landed and there was no sign of Fred. He had obviously had a few drinks while he waited and then gone back to sit in the car. We found him eventually, fast asleep in the driver's seat, flowers and champagne by his side.'

Fred's fears of letting down his friend were unfounded, partly because of the sad demise of Saffron Tartan, who was destined never to defend his Cheltenham title. He was retired with leg trouble in the autumn of 1961, a decision which left Fred free to partner Mandarin in all the major staying chases – when he was fit.

Mandarin won the Hennessy, ridden by the Irishman Willie Robinson, and as Fred watched at home, nursing his injury, he was subjected to those conflicting emotions any sportsman will feel when his team, or one of his horses, wins without him. Pleasure for the connections is tempered by the apprehension, however illogical, that he may now be considered surplus to requirements. But in this case Fred need not have worried. 'There was never any doubt that he would have the ride back as soon as he was fit,' says Cath Walwyn. And so it proved. Worries of form and fitness firmly in the past, Fred settled into a contented groove of winners, culminating in a four-timer at Kempton towards the end of January, which included an impressive Gold Cup warm-up by Mandarin.

Cheltenham's army of organisers live in permanent dread of wintry weather sabotaging the event and, in 1962, it almost happened. Gold Cup day dawned with a thick, mocking frost which refused to budge. A sequence of stewards' inspections followed and when the sun belatedly broke through at one o'clock it was decided, hearts in mouths, that the best day's jumping of this and every season could go ahead provided that the first race was delayed by half an hour. Fred and Fulke were naturally relieved, as both believed that Mandarin had an outstanding chance and that he had been produced ripe for the day; a postponement would have thrown all the planning into confusion. But they were not alone in their confidence. The Irish fancy was Fortria, ridden by Pat Taaffe, and as the shamrock invaders discussed the race for three long nights in the bars, restaurants and hotels of regency Cheltenham, they had plainly convinced themselves that this was the bet to pay for their week. They invested as if a return was plain formality, forcing Fortria down to 3–1, while Pas Seul, once as short as 15–8 on, drifted ominously to 9–4 against.

The market was, if nothing else, an accurate indication that something was amiss with Pas Seul; he could manage no better than a remote fifth place. But Mandarin, sent off at 7–2, was not exactly filling his supporters with confidence either. With half a mile to go,

Fred was hard at work and apparently receiving precious little response. He takes up the story: 'I was driving Mandarin for all I was worth and not making any ground on the leaders. Just at the top of the hill, I could see a gap right down the rails and I thought, if we're going to do any good we've got to go up there. I gave the old fellow a crack with the whip and he simply flew. He went up three places straight away until he got to Fortria.

'We jumped the last but one on his tail and when we got to the elbow Pat Taaffe was not clear enough to move over to the rails in front of us. As soon as we met the rising ground, I thought we might just win but right up to that point Pat was going better than me. It was a hell of a fight up the hill and it was purely Mandarin's courage that won the race.'

The courage of Mandarin had never been in question and, although it was to receive its most punishing examination in France some months hence the public had already taken the horse to their hearts. Mandarin and Fred were given a deafening welcome as they returned to the winners' enclosure, a stark contrast to the reception Fred received later that week when he was beaten in the Triumph Hurdle – which in those days was not run at the Cheltenham Festival but at Hurst Park immediately afterwards.

Fred had needed to choose between Ryan Price's two runners in the race but it had not been a particularly difficult choice. Catapult II, his selection, had much better form than Beaver II, who was consequently ridden by Josh Gifford. Not for the first time, and certainly not for the last, a stable's less fancied runner overturned the hotpot. Inevitably, when this happens, the single-minded punter who has backed the beaten favourite suspects dirty work at hand. Almost invariably, the explanation is much less sinister. Fred Winter, however, was a convenient scapegoat on this occasion, and he does not entirely excuse himself.

'I must admit that I rode rather a bad race,' he recalled. 'I took on the leaders much too soon, going to the front as we turned into the straight, and my horse didn't have much left in him when Josh came sailing along and beat us six lengths . . . the remarks from the crowd you can just imagine.'

Two things can be said in mitigation here. The first is that the entire Price yard, Gifford included, had been guilty of under-rating Beaver. Josh explains: 'Ryan didn't know what to make of this little horse and one morning, as we went out to exercise and I was riding him, the guv'nor said, "Give him a slap when you work him and we'll see if he is good enough to win a seller." I came back and told him he wouldn't. Basically, I thought he was useless. The guv'nor shrugged and said he would give him away to his sister!'

The second point is that this was no fluke win. Beaver went on to win the French equivalent of the Triumph Hurdle on the same day that Mandarin triumphed over incalculable odds. Fred rode him that day, though his physical state was such that he always struggled to recall the details.

Before the drama of Paris, however, came more glory at Aintree, a win which meant more to Fred for the fact that Kilmore, his second National winner, was trained by Ryan Price. Ebullient as ever, Captain Price had declared before the race: 'Barring accidents, Kilmore will win.' Minutes after being proved right, unusually emotional, he labelled it the greatest day of his life.

Kilmore had finished fifth in the race the previous year, having been bought from Ireland with the National specifically in mind. Diana Winter relates how the purchase was not without its amusing side: 'Freddy had been asked to go over to Ireland to school the horse and see what he thought of him. Dave Dick went with him as he also had to school a possible National ride. Well, the two of them had a night out in Dublin and were in bad shape when they turned up for schooling the next morning. Freddy's hangover was not improved by the fact that he then had a crashing fall from Kilmore. His owner was on hand and he turned out to be a doctor. He took one look at Freddy, who was not hurt by the fall, and at Dave and told them they had better come to his surgery to get something to put them right.'

Kilmore came to England in time to run at Cheltenham that season, but trailed in only fifth in an amateurs' race, ridden by Gay Kindersley. Fred, watching from the stands, was unimpressed enough to say to Ryan Price: 'What have you done to me?'

His encouraging run in the 1961 National not only obliged Fred to revise his assessment of the horse but also to review the way he should ride him. He was convinced he had made too much use of him, getting to the bottom of his stamina too soon. Nevertheless, his lead-up to the following year's National was not exactly designed to banish a jockey's doubts. He failed to win any of his five races and, worse still, fell in two of them. On the second occasion, at Lingfield Park just ten days before the National, Fred finally learned, in the act of falling, how this horse should not be ridden. 'I gave him a kick going into the jump and the next moment we were on the floor,' he said. 'It occurred to me that it had been just the same when we fell before, and I really think it was lucky we fell at Lingfield. It opened my eyes, showing me that once I had got him settled it was wrong suddenly to ask him to race faster and jump bigger. When we went to Liverpool, I was determined that one thing I would never do was to make a move on him.'

Sticking rigidly to his plan, and to his beloved inside rail, Fred rode the perfect race on Kilmore in gluepot conditions which counted against many of the more fancied runners. Kilmore won by ten lengths, at 28–1, but even in his moment of euphoria Ryan Price did not linger to host the traditional winners' party, at the Adelphi or in Southport. 'Instead,' recounts his widow Dorothy, who watched the race on television back in Findon, 'he flew straight back and we celebrated in style in the village.'

Snowy Davis, head lad to the yard, missed the party but remembers the day as if it was last year. 'We thought he would win the previous year,' he says, 'but the guv'nor was still confident so we all had a few bob on. Us lads watched from wherever we could push in, but I couldn't see him most of the way round. Freddy, as ever, had a word and a present for us after he had won, and we stayed up in Liverpool before coming back with the horse the following morning.' Then, according to Dorothy Price, everyone involved 'had a good cry – including the trainer!'

Thanks to the wonders of video technology, I watched Kilmore's National many years later and was struck by a number of things – the way the jockeys of the day sat more erect in the saddle than their modern counterparts, and how they sat back at the obstacles; the deadpan face which F. T. Winter seemed to have perfected, then as later betraying none of his inner emotions; and the curiosity, for a relatively recent convert to racing, of jockeys filing out to the parade ring wearing heavy coats over their riding silks and breeches. 'Freddy used to come into the ring in a big sheepskin coat,' confirms Snowy Davis, 'and I would take it from him when it was time to mount. All the jockeys did it in those days, but the custom gradually died out.'

Coats were not, of course, required by the flat-race jockeys, whose season starts in the spring and ends in the autumn, and it was at around this time that Fred took it into his head that he might usefully extend his career by joining their ranks. It was one of the few periods in his racing life that must be termed a complete failure.

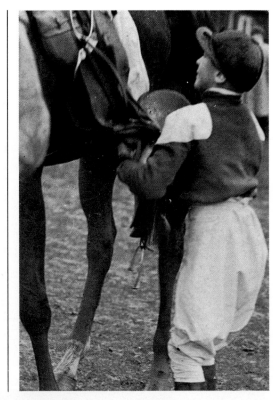

1. *Fred battling with the weight of his saddle after his first ride on the flat, aged 13 . . .*

2. *. . . but by then he was a veteran of many years riding out with his father's string. Here, at Epsom, he is just short of his fifth birthday.*

3. *Carton was the horse which got Fred started over jumps after the war. He is pictured after winning at Kempton in December 1947.*

4. *Fred Winter senior and junior, at the family stables in Southfleet, Kent.*

5. *On his annual pre-season stay at Ryan Price's Sussex yard, Fred found a tame sheep to ride . . .*

6. *But this is a rare sight of the man who hated schooling. Note the lack of jockey caps in those days.*

7. *Jumping the last on Kilmore to win another Grand National.*

8. *Ryan Price welcomes Kilmore and Fred in the winners' enclosure at Aintree.*

9. Fred and his bachelor days holiday friend Dave Dick, showing less familiar sporting skills in the south of France.

10. Wedding day for Fred and Diana . . .

11. . . . and then came the twin daughters.

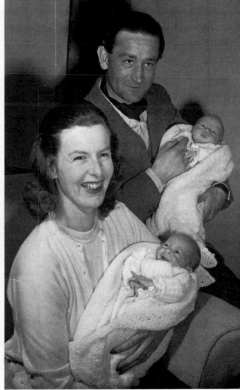

12. *Fred never did enjoy hunting. It was the dressing-up, he said, which seemed such a waste of time.*

13. *Fred and his faithful boxer, Butch, inspecting his daughters on Anglo, Soibina and Steel Bridge. All three horses were in the Grand National that year.*

14. *That inimitable riding style drives Clair Soleil home in the Champion Hurdle, another triumph for Ryan Price.*

15. *Desperate fatigue shows in both horse and jockey after Fred's legendary win on Mandarin at Auteuil.*

16. *Sick and weak, he still came out half-an-hour later to win again on Beaver for Ryan Price.*

17. *Mandarin, back home in Lambourn, received regular visits and lifelong affection from his former rider.*

The theory was fine: by the very nature of the game, flat jockeys can expect to ride longer than their jumping colleagues and to retire with their bodies less battered by regular contact with turf and hoof. Fred was now at an age when he needed to start considering the future and, as he had no wish to sever his racing ties, but had already expressed the adamant view that he would never train, continuing his riding career on the flat was superficially a very attractive idea. What it required of him was some serious wasting, for virtually the only time in his career. The maximum handicap weight in flat races had just been raised to 10 stone, but to have any chance of commanding a competitive supply of rides, Fred reasoned that he must be capable of doing 9 stone 2 lb. Allowing for his silks, boots and saddle, his weight when stripped could therefore not exceed 8 stone 11 lb. To the majority of steeplechase jockeys, this would have presented an impossible assignment, but Fred was smaller, wirier and lighter-framed than most. Without recourse to dieting or sweating, his weight was steady at 9 stone 7 lb, so he set about losing another 10 lb in order to put his plan into operation. Encouragement came from various directions. The Jockey Club rapidly granted his application for a flat-race licence and a number of people offered him advice on weight-loss; even Scobie Breasley's wife wanted to help, and phoned Diana with a run-down of her husband's diet sheet.

By the time he rode Kilmore at Aintree, Fred had lost another 3 lb and was ready for his first rides on the flat in twenty years. It was then that his intentions were stalled by the gradual realisation that 9 stone 4 lb was about as light as he could get. The weight problem was insoluble, leading him to declare reluctantly: 'It's a flop. I'm too heavy, by about a stone, and wasting is bad for me . . . it makes me irritable.' He had only eight rides, none of which won, before abandoning the experiment. He acknowledged that his talent over obstacles, great though it was, did not actually mean very much when transferred to an area in which altogether different specialist skills were employed.

So when the jumping season came to an end in the first week of June, Fred, who had finished third in the jockeys' table, motored down to Cornwall with Diana and the three girls for a summer break. As holidays go, it was to have a great number of interruptions since Fred, far from being off duty, became almost a commuter to France while the ambitious European raids being schemed by Messrs Price and Walwyn took shape.

The racing world was more inhibited in those days; it was a rarity
for British trainers even to venture across the Channel 'on business',
and the instances of British jumping successes overseas can be gauged
from the fact that when Fred won a chase at Auteuil on Ryan Price's
Gold Wire, this was the first wholly British winner of a chase on that
course for more than thirty years. Greater glories, however, were in
the offing, though not without great drama and, in Fred's case,
considerable suffering.

Auteuil's big-race day was 17 June. This was the day on which
Mandarin was to put his British reputation on the line in the Grand
Steeplechase de Paris, run over 4 miles of a deviously unconventional
course which requires the jumping of rails, an awesome water jump
and a notorious bullfinch fence at which the meek will invariably
perish. It was also the day when Beaver II would attempt to complete
the four-year-old hurdling double in the French equivalent of the
'Triumph'.

Beaver was set to carry 9 stone 10 lb, which would not customarily
have caused Fred a great many worries. This, however, was out of
season, when the weight inevitably creeps up for lack of regular race-
riding; he had also been doing himself rather well down in Cornwall,
to the extent that, a week before the meeting, the scales revealed that
he needed to lose 7 lb. This was the dilemma facing Fred, and the
hidden explanation for much of the anguish to come.

Fred's downfall was his love of an evening drink and a decent
meal. His self-discipline saw to it that he lost the excess pounds in
that week prior to Auteuil but then, with his mission accomplished,
he made the mistake of acceding to the demands of his neglected
appetite, and at exactly the wrong moment. For forty-eight hours
before setting off to France, he had fasted. He had eaten and drunk
next to nothing, and the desired effect had been evident on the scales.
He and Diana met at London's Normandy Hotel for the night before
the plane journey to Paris and Fred, consoling his conscience with the
thought that he could always spend his sleeping hours in the Savoy
Turkish baths, proposed a decent dinner, convivially preceded by a
couple of cocktails. He began to enjoy himself. The food was good, if
rich, the wine very palatable and he had a challenging day in France
to contemplate. It was towards the end of the meal that he began to
experience that turbulence in the stomach which, had he only thought
about it in time, must inevitably come from terminating a fast in such
an over-indulgent fashion. Soon he was heartily regretting his

impetuosity, and although he continued with his plan and proceeded, a little unsteadily, to the Turkish baths, the steam only served to make him violently sick. He was ill through the night, hardly sleeping at all, and although he now had no trouble in meeting the required weight, he looked as bad as he felt when he arrived, with Diana, at Heathrow Airport the following morning.

Mrs Cath Walwyn recalls the moment. 'We had a party of sixteen flying over for the race and there was naturally a lot of excitement as we gathered at the airport. Then I saw Fred and my heart sank. He was quite obviously ill – he looked awful.'

In such situations a sick man can either sit and suffer or adopt the kill-or-cure course. Fred, heartily fed up with the way he was feeling and more worried than he would admit about how it might affect his riding of the two British hopes, chose the latter. With a big contingent of racing people ranged around him on the plane, noisily concerned about his condition, Fred ordered half a bottle of champagne. It could have sent him running to the toilet for an indefinite and uncomfortable stay but instead it had the reviving effect he had hoped. When the plane touched down in Paris, he was feeling human again, though it would be a gross exaggeration to claim he was once more in mid-season health. What is more, as the plane taxied to its resting place by the terminal, the British racing folk on board uttered a communal groan when they peered through the windows. It was raining, and the last thing Mandarin wanted was rain-softened ground.

Fortunately, the weather perked up, more comprehensively than could be said for Fred, and the sun was shining warmly by the time Messrs Winter and Walwyn set off to walk the singular Auteuil course. Cath watched them go. 'Fred was still far from well, I could see. But he was so strong-willed, you know. We just hoped and prayed he would be all right.'

The wait seemed interminable. The race was not due off until past four o'clock and Fred, avoiding any further food or drink, was not feeling noticeably better when, at long last, it was time to go to post. He was cheered by the look and feel of Mandarin, and by the sight and sound of the hundreds of Englishmen in the crowd, more than had ever previously attended an overseas jumps meeting. If few of them were cognisant with the health problems of their jockey, many more were to remain ignorant of the drama that followed until the race was over.

From an elevated position on the stands, and to the tutored racing eye with the aid of binoculars, what happened was appallingly plain. As Fulke Walwyn later recalled in his gravelly, matter-of-fact way: 'We could see early on that Mandarin's browband was behind his ear and that the bit was hanging down.' Simply translated, Mandarin was now like a car in motorway rush-hour traffic with no steering. Fred, behind the wheel, was powerless.

Up on the stands, Diana Winter, already anxious over Fred's inevitable lack of strength after so many hours of sickness, viewed the calamity with scarcely concealed horror. 'I saw the bridle break,' she said. 'Monsieur Hennessy was next to me and I instinctively told him what had happened. Looking back, it was quite a comical moment, because he hardly spoke a word of English and I'm sure he didn't understand. I think what followed was the most agonising experience of my life.'

It was not much fun for Fred, either. When the metal bit unaccountably snapped in Mandarin's mouth, just as he was approaching the 6-foot privet hedge which makes up one of Auteuil's most treacherous obstacles, his immediate suspicions would have done credit to the sort of novel that Dick Francis was later to write. 'The first thought that went through my mind was sabotage,' he recounted. 'After that, I was too busy to think much more.'

Cath Walwyn, looking back on the moment twenty-eight years later, expanded on the problems facing Fred. 'Mandarin was an old horse but he had taken on a new lease of life and he always pulled very hard. With this in mind, once the bit had gone we all thought he would run out. He was a bold horse and would always jump what was put before him, but Fred had no proper means of steering him in the right direction. It was a miracle he went round with the others.'

Back on the course Fred was finding to his surprise that Mandarin, far from reacting gleefully to being in complete charge of his destiny, seemed if anything to have responded subserviently to the crisis.

'The amazing thing was that he didn't try to run out. He was normally a free little devil but he never attempted to go mad and he never varied his speed one way or the other. The next thing I thought was: "Well, I'm not going to jump off." I never have done, because I was much too windy! Then I thought that when we reached the end of the straight row of four fences and had to swing to the left, he would probably go straight on anyway. Then I would *have* to jump off because there was an enormous wire barricade.'

But Fred was now over the initial shock of his plight and as close to being in charge of the situation as was possible. A lesser jockey would have had no chance; with Fred Winter there was always a chance. Using his hands on the horse's neck and his knees to guide Mandarin as best he could, he would, however, have been relying heavily on the good sense and good nature of the animal – in other words, on luck – but for the surprising intervention of some unlikely allies. He suddenly realised that, far from gloating over his misfortune and hastening him to his fate, the French jockeys were doing all they could to keep him in the race.

'Several of them realised the jam I was in,' said Fred, 'and one actually helped me round the first bend. He was about a neck behind me and he swung in so that the pressure of his horse, and my own efforts, got us round.'

When the race began in earnest, on the second circuit, Fred's memory is that the other jockeys were no longer actively helping him, but neither were they deliberately hampering him, or running him off the course, which would have been so easy to do. By using all his strength and experience, he somehow kept Mandarin on the correct course and a little less than half a mile from home he began to believe that, despite everything, he might yet win. Then, cruel beyond belief, Mandarin broke down.

'From then on it was a struggle. He had been going terribly easily and I hadn't asked him anything. He faltered in his action and I lost about three or four lengths, a lot of ground to make up at that stage of the race.'

Now, from the skill and strength of a stricken jockey, the focus switched to the unquestioning courage of a little horse who was, in his own way, as reluctant to admit defeat as his rider. Mandarin jumped the last in front and then responded gallantly to all Fred's urgings. A French horse named Lumino, younger and at that particular moment incalculably fitter in every respect, came with a relentless late challenge but Mandarin held on to prevail in a photo-finish, though in the moment they flashed past the post even Winter himself could not be certain if he had won.

'Mandarin was utterly exhausted,' remembered Fred. 'I have never known a horse so tired. I had nothing to pull him up with but he was walking within a few strides of the winning post.'

Fred himself was little better. In the heat of battle he had forgotten his ailments but now, as the tempo slowed, they came sweeping over him once more. Horse and jockey, one lame, one sick, must have made a perversely forlorn picture as they headed for the winners' enclosure.

A picture of a different kind could now be beheld as the stands emptied themselves of jubilant Englishmen, many of them openly weeping in one of those rare, surging moments of sporting magic which one knows, immediately and instinctively, can never quite be repeated. Among the throng were Fulke and Cath Walwyn, lost in their own joy and, just for a minute, lost completely. 'We were going against the crowd to get to the unsaddling enclosure,' recalled Cath. 'It was hard enough to stand up, let alone see anything clearly.' The couple suddenly found themselves facing a locked fire door. Outside the brave old horse was hobbling ever closer to his reception and his resting-place. The trainer and his wife had a problem. Fulke, an uncomplicated man, solved it. 'I gave the door a bloody good kick,' he said, 'and it bust!'

And so the principle connections were able to join up with their exhausted heroes. According to Fulke, 'Fred was in a desperate state. He nearly passed out.' Indeed, he did. The stomach pains were back with a vengeance and it was all he could do to weigh in. As well-meaning jockeys and friends pressed their congratulations upon him he might never have regained the weighing-room at all but for the help of Stan Mellor. 'I have never seen a man in such depths,' said Mellor later. 'You would think he would be too weak to ride again for days, let alone to go out half an hour later.'

Mellor, who was riding against Winter in the four-year-old race, dressed his friend, took him to the scales and then steered him back out to the paddock. Fred only later had the episode pieced together for him by friends; at the time he was barely aware what was happening around him and yet, somehow, he found the resources to ride an impeccable race on Beaver II and win by a length. He might have been doing it from memory, or from instinct; he was too tired to know.

8

Seeing the red light

Within the Findon training yard once populated by Ryan Price and his team there is a steep, grassy bank. One late summer's day during those golden years of Fred Winter's partnership with Price, after the work had been done, a little fun was being had with a children's bicycle. Some of the lads tried to ride the bike up the slope, but none succeeded. Fred watched this for a time before deciding that he would attempt the ascent.

Dorothy Price was among the audience for this impromptu stable-yard version of *It's A Knockout* and she remembers it plainly. 'Nobody could get the bike to the top but that just made Fred more determined. He tried for an hour and kept falling off. Ryan, who was watching, got in a terrible flap in case he injured himself but Fred refused to let this slope beat him and eventually, of course, he was the first and only one of us to do it.'

The story is retold by Mrs Price because somehow it epitomises the indomitable character that has made Fred Winter a winner throughout his life. This was, of course, most pronounced in his race-riding and when he felt he could no longer do it – or, more pertinently, that he was no longer relishing the attempt – he knew with finality that it was a message to stop.

He saw the light during the 1962–63 season, numerically his least successful in thirteen years. As is so often the case, it took an injury to bring it home to Fred that it might be time to seek a more sensible way of approaching middle age. He was thirty-seven years old and, as his brother John later explained: 'He had often said to me that it was sad to see jockeys going on too long. Fortunately, as soon as he was being beaten a short head when he should have won a short head, he recognised the symptoms and decided to pack up. I don't think he found it hard. He rode for longer than most do now.'

If retirement was unsurprising, nothing can have been farther away from Fred's mind in that immortal summer of 1962, when he followed up his pillaging of the Paris spoils with victories in Ireland and America. He became jump-racing's first jet-setter and, at this stage, he was still immensely enjoying the fruits of his talent.

The public acclaim, on both sides of the English Channel, which Fred experienced in the wake of Mandarin's win quite took his breath away. So too, probably, did the party. 'The celebrations were pretty heavy,' declared Fulke Walwyn. Diana Winter was a little more explicit: 'We took over the hotel for the night and things became so noisy that someone sent for the gendarmes. They arrived, discovered the cause of the party and joined in!'

The press, both in France and England, devoted to this extraordinary race the space and superlatives it deserved. Fred was feted in France, and feted once more when, slightly later than planned, he arrived back in England. A mound of letters and telegrams awaited him, the congratulations coming from many people he knew and many more he had never met. One of the letters, from Sir Martin Gilliat, private secretary to the Queen Mother, said: 'Her Majesty arrived back from Canada at midday and the news of your success was a wonderful tonic on her return home.'

Until his successes in France that summer, Fred had never ridden a winner overseas. Jump jockeys, in those days, were not expected to venture far. In the weeks that followed, however, there was a knock-on effect from the Mandarin exploits. First, he was invited to Ireland to ride for 'Phonsie' O'Brien, brother of Vincent, in the Galway Plate.

The Galway Festival, which extends over an entire week at the beginning of August, is a mixed meeting, flat and jumps, but in character and atmosphere it is Ireland's closest equivalent to Cheltenham: socially a test of stamina and in racing terms the gathering of Ireland's best jumpers, sometimes – though because of the summer lay-off and the firm ground not often enough – supplemented by competitive challengers from Britain. The Plate is traditionally the highlight of the meeting. A handicap chase, run over 2 miles 5 furlongs, it carries a lucrative prize and invariably attracts a big field. Fred's mount was Carraroe, bred in Ireland but once trained at Epsom before returning to her native land. More pertinently, so far as

Fred's future was concerned, the mare was owned by Mrs Miles Valentine, one of the wealthiest women in Pennsylvania, a huntswoman and a devotee of jump racing both in America and in Ireland. Fred won the race for her, by a hard-fought half-length; she showed her gratitude by sending horses to Fred, many of them expensive and talented, throughout his training career. Winning at Galway was, it transpired, a very worthwhile day's work.

Soon he had conquered America too. Breaking off from the mundane business of the early-season meetings in England, Fred flew with Diana to New York for a booked ride in the Temple Gwathmey Chase, run at Belmont Park, the most valuable steeplechase in a country where big-city racegoers regard jumping with grave suspicion and minimal enthusiasm. Hunt racing, as they call it in the States, thrives in rural areas, where 'picnic meetings' can attract enormous crowds, often without any betting at all, but the metropolitan tracks have gradually phased jump races out of their programmes.

For Fred this might have very well been a wasted journey. On the morning before the race he schooled his intended ride, the Irish horse Moonsun, on the racecourse, and reluctantly reported to the horse's connections that there was a high risk of breaking down on such hard ground. Equally reluctantly, for quite apart from the adventure of the mission the expense of taking a horse across the Atlantic for nothing is frightening, the owner and trainer agreed. Although this now left Fred without a ride in the chase, he was generously compensated by the offer of a 'spare' in that afternoon's big hurdle race, the New York Turf Writers' Cup. Better still, he not only won the event on Baby Prince but broke the track record into the bargain. Another country had been won over by the brilliance of Winter, still Britain's champion in all but title.

Back on home territory, Fred received honours which had never before come the way of a National Hunt jockey. He was one of the guests of honour at the 'Men of the Year' ceremony, and, before the end of the 1962–63 season, he had been apprised of his nomination for a CBE. Fred's reaction to these tributes is illuminating. At the 'Men of the Year' lunch, a glittering occasion held at London's Savoy Hotel, he spent some time with Francis Chichester, who had just crossed the Atlantic single-handed. To Fred the yachtsman seemed 'a strange, quiet man who didn't look very happy with his surroundings' – a comment, perhaps, which could have applied to Fred himself when, over the years, he was placed in social situations he found unappealing. As for the CBE, Fred was stunned yet proud, feeling that it was conferred not only on himself but on the sport of jump racing too. He accepted promptly and, shortly after the end of the season, yet another rare privilege came his way in the form of an invitation to lunch with the Queen at Buckingham Palace.

Amid this whirl of social graces, a subtle change had overtaken Fred. It was the realisation that the end was near. Ironically, or perhaps significantly, he had received all these honours during a season which brought him more than the accepted share of pain and frustration and markedly less than the share of success to which he had grown accustomed. Retirement to some jockeys is a decision to be taken spontaneously. For Fred it did not happen this way. It was a gradual dawning, a reluctant coming-to-terms with the fact that the years had caught up with him. He explains: 'I began to realise that I was not enjoying it at all that season. I did not enjoy it because I realised that on occasions I was being beaten when I should not have been. I was blowing up 100 yards from the winning post.'

Apart from considerations of physical fitness, Fred, as ever, was honest enough to confess that there was something far greater standing in the way of his continuing. It was the state of what the modern sportsman calls his 'bottle'. 'I gave up because I was losing my nerve,' he admitted. 'It's something which happens gradually. You begin to realise you aren't as brave as you used to be . . . I had always said to myself that when I came to the conclusion that I was not riding as well as I could, it would be a sign that my nerve had gone. You can't give value for money then.' Finally came the comment that was the key to the Winter philosophy of life. 'The only thing I really enjoyed in racing was winning. Being second or third was of no interest at all, and I decided that I was not winning often enough. The period between the start and the finish was not as much fun as it used to be. It was time to turn it in.'

Although this thought process had proceeded virtually throughout the 1962–63 season, and had reached its inevitable conclusion by the end of it, Fred did not make his decision public until 15 November, some way into the following season, which he had decided would be his last. In fact, meticulous as ever, he was even able to tell the racing press that he had nominated Saturday, 11 April 1964, as his final day of riding. There were two reasons for this. He wanted to ride in one last Grand National on his old friend Kilmore, and he had a desire to take his final bow at Cheltenham, scene of so many of his finest moments. For an essentially unemotional man, these decisions revealed a sensitive regard for nostalgia.

Within the time that Fred was privately contemplating his future he continued, of course, to ride as first jockey to Captain Ryan Price. But, although his relationship with the trainer remained as close as ever, and their mutual respect as firm, it was no longer automatic that Fred would have the pick of the rides. Josh Gifford had now served his apprenticeship and was an ambitious and talented member of the senior jockeys. Increasingly, if the Price yard ran two horses in a race, Gifford would ride the more fancied of them. Modestly, however, he insists: 'Although I might be taking the better rides, he would invariably beat me, because he was still so competitive. And although we were now rivals for rides in the yard, and I was being seen as the up-and-coming one, there was never any bad feeling on Fred's side at all.

'A season or so before this, Fred had given me the best advice I ever had. Fred Rimell had approached me to be his stable jockey. It was a big job in an important yard, and as I was constantly in Fred's shadow at Findon, I was very tempted to take it. I told Fred about the offer and asked what he thought, suspecting that, like most people in such a situation, he would be quite happy to see his competition go elsewhere.

'Instead, he said: "Don't be silly, Josh. I've ridden for them all, over the years, and there is only one man to ride for if you have the chance. You stay here." He could so easily have got me off his back, but he is such a gentleman that he considered only what would be best for me. I stayed with Ryan and never regretted it.'

Although Fred's strike-rate of winners to runners was at its lowest ever during the pivotal 1962–63 season, it was an injury, one of the most serious and painful of his career, that gave him the time and motivation to assess his future.

It had been a wretched season for most National Hunt folk. By Christmas the entire country was cloaked in an unforgiving frost. Snow followed, with more frost to top it off. And there was no sign of an end to it. This was one of the worst freezes in British history and one of its damaging side-effects was to cripple the racing industry. Trivial though this may seem when set against the sickness and hypothermia suffered by the nation's old people, in particular, it was not simply a case of a group of people being denied their sport.

Livelihoods were at stake and, in ten weeks virtually devoid of racing, severe hardship resulted in various areas of the industry, the lower and middle-ranking jockeys prominent among them. Fred Winter and family would not starve – the years of success had seen to that – but apart from his retaining contracts, which did not amount to a living wage, he had no income during that period. These days, some of the leading jockeys have supplementary business interests to which they can turn in times of incapacity or inactivity; in the 1960s jockeys rode horses and were not expected to have any higher ideas.

As the miniature ice age maintained its grip on the country, Fred, like everyone else in the racing game, had long since lost any sense of release through an unplanned holiday. Frustration, boredom and anxiety set in. Fitness also became an increasing dilemma as jockeys are never really race-fit unless they are regularly riding horses. Fred employed one of Diana's hunters and hacked around a straw ring he laid in a paddock at home; this, however, was the extent of the available exercise, unless you counted the unusual opportunity to ski and toboggan on the neighbouring Cotswold Hills.

A communal sense of great relief accompanied the thaw. For the jumping fraternity it came only just in time to salvage the Cheltenham Festival, but Fred went through the three days without a winner, finishing third in the Gold Cup behind the emergent star, Mill House. He still had Aintree to contemplate, however, and amongst an attractive book of rides was a third National attempt by Kilmore. Here there were at least some winners – two hurdlers on National day, both trained by Ryan Price – but in the big one Kilmore could only finish sixth behind Ayala, having been kicked by a faller at the water jump.

Despite this disappointment, the month of April continued to revive Fred's season and he rode four winners in a day at Newton Abbot. The fates, being fickle in these matters, decreed that this was quite enough generosity to the old warrior and, the very next day, his season ended in the first race of the card at Chepstow. Riding the favourite, Andy Capp, in the novice chase, Fred was in contention at the final fence when his mount came down heavily. Although the ground was soft, his injuries were plainly bad enough to curtail his engagements for the day. The course doctor allowed him to go home but he was in sufficient pain to cast around for someone to drive him.

Johnny Lehane volunteered. It was not the first time he had driven

Fred around; not being an especially enthusiastic driver, Fred was happier being a passenger and he found a willing chauffeur in Gene Kelly, a middle-of-the-road jockey. Lehane sometimes stood in, and he and Fred were good friends, although complete opposites. Lehane was a weighing-room joker who specialised in nicknames. He himself was generally known as 'Thumper', and he was the man responsible for such enduring nicknames, among others, as 'Duke' (David Nicholson) and 'Bumble' (Michael Scudamore). 'Christening' Fred had presented him with more of a problem but, on discovering the rank to which he had risen in the Parachute Regiment, Lehane decided that F. T. Winter should henceforth be known as 'Lieut'. Fred's gruff response was to tell his friend to 'grow up' but, whether he liked it or not, the name stuck within the confines of the weighing-room.

The journey home to Gloucestershire was an uncomfortable one, sharp pain assaulting Fred's chest. When there was no improvement, indeed a distinct deterioration, by the following morning, it was plainly a wise precaution to visit Bill Tucker, the London orthopaedic surgeon and ally of all stricken sportsmen. His X-rays confirmed that three ribs were cracked, enough to put a jockey on the sidelines for an irritating time but not especially high on the scale of severity. Fred was faintly relieved as he headed home with the injury strapped. It was a short-lived feeling.

This happened to be Diana's birthday and a dinner party had been planned, but Fred did not have the opportunity to enjoy it. Midway through the meal he felt unaccountably unwell. His chest felt as if it were under a great weight; he could not breathe properly. The local doctor was summoned by telephone and after examining the patient gave his view that Fred was suffering from fluid on the chest. Another visit to London was demanded the following day, and there a specialist confirmed the GP's fears. Fred had a punctured lung and required an emergency operation that same evening, in the London Clinic, where more than 5 pints of fluid were drained from the lung.

Not only was Fred's season prematurely ended, he was also in a condition to make him think about the risks, the rewards and the alternatives. On one of his visits to London, during his rehabilitation, he diverted to the Jockey Club offices and made an application to become a National Hunt starter. Astonishingly, he was told that there was no chance whatsoever. What he was effectively being told was that jockeys such as himself should know their place, which was not to have anything to do with the administration of the sport. It was a foolish, elitist attitude which deservedly heaped derision on the organisation when it became known. But it gave Fred the impetus to take a step he had always said he would resist.

Dave Dick later summed up the situation in his customary forthright way. 'Fred wanted to be a starter so that he could do something in racing while having a pretty quiet time. Basically, he just didn't want the hassles and demands of training. Turning him down was one of the few decent mistakes the Jockey Club ever made!'

Rejection not only persuaded Fred to change his mind about training but, paradoxically, had a bearing on extending his riding career too. Although injured, he was still being lauded on all sides and, in many ways, the announcement of his CBE was the perfect cue for a simultaneous retirement speech. Having decided to train, however, Fred now had the intimidating task of finding a suitable property and setting up the operation. This could not be done overnight; besides, he had a sneaking fancy for one last Cheltenham, one last National, one final season among the weighing-room cameraderie that he would miss as much as anything when the moment came to leave for the final time.

And so his plans were laid. His announcement, when it was made in November, commanded a lot of column inches in every newspaper but was greeted without surprise by family and friends. They had seen it coming, not least the perspicacious Snowy Davis, travelling head lad to Ryan Price. 'It was no surprise to me when Freddy gave up,' he recalls. 'When you are in the game, and at racing every day, you learn to spot the signs that tell you a jockey's nerve is going. It is nothing to be ashamed of, because it comes to everybody, and although I would miss him, I was relieved that Freddy was getting out in one piece.'

Diana Winter doubtless offered similar thanks, though her feelings were necessarily coloured by concern over what was to happen next. 'Freddy was noticeably not enjoying his riding so much, so although it seemed to happen quite suddenly, I was prepared for it. He had always said he would stop riding when he began to lose races he should have won. When that time came, he kept his word. In some ways it was a relief, but then I had never been a frightened jockeys' wife, as some were. It probably had something to do with the fact that I had hunted so much, and broken my own back doing so. I knew all the potential hazards at first hand.

'The worry, of course, was what to do afterwards. Freddy had never saved any money as a jockey and I really don't think he knew what he wanted to do – being a starter was just an idea. It was a fact, though, that he did not really want to be a trainer and that I didn't want to be a trainer's wife!'

One of the saddest recipients of Fred's news was Ryan Price. Not that he, like all others in the sport, did not feel relief, for as his wife Dorothy says: 'Ryan could not have stood anything happening to Fred.' It was just that he did not want it to end. 'I wish Fred could have gone on riding for ever and ever,' he said. 'Never mind what he says – at the end he was giving a horse as good a ride as at any stage of his career, and yet he had an inferiority complex and never had real faith in his own remarkable ability. He always thought there were three or four in any race who would go better than him, but he rode me at least a hundred winners that no one else in the world would have won on. He was an inspired rider – a genius.

'Fred was the most useless schooling jockey this world has ever produced,' added Captain Price, 'but once he was engaged in a race, everything clicked into place. Most jockeys don't worry about what makes a particular horse tick, but Fred wanted to learn about each one and find the key to them all.

'Usually, I allowed him tremendous liberty and didn't tie him down with orders. I got a rocket for it once. The stewards called me in at Newbury and asked me what orders I had given Fred in a particular race. They were horrified when I said I hadn't given him any. I mean, what orders would you give Lester Piggott?

'Very few people realise what a great character Fred was. He raised the standard of National Hunt jockeyship higher than it has ever been, and I don't just mean by his riding but by his conduct both on and off the course. I'm sorry it had to come to an end.'

In giving this close-of-play summary of his old friend's attributes, Captain Price also revealed the trust and loyalty which existed between them in their working relationship. For the last ten years that Fred was stable jockey at Findon, no contract existed. What is more, it is plain that Fred did not remain faithful for monetary reasons. 'In the last few years,' explained the trainer, 'he could have had three or four times the retainer he was getting from my stable if he had taken up some of the offers that were made to him, yet he always chose to stay with me.'

This was by no means one-sided admiration. In one of the many press interviews Fred Winter consented to giving during his final months as a jockey, he offered a touching tribute in return. 'I owe Ryan everything,' he said. 'He started me off, stuck to me when I kept falling off, kept putting me back. It's all due to him.'

Very few jockey–trainer partnerships reach such heights of achievement on the course (three Champion Hurdles and a Grand National among them) or such obvious respect off it. It was a very special pairing, which made it all the more sad that its inevitable end should be soured and hastened. For, during Fred's last season, Ryan Price had his licence to train temporarily withdrawn by the Jockey Club.

It was a matter which did not directly involve Fred, though this did not assuage his sense of sadness or lessen his support for Price. The suspension, as it effectively was, arose from the running of a horse called Rosyth, who had won the 1963 Schweppes Gold Trophy hurdle race at Liverpool, and won it again the following season when the race – traditionally a major betting handicap – was staged at the new venue of Newbury. The stewards' interest emanated from the fact that Rosyth had run five times between his first and second Schweppes, finishing unplaced four times. The Newbury stewards were not satisfied with Captain Price's explanations and he was referred to the stewards of the National Hunt committee, who passed sentence.

Rosyth had regularly been ridden by Josh Gifford, who was far more seriously affected than the imminently retiring Winter. It was an indefinite withdrawal of licence but, as it transpired, Captain Price was restored to the training ranks the following year. Later he decided to concentrate almost exclusively on the flat. At the time, however, it was a controversy which left a bad taste and most certainly detracted from the dignified departure of a jockey who would continue to be known as one of the most honest, straightforward and uncontroversial people in this or any other sport.

Before the party was spoiled, however, Fred and Ryan had enjoyed a few last triumphs together, even if the fish they caught were chiefly small. One of the smallest was in a 3-mile chase at bleak and unprepossessing Leicester on a midweek November afternoon. Yet in many ways it was one of their most extraordinary winners. There were only four runners in the race and all four of them fell. Fred's horse actually fell twice and refused once, yet unbelievably won the race, largely through a manic intervention from Ryan Price.

The first casualty, Norwegian and David Nicholson, came down at

the first fence. At the fifth, two more fell, leaving Fred alone. Far
from being sanguine, however, this filled him with anxiety, because
his mount, a horse called Carry On, was notorious for wanting to do
nothing of the sort. All was well up the home straight, as Fred tucked
Carry On in behind the riderless horses. As the course bears right
away from the stands, the stables are clearly visible on the left, and
the fallen horses headed unerringly in that direction, taking Carry
On's attention with them. Fred was expecting this, but was still
unable to do anything about it. Carry On was so keen to join his
mates that he plunged straight into the water jump, the first obstacle
in the back straight. This was uncomfortable but not entirely final.
Fred caught his horse and remounted, to the noisily amused delight
of the crowd. Carry On, though, was now feeling thoroughly mulish
and skidded stubbornly to a standstill before reaching the next fence.
Presented again by the persevering jockey, he somersaulted into the
open ditch by trying for all he was worth to avoid leaving the
ground.

Even Fred was now inclined to call it a day and he had begun to
lead Carry On back across the course when he spied Ryan Price
careering towards him. Ryan had been able to weigh up this whole,
chaotic situation from his place on the stands and, unconventional
though it was, he had now sprinted down the steps and across the
track to tell Fred that two of the other horses were being remounted
where they had come to grief. 'Wait for them to come round,' he told
Fred, 'then drop in behind them. Let them give you a lead.'

Fred's view was that Carry On would still decline to jump the
ditch, but he took his instructions, accepted Ryan's leg-up, and saw.
the evidence of the trainer's wisdom as his horse obediently rejoined
the renewed contest, jumping suddenly with enthusiasm and accuracy.
Biding his time, Fred eventually made his move approaching the last,
and won by three-quarters of a length. One of the toughest and most
bizarre winners of his life had taken thirteen minutes to evolve and
had earned for connections the princely sum of £173. Being the
competitors they were, however, both Fred and Ryan would have
considered it well worthwhile.

As the season continued, Fred left his legion of followers with
other precious memories – not least four brilliantly conceived winners
at the Newbury meeting on 29 February, when his only losing ride
was in the inaugural running of the Mandarin Handicap Chase,
overseen by the great and courageous Mandarin himself, now in

honourable retirement with Fulke Walwyn in Lambourn. Kilmore's last National continued to drive Fred on but, by the time Aintree came around, Ryan Price was a debarred person and Kilmore had been sent to Epsom to be trained by Syd Dale, formerly head lad at the Price yard. If he had to go anywhere, this was at least a yard with connections, and Fred vowed to try to win the race for his old friend. He might have done so, in fact he was himself convinced of this, but Kilmore came down at the twenty-first fence. 'He would have won – I swear he would,' said Fred later. 'He was going easier than at any time in his three other Grand Nationals. We were just hack cantering and I still don't know why he fell. It was the only time at Liverpool that he made a serious mistake of his own accord.'

To the very end, Fred remained as competitive as he had ever been, and as encouraging to younger jockeys. Jeff King, who was to become one of the finest riders of the next fifteen years, recalls sitting in a bar with Fred at a social function just before his retirement. To King, as to most of his generation, Fred was a figure to be regarded with some awe, so what followed has it humorous side. 'Fred was telling me that to be any good as a jockey you needed to be very strong. I kept replying that I was strong. To prove it, we started arm-wrestling and before I knew what was happening, we were rolling about on the floor!'

Fred Winter's last winner came in the modest and unlovely sur-roundings of Wolverhampton, on 25 March 1964. It was on a horse called Vultrix in an undistinguished handicap chase. Even the greatest of careers do not necessarily have the endings they deserve and the farewell day at Cheltenham that he had selected for himself passed off entirely without success. It did not, however, pass off without much dewy-eyed emotion from all of those who had known him, either intimately or from afar, during his peerless years as a jockey. It was not the end of a story, but it was the end of an unrepeatable chapter.

9

A new life at Uplands

It is all very well deciding that one is, after all, going to become a trainer. Certain tools of the trade are required to make the notion viable – like an adequate number of capable racehorses and the facilities needed to train them. Racing being a highly competitive arena, there is limited scope for sentiment or speculation. History dictates that some of the greatest jockeys have made no impact in the training ranks and in general it has been the well-heeled and well-connected, rather than the most successful, who have found the transition easy. Fred Winter was under no illusions. He did not expect any favours, which was just as well because he did not receive any. He launched his training career in primitive surroundings and with only five horses. His eminence as a jockey counted for next to nothing.

Despite all his distinguished years in racing, Fred was not helped by the way he had chosen to go about his life as a rider. John Winter, who followed and chronicled his brother's career more closely than anyone, explains: 'Fred had no grounding in the skills of training because, as a jockey, he had never taken any interest in schooling or in stables. He had to start from scratch, and it was not put on his plate. He did eventually get some nice owners, but they were not rushing to send him horses when he started out.'

It was undoubtedly to Winter's advantage at this time that his nature eschewed arrogance of any kind. He had never believed that racing, or those involved in it, owed him a thing, no matter how much and for how long he had elevated the public image and awareness of the game. What did occasionally rile him was the jealous pomposity of those who ran racing, their determination to protect their elitist ranks from commoners with vulgar virtues such as wisdom and experience. But it was this, indirectly, which had driven him away from his solid intentions to avoid training at all costs. He had made his bed, and now he had to lie in it.

At first he found it difficult to leave his previous existence behind. People would not allow it. To the public, indeed to many of his riding and training friends and perhaps also to his family, he was still Fred Winter, jockey, until they could be convinced otherwise by the following season beginning without his familiar name-plate on the number-boards at Newton Abbot and Devon and Exeter. There was a temptation, as is often the case when one of the legends hands in his magic wand, to believe that it was no more than a temporary disenchantment and that he would be back again, large as life, when autumn came around and the jumpers began to stretch their legs.

His retirement, however, was accorded show-business status, Sinatra-style, when the Variety Club of Great Britain laid on a 'Fred Winter Tribute Luncheon' at London's Savoy Hotel. Fred was honoured, of course, but also a shade daunted. This was the racing party to end all racing parties; of those who had closely shared his years in the jockeys' weighing-room, there were very few absentees, and as the whole idea of the day was to honour one man's achievements, that man had to sit through a great deal of flattery. Peter Cazalet, who then trained the Queen Mother's horses, perhaps summed up the communal feeling most precisely in his speech, when he thanked Fred for 'your splendid example to all the young jockeys. Few individuals stand out in leadership as you do, and during the last ten years you have stood out alone.'

Fred was now conspicuously alone. The buck stops with a trainer and the demands on his time, energy, tact and patience are incessant. Fred was very soon to appreciate the difference between riding and training. 'As a jockey, you have to watch your weight, of course, and there's the odd bit of schooling and riding gallops [in Fred's case, a very odd bit!] . . . You get your Racing Calendar and mark your rides off at the beginning of the week. You drive to the course and ride them, and that's the end of your responsibility. With training you really have to use your brain the whole time, dealing with people as well as horses, doing the entries, buying hay, entertaining owners and keeping them informed about their horses, worrying about staff, finding new horses. And the telephone . . . it never stops.'

This, plainly, was a judgement issued from experience rather than expectation. The comments were made some years into Fred's training career, and from a position of success. Back in 1964 his most pressing problem was finding somewhere to train. Until he had solved that, his consolation was being spared any worries about horses, owners, staff and jockeys.

In his seventeen seasons as a professional jockey Fred had ridden 929 winners at a strike-rate of almost one in every four rides. He had won the Gold Cup and Grand National twice each and the Champion Hurdle three times. He had earned an unshakeable reputation for his integrity and had, by general consent, uplifted the sport and its standards. He had earned the thanks and admiration of some of the wealthiest and most influential men in the country. And yet none of them now stepped forward flourishing a cheque book and an expansive smile, inviting him to help himself to the best yard, gallops and racehorses available. Only those who still have the influence of the silver spoon command such privileged treatment, and Fred never had been one for that route. His father had made his way in racing through hard work and knowledge; he would do the same. But for all that, the search for property was a prolonged and frustrating business.

Ideally Fred and Diana would have liked to stay where they were, in the Cotswolds. Not only was it conveniently central, within an hour or so of a great many racecourses, but it had also come to seem very much a home to them. 'We had lived well in Gloucestershire,' says Diana. 'We had employed a cook and a nanny and had made plenty of friends. I still hunted in the area and the girls had space to ride their ponies. All three of them were also now at school; we had their education to think about.'

Regretfully, and after much discussion, they agreed that remaining was out of the question, because there were simply no suitable training grounds in the vicinity. One can build stable boxes on spare land almost anywhere, but if the adjacent ground cannot be turned into workable gallops, even the masters of the profession will not train any winners. At around this time Ryan Price, his licence still suspended and his stock being dispersed, asked Fred if he would like to take over at Findon. Fred declined, possibly because of the prevailing circumstances but perhaps also because, no matter whether he succeeded or failed at Findon, his progress would inevitably be compared with that of his long-time 'guv'nor'. He did not want it to be.

Fred's mind had long been on a move to Lambourn. He knew the area, notably through his association with Fulke Walwyn, and regarded it as the best place to train jumpers. Its gallops and schooling grounds, on the downs behind the village, were superb. Back in the autumn of 1963, soon after Fred had concluded his debate with himself and decided to train (but before his decision was widely known), he and Diana had heard of a yard for sale in Upper Lambourn. By strange coincidence, the property, Uplands, was immediately next door to Saxon House, where Fulke Walwyn trained. This had its attractions. The house had potential and the gallops were nearby. All of this was encouraging. The problem was the time factor. Fred was now committed to riding for one last full season and they would not be able to move into anywhere new, much less organise any essential work on it, until that season was over, retirement papers complete. The sale of this property was imminent and urgent, brought about by the tragic death of its previous incumbents, trainer Charlie Pratt and his wife, when the light aircraft bringing them home from a race meeting in the north crashed in stormy weather.

Reluctantly the Winters accepted that their funds would not stretch to purchasing this place at the planned auction and having it as an unoccupied 'second home' for eight or nine months. They turned their attention elsewhere, inspecting most of the yards which came on the market. Uplands, meanwhile, was bought by Douglas Marks, hoping to expand his training operation from its current base near Ascot. Fred and Doug knew each other well enough; later they were to become close friends and regular golf partners. At the time, however, Fred simply acknowledged another person's good fortune and filed away his impression of the yard at the back of his mind.

Christmas came and went and still there was no sign of a solution. 'It really was very hard to find a place where Fred could train and where we both thought we would be happy,' recalls Diana. 'We had relatively little money and we were beginning to get quite anxious.'

In January, Fred encountered Doug Marks at the races. Marks had still not moved to Lambourn and Fred flippantly asked if he would sell him his new yard privately. Marks appreciated the joke; no more, no less. But the seeds were now sown and, some days later, when the two men met up again, he astonished Fred by reminding him of his offer and telling him that, if he really meant it, he had a deal. Marks had by this time come to the conclusion that he had taken on more than he either needed or wanted when he successfully bid for Uplands at auction. He was now intending to set his sights somewhat lower and, subsequently, he would take over the Lethornes stables on the main road connecting Lambourn village with the hamlet-cum-training-centre of Upper Lambourn, where horses tend to have priority over all other forms of life.

Fred was happy to have secured the only property he had yet seen which met all his requirements, and he was entitled to be pleased. He was to train steeplechasers, generally contentedly and with huge success, for the next twenty-three years at Uplands and would love the place as an idyllic home as much as he respected it as a place of work. It was not, however, merely a case of moving in and the job taking off of its own accord. Uplands had now been empty for several months; it was also in a state of disrepair. Diana describes her next sight of it as 'a nightmare'. She explains: 'The house really needed to be gutted and the garden was one big bed of nettles.'

At the end of the season, when the Winters had arranged to move out of Kitsbury Orchard at Stow, Uplands was still some way from being habitable. While the work was being done, Fred, Diana and the girls stayed next door with the great friends who were soon to become the closest but friendliest of rivals. Fulke Walwyn was quietly delighted that Fred, with whom he had shared many French holidays quite apart from many winners on the racecourse, was about to become his neighbour. There was hardly a man alive for whom he had greater respect, as his wife Cath explains.

'Fred and Fulke always got along so well, perhaps because they were similar types. One of the greatest compliments Fulke could have paid Fred was to accept that he was the worst schooling jockey in the world and yet still believe he was the best race-rider he had ever seen. It was a waste of time having Fred to school and Fulke just acknowledged it and allowed him to get on with the business end of the job. I do remember, though, that Fred was the first jockey we had ever seen wearing a helmet. He was wearing it on one of the rare days when he did come schooling. Dave Dick scoffed and laughed his head off – told Fred he looked like a spaceman. He became so hysterical about the sight of his chum that he could barely ride. But Fred had a fall schooling – as he often did – and the helmet helped him. Soon, of course, everyone was wearing them.

'While he was still riding, we sometimes used to pick Fred up at Oddington if we were heading for a meeting in the midlands or the north. Di hardly ever came, in fact she would often be out hunting. After racing we would drop in for tea, and Fred would get it. If we stopped on to the cocktail hour, Fred would fuss around putting ice in the drinks. He really was very domesticated, apart from all his other qualities.

'We were close enough to him to be concerned over what he would do when he stopped riding, especially as he had always said he would not train. Somehow we could not see Fred away from racing, and we were both delighted when he decided to train next door. We were to have plenty of competition over the years but we never once fell out.'

The goodwill emanating from 'over the wall', as the Walwyn establishment was to become known among the Winter lads in years to come, was utterly genuine and did not begin and end with the offer of a spare room while they literally put their house in order. It extended to practical assistance too.

Fred was disarmingly frank about his qualifications for this new life. 'At the beginning I had no idea whether I could train or not. There is no law which states a successful jockey will make the grade as a trainer and I had never taken much notice of stable routines. The only practice I'd had was when my father was slightly ill and I helped out at his yard in Kent.'

Help and advice was forthcoming from a good source – Walwyn's capable head lad, Joe Lammin. Most evenings, when he had finished his duties at Saxon House, he would go down the lane to Uplands, where Fred was working on the basic geography of the place. Lammin was able to assist on the siting of tack-room, feed-room and so on, quite apart from more detailed matters relating to the smooth working of a stable.

The Walwyn yard, however, was working to capacity, with more than fifty horses. Fred had no more than a handful. Part of his reason for announcing his retirement fully five months before it would be actioned was to alert potential owners to the fact that he was about to start training. He did not expect an avalanche but he was fully entitled to his disappointment when only one man, of all of those for whom he had ridden winners down the years, came forward as a patron of the new yard. 'Fred was amazed,' confirms Diana, nodding her head at the memory, 'but he would never say anything.'

Winter, in fact, was proudly applying the same principles to training that he had followed as a rider. Paramount among them was never to beg for business. 'I've never touted for owners,' he said later. 'It was the same when I was riding. I never phoned round trainers, other than those who regularly put me up. I never asked for rides. Some people do, but I don't think it is ethical.'

There are any number of jockeys, trainers too for that matter, who might consider such regard for ethics as unwise and unbusinesslike and promote the alternative view that nothing comes to those who do not ask. Fred, however, had achieved boundless respect in his riding years by refusing to poach other jockeys' regular rides. Had he been so inclined, few trainers in the land would have rebuffed his offer, but he stuck determinedly by what he thought was right. His principle in such matters went even further. On one occasion a trainer for whom he rode regularly had two good horses taken away. The owners were dissatisfied for reasons best known to themselves, as both the horses had been winning their share of races, but when Fred was asked by the owners, to continue riding them from their new yard, he quietly declined. Again, he simply felt it would not be right.

One might cynically respond to all this by pointing out that Fred Winter the jockey was in a position to pick and choose. He did not need to scramble for spare rides, being attached to some of the most successful stables in Britain. He could turn down rides for which lesser jockeys would have happily begged. All this, of course, is true. As he set up in training, however, different rules applied. He was once more at the bottom of the pile and few were willing to haul him upwards.

The one man who did give Fred the chance even to move off the starting grid as a trainer was Michael Sobell, the television magnate later to be knighted. Sobell had part-owned some extremely useful racehorses including Flame Gun, whom Fred had declared to be 'the best 2-mile chaser I have ridden' when he won on him at the Cheltenham Festival of half a dozen years earlier. On hearing of Fred's training plans, Sir Michael bought two horses from Ireland named Solbina and One Seven Seven, registered them in his wife's name and asked his former jockey to train them for her. They arrived at Kitsbury Orchard for a peaceful summer at grass, and when the family finally uprooted and moved to Lambourn, they formed two-fifths of the stable strength. One horse, Royal Sanction, had been sent up from his father's yard in Kent, and another two arrived from Ryan Price's Findon yard, which was soon to provide two further inmates – including, notably, Anglo.

It was not exactly a formidable team with which to let battle commence but, in a perverse way, it may easily have hardened Winter's resolve. If his previous ambivalence towards training had been banished – for it is hard to conceive Fred entering into any such venture half-heartedly – some doubts and apprehensions must naturally have remained. Far from increasing them, the meagreness of his start could have acted as a spur. He now knew that nobody intended to present him with a yard of talented horses to train, so he must persuade potential owners in the best of all ways – by proving his worth in the job.

To give himself the best chance of success, Fred first had to surround himself with the right people. Here, he was lucky – or perhaps that under-estimates him. For Fred, like Ryan Price before him, was to prove not only a fine judge of a horse but also a very good judge of human character. He might not have been able to describe in detail the sort of people he was seeking to join the Uplands adventure but, when they came along, he was in no doubt. Two men, in particular, fitted the bill. They were opposites in many ways but they slotted into the machine as it began, slowly at first but with ever-increasing speed and certainty, to produce the goods. They were Brian Delaney and Lawrence Eliot and, until Eliot's death more than twenty years later, they were together responsible for the day-to-day workings of the enterprise – Delaney among the lads in the yard, Eliot among the paperwork in the office.

Delaney had made Fred's acquaintance by one of those happy coincidences. He is one of five sons born to Jack Delaney, a prolific rider of winners in Ireland; all five brothers went into racing but the youngest was killed in a motoring accident while working for the late Fred Rimell. Brian served his apprenticeship with Jeremy Tree and then signed up for two years with the King's Troop Artillery, based in London's St John's Wood. Soldiering, even on horseback, did not agree with him. It gave him an ulcer, which he insists to this day was caused by Army food; it also, however, gave him skills of horsemanship which he might not have gained from a racing apprenticeship. Once out of the Army Brian wanted nothing other than to be a jockey. On the suggestion of his father he went to work for a trainer named Hector Smith, based in the village of Snowshill, near Broadway in picture-postcard Cotswold countryside. There, Brian had upwards of fifty rides but, far more pertinent so far as his future was concerned, he came into regular contact with Fred Winter. Although during his racing days he hardly ever travelled south to ride out for his retaining stable in Findon, Fred naturally kept himself race-fit, and would quite often ride work, or even schooling, for Hector Smith, whose stables were only a few miles from Oddington. 'It was a chance to meet the guv'nor that I would not have had otherwise,' reflects Delaney – a fortunate chance, too, for he plainly left something of an impression on the retentive mind of Winter. When Hector Smith retired, Brian wrote to Fred to ask if he could join him when he began training. He received a swift reply in the affirmative.

Lawrence Eliot's route to the Uplands yard was more complicated, in a number of respects, not least in that he had been due to join the Walwyn stable next door. Fulke had appointed him to succeed his existing female secretary, who was about to leave. The lady changed her mind and so Lawrence was out of a job – until Fulke suggested to his new neighbour and old friend that he would soon be needing a secretary and this might be the ideal answer to his own slight embarrassment as well.

Whereas Delaney's time in the military was never intended as more than a temporary diversion from racing, Eliot's life – almost his death – had belonged in the Army. A turbulent life it had been, too. As an officer in Malaya he had coincidentally been posted away from his job in beach defence on the very day the Japanese invaded. He was then taken prisoner by the Japanese when in Singapore and there must have been times in the ensuing years when he almost wished he had stayed on that beach and numbered among the casualties. After a spell in Changi prison he was one of 100 British officers sent to a camp to build railway lines. He became sick, sometimes it seemed terminally so, but although he recalls, horrifically, that much of his time was taken up with digging graves for his colleagues, he was one of the fortunate and resilient men who came through the hideous experience to tell the tale.

His military career continued, after the war, in Cyprus and it was there that he met Sheilah Davis, later to become Mrs Dick Hern. This was Lawrence's link with racing, for when he returned to England, seeking a change of life, he visited Sheilah and Dick, who suggested he might get a job in racing. Until then he had maintained the vague interest of an infrequent racegoer but now, after learning to type, he first joined Bob Turnell in Wiltshire before applying successfully – or so he thought – for the post with Fulke Walwyn. He was passed 'over the wall' and became a stalwart of the Winter operation, his military mind of constant use in the organisation of bills, entries and everything else which the trainer himself was too busy to do.

Eliot and Delaney made an odd couple but an extremely effective one. In the two decades to follow they were to be invaluable to Fred as he built and then maintained his marvellous reputation at the head of National Hunt trainers.

If there was reflected glory to come, even perhaps a little hectic glamour, there was, however, precious little about in that first autumn of 1964. The five horses in the yard, when the season began, were looked after by a staff of four. Head lad at this point was Tommy Carey, who lived in digs in the village. Lawrence Eliot, a bachelor, also had a flat in Lambourn, which left three stable staff on site at Uplands – Delaney, Derek King and Richard Pitman. Their home was a shared caravan.

Delaney recalls how their meals were brought up to the caravan in a wheelbarrow, how the caravan was surrounded by thick beds of nettles and how, if they needed a loo, they had a straightforward choice. 'The woods were right behind us,' he said, 'or we could walk down to the Maltshovel pub for a pint and use their toilets.'

It was rough, no argument. Precious few lads of today would tolerate such conditions, but these three felt, for whatever reason, that they had a future with Fred Winter. In the case of Delaney and Pitman, at least, their fortitude was richly rewarded.

IO

The improbable dream

Jay Trump's life as a racehorse was unplanned. It might also have been extremely short. Bred through a chapter of accident and circumstance, he met with disaster and near-death on his first racecourse trial. He was also widely considered to be a useless rogue. This, however, is the horse responsible for one of the greatest romantic adventures that even the vivid history of the Grand National can boast. He is also the horse responsible for launching Fred Winter's training career in the most spectacular fashion, from which he was never to look back.

Jay Trump's National defied the dictates of record and reason. There was so much evidence for regarding it as an impossible dream and yet, as we have seen so often, the very word is anathema to Fred Winter. In this project he was helped by having as his partner a young American of similarly indomitable spirit. Tommy Smith's mother is quoted as saying of her son: 'Tell him he can't do something and he'll set out to prove to you that he can.' Fred's mother doubtless said much the same of her elder son; it is the sort of thing mothers are apt to say of wilful offspring. But in these two cases the words were prophetic.

Fred was still living at Oddington, seeing out the final days of his farewell riding season, when he took a transatlantic phone call. On the American end of the line was one Crompton Smith Junior, commonly known as Tommy. Fred had never heard of him. Tommy knew Fred only by reputation and through a newsreel of Mandarin's astonishing win in Paris, which he had watched, spellbound, while at the movies with his fiancée, Frances. On the way out of the cinema he had said to Frances: 'Of all the people in the world, I would most like to meet Fred Winter.'

The subject of the call was a scheme to aim an American horse at the Grand National. The horse's name was Jay Trump and Fred had heard of *him*. Only shortly before the call was placed Jay Trump had won the Maryland Hunt Cup for the second time. Fred, while far from intimate with the American racing scene (his one, whistle-stop riding trip to New York having given him no conception of the country Hunt circuit), knew enough to be confident that any horse capable of winning the Hunt Cup twice could, at the very least, jump and gallop.

At this trime Fred's training plans were seriously inhibited by lack of takers. He had precisely three horses, all at grass in his paddocks at Kitsbury. While his strict principles precluded touting for owners, here was a customer phoning him personally to seek a home for his obviously talented horse. It was not an opportunity to be lightly passed up. Tommy had begun by tentatively suggesting that he might send the horse to Ireland to be trained by his cousin, Dan Moore. Fred, realistically, said that if Jay Trump was a fast-ground horse, which virtually all American chasers are, the going in Ireland would not suit him. He added that it would also be more difficult, in Ireland, to qualify him for the National. He said he could take the horse himself and, as he was only just starting to train, could devote individual attention to the project. This, privately, was what Tommy had wanted him to say all along. He was now going to meet, even work with, his newsreel hero, even if the ultimate ambition at Aintree did prove inaccessible.

Arrangements were agreed there and then. The horse, and jockey, would come to England in July, by which time the Winters would be ensconced, if not exactly settled, at Uplands. Fred looked forward to seeing his new acquisition and to the prospect, albeit a distant one, of a National runner in his first season as a trainer. Had he known something of the Jay Trump story, he might have had serious misgivings.

Tommy Smith's bid to win at Aintree was much more than just the frivolous fancy of a privileged American to take home a slice of England's heritage. It was an obsession, passed down through the Smith generations. In the spring of 1965 Tommy was to attain the prize first sought by his grandfather more than half a century earlier.

Harry Worcester Smith could plainly be described as a wealthy mill owner from Massachusetts. This does him scant justice. He did, indeed, inherit a loom works previously owned by his father-in-law.

He added to it, acquisitively and ambitiously. Then, in mid-life, he invented and patented an automatic colour-weaving loom of incalculable use to the rag trade. This made him a very rich man and he cashed in his chips in the style of a gambler getting out on the crest of a run. His asking price for all his business concerns, and the patents, was $6 million and a major national concern happily paid up.

Harry Worcester was thus left, at the age of forty-five, with time and money to burn. He had no wish to invest in any other business; instead, he devoted himself to half a lifetime of horses. He would hunt, he would ride steeplechasing. He would go to England and win the Grand National. In truth he had never stinted himself on the horse front. For the previous twenty-five years he had been to the fore of American foxhunting and had done much to popularise steeplechasing. Fearless on horseback and intimidating to meet, he was one of the enduring characters of middle-American sporting society. Intolerant of any, horses or humans, who failed to meet his exacting standards, he was also demanding of himself in a gung-ho style. It is said he once rode an entire hunting season with a broken and plastered foot in a carpet slipper. He was equally dismissive when he suffered a punctured lung, quite determined that it should not curtail his life's passion. But, although he continued to ride to hounds, he was reluctantly obliged to accept that a man with a punctured lung, especially a man approaching the age of fifty, could not ride in the world's most punishing steeplechase. Having accepted this, Harry Worcester modified his Aintree plan. He would provide and prepare the horse, and his son, Crompton, would ride.

With this settled, a curious entourage of men and beasts disembarked from the *Lusitania* at Liverpool docks in the late summer of 1912. The Smiths, Harry Worcester and son Crompton, were accompanied by seventeen horses and seven negro handlers. For good measure they had a gamecock (presumably a family pet) and a sleek American car of a type seldom seen in England. They were bound for Ireland, where the idea was to train the horses for the Aintree race before selecting which of them should be ridden by Crompton. The carefully laid plan came to nothing, however. Crompton had a hunting accident, badly breaking a leg. Any other owner-trainer could have proceeded with preparations, simply substituting another jockey. The obsession of Harry Worcester Smith, however, debarred this, for he was interested only in having the first all-American runner in the great race. An English or Irish jockey would relegate the deed close to the commonplace. There was nothing for it but to abandon the project, yet Harry Worcester, being the man he was, did not allow his son to escape uncensured for his perceived stupidity in allowing a hunting horse to unship him so disastrously. He sent him home on a cattle ship!

It was not for another twenty-three years that the Smith family tree was extended and a new candidate for the Aintree dream came under orders. One of the first vivid memories in Tommy Smith's life is of the drawing-room at his parents' home in Middleburg, Virginia, and his grandfather standing, dauntingly erect, in front of the fireplace, above which hung a large, illustrated map of the Grand National course. His destiny was depicted in that memory, though for some years he rebelled against the force.

As a child Tommy was almost certainly scared of his grandfather, who spent a lot of time at their home, Featherbed Farm, and never hesitated to impose himself upon the scene. His ideas of living were spartan – no drinking or smoking and endless fish to eat – and his ideas of discipline were harsh. He would rap young Tommy's knuckles with a hunting crop at the first sign of insubordination.

The family obsession lived on, and Tommy could not avoid its grip. Probably against his will, although he was not old or strong enough to express it, he was introduced to foxhunting at the age of three. He recalled, years later, the sight of his grandfather setting off after the hounds with a sign pinned on his back proclaiming: '75 and still ticking'. Worse, there was constant teasing aimed in his direction by Harry Worcester, which riled Tommy's father and began to harden young Tommy's heart against this eccentric pursuit so beloved of his ancestors.

In 1945, at the age of eighty, Harry Worcester Smith died of a heart attack. Tommy was eight years old and his family life began to disintegrate. The days of prosperity were long gone and, amid the tightening of belts and anxieties over the future, his parents divorced. His father, invalided out of the military and a failure in steeplechasing administration, turned brokenly to drink before the inevitable split. He left Virginia and went back to Massachusetts. Tomy and his mother, Margot, heard from him only once, when he sent a messenger asking for one, much-missed possession. It was the map of Aintree, which still hung over the fireplace at Featherbed Farm, and it was amicably sent on to him.

This might have been the end of the story. With his grandfather dead, his father departed and even the constant reminder in the drawing-room gone for good, Tommy might have forgotten all about the Grand National, especially as his mother had been forced to sell the family's remaining horses and try to eke a living as a dairy farmer. Even Tommy's pony had passed away. He had to help with the milking when not at school and developed an aversion to cows to match his feelings about horses. He wanted nothing further to do with either farming or riding and buried himself in academic studies, at which he was more than adequately bright.

The rebellion began to relax when Margot remarried. Her new husband was steeped in hunting and racing and, to the family's audible relief, the cows disappeared from the farm and horses returned. Tommy's stepfather began to gently wean the boy back to riding. At first it was a difficult and delicate process, but eventually he interested him in showjumping and, on a horse called Golden Jane, Tommy Smith began to enjoy and succeed at competitive riding for the first time. In 1957, at the age of twenty, he rode in his first point-to-point. He fell and remounted twice. The third fall shook him up just too badly to continue. Only later did Tommy discover that his ride, offered to him when he turned up to spectate, had never jumped a fence before, and a week earlier had broken its owner's leg.

Far from deterring him, the experience instilled in Harry Worcester's grandson an absolute commitment to succeed at the game. He continued to ride bad horses because he convinced himself it was the best way to learn. He punished himself and he punished the horses by being excessively hard on them. He did it all with a swaggering cockiness which did not endear him to some; but he did it, in all probability, because he was still trying to break out of the inhibiting shadow of his grandfather and to establish his own identity.

He took up riding on pretty much a full-time basis in 1958. The next year he won the Maryland Hunt Cup on the first of four occasions. Now he was unarguably hooked on the game, and when an old friend of his mother's, Mary Stephenson, asked him to find her a horse to win the Hunt Cup, he immediately agreed. At the back of his mind, you may be sure, was the possibility, however remote, that if he was to find the right horse, Maryland might just lead to Liverpool.

Tommy chose to seek his horse in an area where the volume was plentiful but the talent was in poverty. He went to West Virginia, to the Charles Town track where his father had briefly been a patrol judge. He booked into a motel and began, with the thoroughness that

was to mark this story, to select by process of elimination. It proved
to be a prolonged and thankless task.

There are two racetracks in this racing 'commune' beneath the
Shenandoah Hills; they share 250 days of racing a year. The quality,
however, is poor. The line of training establishments attached to the
tracks housed such a proportion of lame, patched-up and over-raced
misfits that it was known locally as 'Cannery Row'.

Tommy inspected any number of candidates, and struck them off
his list, before one morning spotting a notice in the office of the
course secretary. It advertised a horse called Jay Trump. He asked
one or two people he had come to know and trust what they knew of
the horse and was instantly warned off. Jay Trump, they said, was a
villain and no self-respecting jockey would ride him after what he had
done to a popular and experienced rider called Willie Liddle. Gradually
Tommy was to piece together the story of Jay Trump, but it was a
long while before he learned all the more intimate details, such as the
accident of his conception. His dam, Be Trump, had exasperated
connections by returning barren from stud farms on several occasions.
Accorded one final mission, she refused even to board the horse box
and so was disgustedly turned out in a field where she had a resting
stallion, Tonga Prince, for company. Some while later the owner of
these two undistinguished horses noticed that Be Trump had developed a belly. She was confirmed to be in foal and the progeny was
named by the wife of the surprised handler. His name was Jay
Sensenich and, but for him, Jay Trump would never have got as far
as Maryland, let alone Lambourn.

Jay was evidently a man who devoted every hour of the day to
looking after his horses, regarding it as a lifestyle rather than a job,
and he brought his equine namesake along quietly. When the animal
was two years old, he sent him out on the Shenandoah track, telling
jockey Liddle that his ride was well-mannered and equable. Liddle,
just returning from a serious back injury, chose to believe him and
lived – just – to regret it.

Jay Trump had never encountered a whip before. Liddle did not
know this, and when he used his stick to correct some 'green'
wandering across the course, he accidently struck the horse in the
right eye, which was not a help. Half-blinded by the blow, not to
mention affronted and frightened, Jay Trump veered sharply left. The
running rail loomed up ahead and, instead of correcting course, he
elected to jump it, an achievement in itself for a raw two-year-old; as

he landed he made sickening, head-on contact with a floodlight pylon. Liddle was seriously injured and hospitalised for several months. Jay Trump was so badly lacerated, his joints so hideously severed, that many of those who gathered at the scene thought the only humane course was to put him down immediately. But Jay Sensenich had never lost a horse and did not wish to start now. The course vet saved Jay Trump's life in a delicate two-and-a-half-hour operation; Jay himself then made the horse's life worth living.

It was many months before he was fit to race. Then, of course, no one wanted to ride him. Jay Trump had been blacklisted for his treatment of Liddle. When Sensenich did persuade the young, the ignorant or the simply useless to get on board, his horse showed him nothing, not least because the other jockeys would force him out of the race. In fours starts as a two-year-old, he beat only one horse home.

Things were not going well for Sensenich. He now had to sell to survive and, regretfully aware that Jay Trump was a liability, he posted the 'for sale' notice in the secretary's office. It was then that Tommy Smith heard the alarming – and probably embellished – details of Jay Trump's career and struck him off his list of potential purchases.

Smith's search went fruitlessly on, taking him through the barns of one lame animal after another and, on every race day, down to the starting stalls to scrutinise the build, head and walk of the runners. On one such day he was attracted by a particular horse – not by his coat, for this featured a long and dreadful scar, or by his health, for he was bony and grimy. It was his head, intelligent and honest, and his superior eye which singled out the animal. Tommy was vaguely startled, when he checked the animal against his racecard, to find that it was Jay Trump.

The upshot was that Jay Trump ran his best race so far, finishing second over a mile, and that despite all the discouraging noises made by everyone whose opinion he sought, Tommy paid Jay Sensenich $2,000 – not insubstantial, thirty years ago, for a horse of little known ability. The truth of it was that Tommy had fallen in love with the horse, a state of affairs which was to continue for some years.

Back in Maryland, Mrs Stephenson was at least superficially satisfied with the horse Tommy brought back for her, reasoning that he might make do as a hunter if the main objective proved out of the question. Initially this seemed likely to be the case. Jay Trump's first race over

obstacles was in a ladies' point-to-point, in which he was beaten sixty
lengths by the only other runner. This was the first and only time that
Mrs Stephenson allowed anyone other than Tommy Smith to ride the
horse; a week later, on the racecourse in the foothills of the Blue
Ridge Mountains, where once his grandfather had hunted, Tommy
won a steeplechase of some local prestige on Jay Trump. Those who
had seen his two races, seven days apart, could scarcely credit the
transformation. What became clear, as the races passed and the
victories increased in volume and value, was that these two, horse and
jockey, were a partnership with that indefinable something which
made them extremely hard to beat.

It was April 1963 when Jay Tump won his first Maryland Hunt
Cup, in a course record time. A year later, despite rain-softened
ground which was thought to be against him, he won both the Hunt
Cup and Maryland's two other major steeplechasing prizes. There was
nothing left to achieve in America and, to Tommy's great relief, Mrs
Stephenson proposed an assault on Aintree before he could raise the
subject himself. There was now a sense of increased urgency about
the idea, too, for although, in 1965, Jay Trump would still be young
for an Aintree horse at eight, it had been announced that the course
was to be sold off to make way for a housing development. Un-
thinkably, this next Grand National was to be the last. This, of
course, is a threat which was uttered several times in subsequent years
and always the course and the race survived. Tommy Smith was not
to know that, and he launched into his plans with a gusto that made
onlookers feel tired.

Having, to his great delight, acquired F. T. Winter as trainer, he
researched in detail such subjects as nutrition and the comparability of
horse feeds in America and Britain. Then he organised the transport
and struck a hitch. Pan-Am had agreed to fly Jay Trump and his rider
to London on the maiden transatlantic flight of their new 707 aircraft.
They built a special stall for their famous horse ... but it was too
small. The error was only discovered when the would-be passengers
arrived at New York's Kennedy Airport, which meant simply that the
plane had to leave without them. Tommy and his horse squatted for
two nights in the airport's animal shelter, with some noisy African
monkeys as their fellow guests, before BOAC could be persuaded to
construct another stall, this one made to measure, and take them on
their next flight to London.

After twenty-four hours cooped up in the aircraft, the precious cargo landed at Heathrow close to midnight in a soft, English midsummer. Frances, who had recently become Mrs Smith, awaited the arrival, and a horse box was at hand for the short journey to Lambourn. Despite the hour, Tommy Carey, the Winter's experienced head lad, was up and about to greet them at Uplands. The horse was assigned a box and bedded down for the night; his exhausted jockey retired, with his new wife, to their pre-booked room at the Red Lion Hotel, a white-painted pub which faces the church in Lambourn's village square.

If, for Tommy Smith, fulfilment was now closer at hand than he had ever realistically expected, it remained in the middle distance so far as Fred Winter was concerned. His position was simply this: with his training career in its infancy, he considered himself fortunate to be sent any horse, let alone a Maryland Hunt Cup winner. It was not now, however, simply a case of filling in the hours and days before the National, putting the jockey on top and awaiting the acclaim. As Brian Delaney later observed: 'Of all the things the guv'nor achieved, winning the National with Jay Trump in his first year was the best. He not only had to train the horse to jump round Aintree, he had to train the jockey as well . . . and Tommy Smith was not the easiest to get along with.'

Fred, having made some discreet enquiries about the human and equine visitors he had agreed to take on, was expecting the worst. He recalled: 'I had been pre-warned about Tommy. I'd been told he was rather difficult to deal with and very self-opinionated, had his own ideas. So when he first came over I must admit that I rather had my back up before we met. The yard was in a complete shambles, because we had only just moved in, and I think I had eight or ten horses. I had told Tommy that if he wished to ride out, we would go out at 7.30 am. That morning, by the time he arrived, we had been walking round the yard for two or three minutes, all mounted. I said to him: "Mr Smith, when we say 7.30, we mean 7.30 and not 7.35."'

Fred Winter always has had the ability to narrow his eyes and deliver a truly withering remark without raising his voice. This, evidently, was such an instance. Mr T. Smith, in fact, quickly felt thoroughly out of place on his first morning at Uplands – as one would, dressed in cords, scuffed cowboy boots and a felt sombrero. Not only this, but the first horse he was asked to sit on tolerated him for a matter of seconds before, with one buck, depositing him unceremoniously on the stable yard under the unsympathetic gaze of the lads. By a quirky coincidence, this horse was Anglo, recently sent up from Ryan Price's dispersed stable and not thought to be anything out of the ordinary. He was to win the 1966 Grand National. Tommy's discomfort was complete when, to calm his fluttering nerves, he lit a cigarette as the little string of horses walked up the lane towards the downs. That withering voice penetrated his eardrums again: 'Mr Smith, when we ride, we don't smoke.'

There were good reasons, on both sides, that first morning for believing that this was an ill-fated project, doomed to acrimonious failure. But things could only improve and, gratifyingly quickly, they did so. Fred came round to seeing that Tommy, for all his Americanisms, was a bright and analytical young man who was going into this unusual venture in complete earnest. Tommy, like so many before and since, came to know Fred as a kind, thoughtful and thorough man whose gruffness was a veneer but who, nonetheless, would never suffer fools.

They had their differences, of course. No matter the weather, Tommy insisted on continuing to wear corduroy trousers rather than jodphurs for riding out; he said that jodphurs made him uncomfortable. He did make concessions, however. The sombrero went – and the cowboy boots were replaced by new, expensive and gleaming riding boots. Tommy had been struck by the trim, polished image of his tutor and had no wish to be considered a vagabond.

For the first two months of their stay, Tommy and Frances lived in the Red Lion. It was a genial place and comfortable enough, although, as Fred mused afterwards: 'Not quite what a young American lady would be used to.' They were given a room on the top floor, beamed and quaint, but it is unlikely they were taken in by its description as the bridal suite. Now and again they spent an evening at one of the other local pubs, notably the Maltshovel, hidden away on one of the dead-end roads into Upper Lambourn village and, for decades now, the haunt of lads from the Walwyn yard, and more recently from Winter's too. It seemed to Tommy that, no matter what the make-up of the evening's gathering in 'the Malt', the conversation would, inevitably and eventually, get around to Fred Winter and Mandarin. It was a local obsession to match his own, not-so-local obsession.

In September, or what he would have called the start of the fall, Tommy and his wife moved out of the Red Lion (seen off royally by all accounts) and into a rented cottage at the far end of Upper Lambourn. They could make a home there, and with two dogs and a

Grand National painting or two they were contented. Frances had overcome her initial unease in England and grown to enjoy the village lifestyle; Tommy was happy just riding to Uplands each morning on his newly acquired bicycle and immersing himself in the Jay Trump mission.

Things, at first, moved too slowly for Tommy's liking and this might easily have been a source of discord between him and Fred. It had been Britain's driest July in half a century; all racecourses were too firm for comfort and most were like roads. Fred did not have many horses and he refused to risk any of them on hard ground. Tommy failed, initially, to understand this. So far as he could ascertain, this was just the sort of ground on which Jay Trump had done almost all of his racing and winning in the States. He was impatient to get an English run under his belt but Fred, intent on building a stable of fit horses rather than knocking them down for no reason, insisted on waiting.

The race he had in mind for Jay Trump was the Autumn Trial Chase at Sandown Park in late October. By then, he reasoned, there would be some give in the ground. As it transpired, any change from the drought conditions which had rendered the previous two months of racing so prohibitive was marginal, but the plan was allowed to proceed. Two weekends before the race – enough time, Fred thought, to allow it all to digest – Fred and Tommy went to the Sandown course, set enviably in the heart of London's stockbroker belt, and walked every inch of it, the trainer giving his jockey a complete insight as to the way each fence and each turn should be approached. Tommy found the procedure both fascinating and invaluable; it was a routine they were to perpetuate, each time Jay Trump was due to run. It was also symptomatic of the depth of planning which went into this operation.

Tommy had taken to travelling to race meetings with Fred. In the car he would press him on various aspects of riding. This, to those who know the Winter mentality, is a particularly fascinating part of this story, for normally Fred would shrink away from much car conversation at all, let alone at such a philosophical level. Yet with Tommy, his American pupil, it was evidently different. Once, according to Smith, Fred said to him on the subject of a jockey's nerve: 'Courage is like a bank account. If you draw too many cheques, sooner or later one bounces.'

The American became increasingly impatient for some activity and taxed Fred on the subject of foxhunting. He was implicitly banned forthwith. 'Far too dangerous,' was the trainer's assessment, plain indication that, even at this early stage, he had begun to see that the feasibility level of this crazy plan was remarkably high.

Came the night before the Sandown Park race, and Fred and Tommy sat down together in the kitchen at Uplands to go through the form of the rest of the field. It did not take them long – there were only two other runners and one, by all known evidence, was next to useless. The press and bookmakers sided with a horse called Comforting Wave. They tended to denigrate the American reputation of Jay Trump and cast grave aspersions on his credentials for jumping a course like Sandown. They were proved emphatically wrong.

Fred had given his jockey copious instructions, as Tommy recalls: 'I never asked him how he thought the horse was going to run. He told me to let him get the feel of racing over British fences but not to worry if he lost ground and not to push him. If he seemed to like what was happening, Fred said, then you might think about doing something after the three quick fences down by the station, but if he doesn't seem to get the knack of it, then wait for another day.'

However, as Fred later reported: 'He was a bit sticky over the first four fences but after that he was brilliant. Everything went smoothly. Tommy did everything I told him.' This, of course, was very high praise for Fred Winter to be handing out, both to horse and jockey, and he admitted to being surprised by the cosy way in which they won by five lengths. What surprised Tommy was the deafening reception which greeted him as he walked Jay Trump into Sandown's prettily kept winners' enclosure. He knew his horse had come to England with a bit of a reputation, but surely this was overdoing English emotion, after a relatively bloodless win in a three-horse race? What he did not immediately appreciate, which the crowd and his trainer most certainly had, was that he had just ridden Fred Winter's first winner as a trainer.

11

Jay Trump's National

'Looking back on it,' says Brian Delaney, a pleasurable nostalgia in his voice, 'there were plenty of times when we thought Jay Trump would never even go to the National, let alone win it.'

During the course of this first season at Uplands, Delaney had been assigned to the American horse. He 'did' him whenever Tommy Smith was not there to supervise Jay Trump himself; he took him to the races and led him up; he formed, in fact, a close attachment to the horse and a relationship of mutual respect with the rider which subsequently prompted Smith to offer him a job back in Maryland.

Still living rough in the caravan which made do as a lads' hostel, Delaney was very much a part of the team which, under Fred Winter's calm and organised direction, overcame all manner of obstacles to the Aintree dream. Even Fred, however, could do next to nothing about the virus which, with a pitiless sense of timing, swept through Lambourn in early March. In these enlightened times of constant advances in medical science, still no one has found a solid protection against equine flu, or even a rapid cure. It attacks without warning, summarily demobilising the grandest and the most modest of stable yards. This is one area of horse racing which is totally democratic: class and wealth count for nothing against the onset of the virus. Frequently trainers will know nothing of the menace in their midst until a horse, or probably several horses, run unaccountably badly. Only then will the veterinary tests reveal the worst. The 1965 virus in Lambourn, however, was a particularly virulent strain. There was no mistaking its effect.

'We did not have flu vaccine in those days,' explains Delaney. 'Almost every horse in the yard was laid low, candles hanging from their noses. There was nothing for it but to let the thing run its course. At first only two of the horses escaped – Solbina and Jay Trump, and with the National only a few weeks away, the American horse had to be isolated.'

And so a story already overloaded with drama stood threatened by a tragic end, the sabotaging of many months of scrupulous effort by a malevolent visitor, unseen and unwelcome. Tommy Smith, from whom all cockiness had long since evaporated in a regime of single-minded self-denial, saw his dream about to die, not through an unfit jockey (as had befallen his grandfather) but a sick horse. As the days passed and he waited for the virus to strike at Jay Trump, Tommy himself became sick with worry.

To this point everything had been going well, horse and jockey learning together in an unfamiliar environment to which, after the inevitable acclimatisation, both had adjusted remarkably readily. Tommy had initially been completely ignorant of English racing routines, and there was a limit to how many situations even Fred could foresee. So, for instance, when he weighed out before the Sandown Park race which was Jay Trump's British debut, he walked directly to the parade ring with his saddle, and stood alone there for a good ten minutes, quite bemused. Nobody had told him that, unlike in America, British riders give their saddles to a stable representative and then wait to be called communally to the ring, shortly before the off-time. He was a fast learner, though. He was also aware that, in Fred Winter, he had acquired the best possible tutor for his chosen ambition. Indeed, when he jumped off Jay Trump in the Sandown winners' enclosure that October afternoon, the crowd still cheering the first Winter training success, he told the assembled press: 'It was Fred's race. Fred was riding all the way.'

Fred had formulated a provisional plan to take Jay Trump to Aintree for the November meeting which still existed at the time. There he thought he could run in the Becher Chase over the National fences and all concerned would find out a great deal more about the viability of a Grand National bid. After Sandown, he abandoned the plan. Jay Trump had shown him just how well he could jump English-style fences – and Sandown has some of the trappiest in the country – so he saw nothing to be gained, and quite a bit to be lost, by subjecting horse and rider to the Aintree experience at such a comparatively early stage of the enterprise.

Tommy's analytical mind did not agree with everything that Fred proposed – at least, not at once – but he had rapidly come to terms with the fact that his trainer was the boss. He was grateful, too, for Fred's style, which was to offer a few, well-chosen words when he deemed it necessary. Neither of them was the sort to be frivolous with conversation, but Smith said: 'I have never worked with anyone in my life who could instil you with so much confidence by being so helpful and determined. He, at least, appeared to be confident that the job was going to be done properly. He had a marvellous understanding of what a rider is feeling in the paddock as he gets up to go out. We would have worked it all out the night before a race and Fred would be relaxed and would never give any further instructions.'

This, of course, dated in part back to Fred's own riding career and his dislike of being tied down by complicated orders in the parade ring. Ryan Price had always respected this. One day at Sandown, when Price let Fred off one of his runners to ride for a particularly prestigious owner, there had been another example of it. Dorothy Price recalls: 'The trainer of this horse was babbling on at Fred when he was loudly interrupted by his owner saying: "You needn't say any more. Winter is a master of his craft."' The speaker was the then Prime Minister, Winston Churchill.

And so, as a trainer, Fred had developed a relaxed style with his jockey in the paddock, which might involve a little idle banter with the owners and would invariably conclude, as the call came to mount, with a simple yet heartfelt 'God bless'. It was a style much appreciated by Mr C. Smith Junior during these educational outings on various of England's racecourses.

After Sandown came Windsor in November. The ground was still too fast for many of the leading staying chasers and Jay Trump had only four opponents, none of whom could match his relentless jumping and galloping. He won, comfortably, by a length and a half, and although a significant lobby in the racing media still felt, and wrote, that he seemed short of speed, the bookmakers' reaction was more positive. Jay Trump was installed as the ante-post favourite to win the Grand National, at 18–1. Tommy Smith could not believe it. The mission ahead remained enormous, in his mind, and he probably regarded it as more like 18–1 against getting round Aintree – if, that is, they even got to the race.

Four months still remained before the Aintree meeting, and an awful lot could go wrong in that time. The weather was just one of the imponderables which complicated life for Fred and Tommy. In order to be fairly handicapped for the National, Jay Trump had to run three times in Britain before the end of the calendar year. A month of unsuitably soft ground after the Windsor race persuaded Fred to wait for Christmas and aim high – at Kempton's King George VI Chase on Boxing Day. But on Christmas Eve there was snow, and on Christmas night a thick frost. Boxing Day dawned with London frozen up and the stewards at Kempton Park facing a serious dilemma – abandon the card and sacrifice their biggest and best meeting of the year or take a chance, pass the course fit and risk a stream of non-runners? They opted for the latter course, to the enormous relief of Winter, who had no other engagements for Jay Trump before the handicap deadline. If Kempton had been abandoned, he would have carried automatic top weight at Aintree, which might easily have put paid to all the hopes.

The surface at Kempton was barely raceable. Some plainly felt it was unfit, for the feared flood of withdrawals duly materialised. Only two runners stood their ground for the King George, and to this extent the big race was a mockery. To this day it has never had so few runners. So far as Fred was concerned, however, more important than winning, even against one opponent, were the benefits from simply taking part. He was not dismayed that Jay Trump was well beaten by the favourite, Frenchman's Cove, for he had never raced in such conditions and was unsuited to a right-handed course. He was irritated and said so, when, in trying to make up an improbable deficit on the leader, Tommy drove Jay Trump into the third last fence, the horse predictably slipping and almost falling. 'Get round safely and come back wiser' was how Fred viewed the day, and Tommy was sharply apprised of his error. 'If you did something in a race he didn't like,' he later confessed, 'Fred didn't wait until tomorrow to tell you.'

The frost lingered stubbornly. It was not a freeze-up to rival that of two winters earlier, but it was sufficient to wipe out the racing programme for much of January. Fred's string had steadily grown through the course of this initial term and he had begun to turn out regular winners. When racing resumed, he had it in mind to give Jay Trump two further runs before the National (for which he had been allotted a reasonable 11 stone 6 lb) and he first found a good opportunity for him at Newbury. It was an amateur riders' race, competitive enough with fourteen runners, but Jay Trump just out-jumped and outclassed them all. Tommy, who had fretted so much during the enforced inactivity that he had booked a ski-ing trip, indignantly vetoed by his trainer, was pleased and relieved to be back in the thick of things.

It was about now that the concentrated coaching began, with Aintree specifically in mind. It was also about now that Fred had some fleeting misgivings about the nerve of his pupil. He explains: 'Tommy refused to ride any horse other than Jay Trump, though he was offered a number of rides. One began to have doubts about his courage and I remember a day at Windsor when he saw seven or eight falls and made a remark which sort of strengthened one's suspicions. But in fact I came to realise he actually had more guts in refusing to take other rides. He believed he had come for only one reason, to win the Grand National, and he was not going to take a chance until he had fulfilled that.'

Perhaps with this in mind, Fred gave an interesting quote to the press following the Newbury race. He had, hitherto, been deliberately low-key about Jay Trump's prospects in the National, but this fluent victory had plainly enthused him. 'If I still had my nerves,' said Fred, 'I would like to ride him at Aintree myself.'

All of Fred's tutorage regarding the big race concentrated on one essential. He insisted that Tommy should keep Jay Trump to the inside rail, just as he had done in his riding days. There, he told Tommy, the drops may be slightly bigger but you are always saving ground and, in addition, you invariably avoid the carnage of fallen horses and jockeys. Help came from other sources, too. Bryan Marshall, whose jockeyship had once been idolised by Fred himself, was training in Lambourn now, and a neighbour of Tommy's. As genial and approachable then as he is today, and as committed as ever to promoting the art of race-riding, Bryan offered his new, young, American friend some wise and well-meant advice on the use of the whip, riding a finish and general positioning – this despite the fact that he had recently acquired a horse to run in his wife's colours at Aintree, against Jay Trump.

Tommy also got to know and like Keith Piggott, the training brother of Lester. Keith had a film projector and a collection of recordings of recent Grand Nationals. He lent Tommy the whole package and, night after night, he and Fred would pore over the films. 'Fred would point out people doing things right or making mistakes,' said Tommy. His attention was specifically drawn to Bobby Beasley's riding of Nicolaus Silver in 1961, Winter's role model of how to ride Aintree.

'Fred would say to me: "They will go a terrific gallop the first mile. This is because they are mad,"' related Smith. '"You get your horse in a nice, comfortable pace. Just sit there and hunt. The object of the game is to get round." I used to say I would never make it, but Fred always managed to minimise the tension somehow. It's a fact that very few great people, especially sportsmen, are articulate and very few of them know why they do what they do. We all know that Fred is a great rider but he is also a great teacher, and he makes you understand what you've got to do and why.'

But then the cough struck. It came with devastating speed, eighteen days before the Grand National. In next to no time, operations at Uplands had virtually ceased. Fred knew he had to work fast to protect his healthy horses – all two of them! 'As soon as the coughing broke out, and it was really bad that year, I put Jay Trump in some separate boxes out at the back of the stables, with Solbina for company. I was going round the yard twice a day to see the patients. It took about ten days for a horse to lose the cough, and they were very weak afterwards.' In other words, if Jay Trump had contracted it then, the Grand National could be forgotten.

Brian Delaney, who was as anxious as anyone about the impending disaster, takes up the story. 'We all felt helpless, really, having put in so much work towards this one end. Then one morning Solbina coughed. We all thought that there was no escape at that point. Ten days before the National Jay Trump went to Worcester for his final prep-race, and ran well below par. It seemed that he had gone down just like the others.'

There was a gloomy silence in the group which stood around Jay Trump that day. Words were unnecessary. Everybody sensed that the worst sort of defeat, the one over which you have no control, was now confronting them. Tommy Smith was as downcast as anyone, as he was entitled to be after his horse had trailed in a listless and remote fifth. But he was not about to give up on the dream just yet.

Across the lane from his cottage in Upper Lambourn, Tommy had located a disused barn within the property that, these days, forms part of Jenny Pitman's training set-up at Weathercock House. Jay Trump was moved in there on the night following his flop at Worcester. Before he entered, Tommy thoroughly disinfected the place. For the next ten days he allowed nobody near his horse, with the occasional exception of the trainer. Fred related: 'Tommy looked after the horse entirely. I used to go down each morning and evening, and stand in a tray of disinfectant. If Tommy gave the thumbs-up sign, I wouldn't go near him. He used to go up the gallops by himself and, on work mornings, we used to rustle up what we could to do a gallop with Jay Trump.'

Although the Worcester race and the appearance of the horse convinced Fred that he had, indeed, contracted 'a slight touch of the virus', the splendid isolation was a success in that his health did not deteriorate. Which is more than could be said of Tommy Smith. Racked by the stress of crossing the road each morning with the constant dread of hearing that barking cough which would have signalled the end of the line, Tommy lost more weight than was good for him, developed a sinus condition and suffered headaches and insomnia. When the time finally came to make the long journey north-west to Liverpool, he was feeling thoroughly ill.

Jay Trump had been pushed out in the betting to 25-1 following the Worcester race. When Fred and Tommy arrived at Aintree on the Thursday, the opening day of the meeting, they privately thought the bookies would be far from incautious in lengthening the odds still further. It was snowing and the course was riding soft. Jay Trump would hate it. Tommy looked crestfallen, the worries of the past fortnight now pressing down upon him, and even the encouraging words of Brian Delaney could not restore his lost confidence.

On Friday the weather improved; but Tommy Smith's opinion of his victory prospects did not. This was the day, captured for posterity on TV news and by many still photographers, when Fred Winter held his teach-in on the Aintree course. Fence by fence they went around, the jockey not bothering to conceal his horror at the size and scope of these mighty obstacles that he was seeing for the first time. At Bechers his face fell to his cowboy boots. 'Right then,' he said later, 'I think we all decided we were in way over our heads.'

There was nothing private about this vital walk of the course. Along with Fred, who led the way like a pied piper, Tommy and the horse's American owner, Mrs Stephenson, walked a procession of cameramen, news reporters, Fred Winter fans, visiting Americans and curious hangers-on. Those who were within earshot would have heard Fred's repeated message – keep to the inside – interspersed with comments about how best to approach each particular fence.

On Friday afternoon Tommy did not attend the racing. He went instead to a cinema in Liverpool. His choice of film was illuminating – it was Frank Sinatra in *None but the Brave*.

The Adelphi Hotel was, as usual, crammed to its ancient and elegant chandeliers with the racing fraternity, from nobility to nobodies. Tommy Smith's mother Margot had flown over for the race and she was staying there. So too was Mrs Stephenson, her oldest friend, installed in a suite and awaiting her most exciting day. But Tommy and Frances had opted for somewhere quieter, a small bed-and-breakfast hotel far from the Adelphi's madding crowd. They might as well not have bothered. The sleep that Tommy craved was reluctant to come. His sinuses were still playing up. His head ached. He probably wanted, more than anything, for the next twenty-four hours to be over.

Saturday morning began dry, bright and breezy. The course was drying. More good news was evident when Tommy, with some trepidation, made his way into Jay Trump's box, shortly after 7 am. There was neither sign nor sound of the virus. They had escaped. His heart and hopes began to lift as he gave the horse his final, gentle exercise, watched over all the while by Fred. Then Tommy returned to rest for an hour or two. Fred told him that when he himself had ridden in the race, he always thought it a good idea to share a bottle of champagne with a couple of the other jockeys before leaving for the course. 'It won't do you any harm,' he said, 'and might do away with some of the tension.' His jockey politely declined the offer.

In the weeks leading up to Aintree, Tommy Smith had put himself through a rigorous training regime. He did an exercise routine every morning, went running on the Berkshire roads each afternoon, and found time to cycle almost 20 miles a day. He had severely cut down his smoking. And he had drunk no alcohol at all. He did not intend to break with discipline just yet. He had only to look, and listen, when he finally entered the Aintree weighing-room, to know that not all the jockeys had been so abstemious. Some, in the great tradition of pre-National binges, had apparently been up most of the night. Dave Dick, indomitably cheerful and nervelessly anecdotal as he awaited his thirteenth Grand National ride, was undoubtedly among them. Tommy sat silently. His hands were shaking.

Alongside him on the bench sat John Ciechanowski, a Polish expatriate later to begin training in England. He was well into his forties and extremely short-sighted, yet proud and excited enough about this, his first National ride, to make an impromptu speech about the glories of the day. Few might have listened to him, too immersed in their own worries. But Tommy listened, and suddenly recalled a story Fred Winter had told, against himself.

It related to 1948, to the disjointed start of his jump-racing career, when he was struggling to resume after his long lay-off with a broken back and suffering nothing more sharply than sheer, hollow fear. It related particularly to a day at Hereford when Fred sat in a funk, as Tommy was now, waiting to go out for a hurdle race and genuinely frightened of a fall. Alongside him in the stark weighing-room was the man who was to win the race, Jack Moloney. He was well past the age of fifty yet remained unshakeably brave and enthusiastic. He would not have known it, but Jack Moloney shamed Fred into action when he was first out of the door as the jockeys were called. 'If that man can get up and walk out like that with no nerves at all,' he demanded of himself, 'what the hell is wrong with you, Winter?'

The memory of that tale, and the sight of the short-sighted, animated Pole next to him, drove the fear away from Tommy Smith. He became calmer, more rational and altogether more content as he contemplated the ride he had dreamed of for so many years.

After all this preparation, all the striving of the Smiths over three generations, all the hazards that Fred and his team had somehow overcome in their young but now trim and developing yard, the race itself was odds-on to be an anti-climax. But it was not. All those who were there, or who saw it on television, or who have watched it on video since (as I have done many times) will concur that it was one of the most stirring, gut-wrenching Nationals there has ever been. And, in a quite quirky coincidence, the horse which Jay Trump held off, in a desperate finish, was called Freddie!

There were many Americans in the crowd, almost all of whom had invested in Jay Trump. There were many reminders for Tommy, had he paid heed to them, of the family obsession which had been the original driving force behind this crazy plan. But he put them all out of his head. 'Anyone who has time to think romantic thoughts has no business riding in this race,' he said later. He was blinkered, single-minded, his nerve now cool but his will to win hot. He was matched in this by the horse underneath him. Together they put the carefully laid plan into glorious operation.

Tommy Smith later explained: 'I had spent so much time with Fred and we had gone over it so much that it was as if I was not really riding that horse. Fred had impressed himself so much on my personality, it was as if the whole thing was detached and separate from me and as if he rode in the race himself. I just watched it happen.'

Prosaic it may sound but the pair, an improbable match, certainly had developed such an understanding that, during the race itself, it sometimes seemed as if telepathy existed between them. Fred Winter once told me, much later in his training career, that he was an unemotional sort when at the races: 'It's not very professional for a trainer to scream and shout, is it?' That day at Aintree, however, Fred did his share of shouting from the grandstands, and although there was no way that Tommy Smith, far down below, could hear his master, he responded – never more so than in the final, churning yards of the run-in with the favourite, Freddie, closing valiantly yet again. There were 200 yards to run and Tommy had just hit Jay Trump, with the whip in his right hand. Whether or not it is possible that the horse remembered his racecourse debut at Shenandoah all those years earlier, he resented it, shying away and flashing his tail. He was going to be beaten, and certainly would have been if Tommy had hit him even once more.

Up on the stand an anguished Fred bellowed instinctively: 'Put the whip down!' Obediently, 200 yards from the winning post, Tommy Smith put down the stick and pushed out Jay Trump with what remained of his strength. The horse, confronting failure, stretched out once more and the triumph was his – and Tommy's, and Fred's. The most protracted, dramatic story in Grand National history was over.

12

For the second time, and the last . . .

Fred Winter undoubtedly would have attracted the patrons to fill his yard anyway; his gift with horses would have seen to that. But the Jay Trump adventure certainly cut down the anxious hours of waiting. Soon after the Grand National was won, Uplands had the 'No vacancies' sign up, all forty-three boxes occupied.

The yard that Fred had hovered over, declined and then fortuitously inherited from a friend whose outlook had lowered was a thriving concern well before its logical time. The progression from riding to training is fraught, as several household names have discovered in more recent years. Jonjo O'Neill trained only three winners in his first season, Bob Champion struggled on with poor horses and few returns and John Francome gave up, admitting that it was 'the first thing at which I have ever felt a failure'.

Fred had no time for self-doubt. That initial season he was hectic on two fronts – converting the jungle and jumble into a stable yard to satisfy his tidy mind, and piloting the Jay Trump team into uncharted territory. Most men would have fallen down on at least one side of the job, but not this man. 'Di and I never knew what hard work was until that season,' he later admitted. But it was work which he was never to resent or regret, for it set him up in a home and yard from which he was never to move, or have any inclination to move, until his training days ended.

As Diana confirms: 'Jay Trump really set it up for us. The first year had been hard, especially getting the house and garden into any sort of shape, and we had both been surprised at how few horses we were sent. It all changed after the National, and soon it was a case of having to be selective.'

Fred was to be selective for the rest of his long years in the game. He did not, unlike some trainers, enjoy taking in horses whose pot-hunting owners were simply dissatisfied with their lack of success in their present yard; on a number of occasions, indeed, he turned down a consignment of fresh blood, some of it unquestionably with ability. Fickle owners who came on the telephone to Uplands expecting their horses to be welcomed enthusiastically by Winter were, more often than not, given a curt, dismissive reply.

Fred liked owners, or prospective owners, who asked him to find them a horse, gave him a ceiling price and left him to do the rest. He was not infallible but he had some notable successes in the buying department, not always with the limitless resources that jealous rivals might assume he had at his disposal. In 1968 he was asked by a woman in Oxfordshire to find her a horse, with the proviso that she could not stretch to more than £1,000. Even in those days this was a pittance with which to go searching for a horse which might win a race or two and Fred might have been entitled to tell the woman so. But whereas Fred could be brusque to the point of rudeness with men who he felt were wasting his time, he always could both charm and be charmed by the ladies. He went to Ascot Sales and picked out a three-year-old who had won a bad seller on the flat. He paid a mere 500 guineas for Soloning and likened his appearance, at the time, to 'a rabbit'. But Fred had seen that indefinable something in the look of this modest animal, and his intuition, and the owner's brave outlay, were triumphantly vindicated. At the 1970 Cheltenham Festival, Soloning won the Arkle Chase, the 2-mile championship race for novices. Two seasons later, carrying 12 stone 1 lb, he returned to the festival and won the Cathcart Chase. In four seasons of racing he won his grateful owner more than £13,000.

'To be a top trainer,' observed Fred's bother John, 'you have to possess an inborn instinct to know a horse's mind. It is not a skill you can learn, it is a gift – and Fred relied on his instinct to the full.'

Nobody was more pleased than John about Fred's successful switch to training. The year of 1965 was a momentous one for him too – in July he took out a licence to train on the flat, which he was to do for twenty years, and in November he married and moved to Newmarket. John remained, however, his elder brother's greatest fan, and there was not a trace of resentment about being in Fred's shadow. 'I remember being at a party one evening,' explains John, 'when I found myself talking to a man who turned out to be Dirk Bogarde's brother. He was full of jealousy because he was not rich and famous. That sort of jealousy never occurred to me.'

In Fred's first season, 1964–65, he trained twenty-five winners, a princely figure for anyone's debut. The number of winners was to rise each season until 1971 when, for the first time, F. T. Winter was champion trainer. Still, perfectionist that he was, Fred intently picked holes in his own performance during the early years. 'I think I made a lot of mistakes through hurrying too much at first,' he confessed. 'All owners want quick results, but some horses need much more time than you realise.'

Back in 1965, however, no one would have listened to Fred's self-recriminations after his remarkable feat with Jay Trump. John Law-rence, drawing on his own experiences as an amateur rider, had been very sceptical about Tommy Smith's insistence on riding only one horse. He did not believe he would be sufficiently race-fit. After the National, however, he wrote: 'Tommy Smith and Jay Trump proved once again that to those who dare, nothing is impossible . . . seldom in all its long history has the Grand National been won more gloriously or in the face of greater odds.'

Those in Lambourn who had harboured similar reservations about the amateur rider and his dubiously bred American horse, reasoning that even Fred Winter could not work miracles, quickly forgot any such heresy as they launched into the village's biggest celebration since Mandarin had won in France. As the horse returned to Uplands an American flag, borrowed from a nearby military base, fluttered proudly and a banner proclaimed: 'Welcome home the mighty Trump'.

In the Maltshovel pub, landlord Tommy Dearie, a Scotsman who rode on the flat until breaking his spine, and his wife Di prepared for an invasion in their curiously clubby establishment, inhabited almost exclusively by stable-lads. They were not disappointed. There are racing lads in Lambourn who drink ritually in 'the Malt' every lunchtime and evening, and then there are those who will go through the doors of this converted seventeenth-century bakehouse once or twice a season. That night there were no absentees. 'We drank the pub dry,' recalls Brian Delaney with the satisfaction of a job well done.

There was a postscript to the Jay Trump story. He had already conquered Maryland and Aintree, and Fred believed him capable of completing an unimaginable treble in Paris. The Grand Steeplechase de Paris, to this day known disrespectfully in England as 'Mandarin's race', was scheduled for late June. Having satisfied himself, in the space of two or three weeks, that Jay Trump's health and spirits had not suffered the common post-National depression, Fred proposed this new, audacious, international challenge. Tommy Smith was entitled to decline and settle for what he had achieved, but he was not that kind of man. The plans were hatched in the now customary Winter–Smith detail.

This project did not have a glorious ending, merely a gallant one, but it was probably the making of Brian Delaney. Jay Trump was to go to France six weeks before the big race in order to acclimatise, school over the very different French fences and have a run, at Auteuil, as part of his education. Well-travelled though the former rogue of Shenandoah now was, he needed an escort and Brian was delegated to travel with him. Jay Trump was stabled at Chantilly and, for a fortnight, Brian was in sole charge. Then, four weeks before the race, Fred, Tommy and Frances moved into the Hotel du Parc and began the process of teaching their willing charge to forget about the brooks and steep drops of Aintree and, instead, jump the singular Auteuil obstacles. Few horses from outside France learn in time to cover this course with any fluency; consequently, they lose ground at too many fences to have a serious chance of winning. Jay Trump was given a spin in a prep-race ten days before the big one (the same time-span used prior to the National) and, by finishing fourth and jumping confidently enough, filled Fred with hope.

The greatest problem was with the rider. It was not his tenacity or his will to win which were at question, for these were as impressive as ever. It was the fact that, to meet the weight Jay Trump was set to carry, Tommy had to be lighter than he had been since his college days. Gymnasium work and a fiercely controlled diet took off the required 16 lb, but this is too much for any athlete to shed without suffering a certain weakness and dehydration. On the day Jay Trump jumped the course impeccably but his jockey did not make the best use of him. In front over the last, his perennial lack of finishing speed told and he was only a close third at the line. Fred, while phlegmatic and sympathetic, was in no doubt about the cause of defeat. 'Tommy was too dedicated for his own good. He had got down to a ridiculous weight for someone of his build and, because of all the wasting, I don't think he was capable of thinking clearly. If he had kicked on when he took up the running, three-quarters of a mile out, they would never have caught him. I know Tommy felt the same afterwards. Then he didn't ride a finish at all. He could hardly move on the horse. He was too dried up.'

Jay Trump was to win one more Maryland Hunt Cup, making it a record three, and Fred and Diana flew to America to see him do it. The horse did not return to Lambourn after his race in France, however, and the 1966 Hunt Cup was his swansong. Tommy Smith, perhaps inspired by his time in Upper Lambourn, was setting up as a trainer. As his first acquisition he wanted Brian Delaney as head lad. Fred, reluctant to lose a good man but unwilling to stand in the way of advancement, gave his blessing and Brian was duly approached.

'It was a good offer,' Delaney recalls, 'and the guv'nor told me I should go, if only to get a couple of years' experience. I had no real wish to leave Lambourn but I had just married my wife, Jill, and we were living with her parents in the village. We had no money to buy a house of our own and so America, with somewhere to live thrown in, looked like an offer I couldn't refuse.'

What he now sees unequivocally as a great stroke of luck detained Brian at Uplands. He had great problems obtaining a work permit for the United States and, as the months of waiting accumulated, Tommy Carey left his job as Fred's head lad. It had not, reading between the lines and the frowns, been a smooth relationship and, as Delaney says: 'He was a bit of an oddball . . . never mentioned to me that he might be going.'

So it came as a complete surprise to Brian when, one morning on the downs, Winter instructed him to proceed to 'the Folly' and wait for him. This was sheer Fred. He was happier making even business arrangements on horseback. 'He asked me straight out if I would like to stay and take over as head lad. I never hesitated. A bungalow came with the job and, as I had now pretty much given up all thoughts of being a jockey, I could not think of anything better. I said to the guv'nor that I hoped I could justify his confidence. He replied that we would learn together.'

Fred had been impressed by Delaney's efforts with Jay Trump, both at home and in France, and he now saw in him that certain something he required of those whom he gave authority. Brian, one of eleven children, had set his heart at an early age on following his father's example as a jockey; he had come to Uplands with that ambition still burning. But, passed over for the precarious life he craved, he had found instead a position of far greater security and, as he was to discover, constant rewards to compensate for its punishing routine. In the years to come Fred and Brian worked contentedly, harmoniously together. Fred described it like this: 'I hated the Army, but I agree with their principle of delegation and use it here. I am the company commander, my assistant trainer is platoon commander. Brian is the sergeant-major who sets the example to the troops and brings the inevitable few stragglers into line.'

There was, indeed, a milatary feel about the way in which Fred Winter ran his training establishment, and the example came from the top. Fred could forgive most things, but he would not tolerate those who were tardy, slovenly or, worst of all, both. Diana has no doubt as to the reasons. 'It is the discipline of his Army days,' she explains. 'Whatever he does in life, he has always insisted on being punctual and looking immaculate. Do you know, every morning, before riding out, he would clean and polish his boots?'

In building the sort of team he wanted, Fred was naturally anxious to secure a suitable stable jockey, loyal, talented and able to communicate with the trainer on his terms. It would be fair to say that this took him longer than virtually anything else in the operation. Richard Pitman, who was at Uplands from the very start, sharing the makeshift caravan with Delaney and King, had to wait patiently for eight years before becoming first jockey. In the meantime there were several short-lived arrangements of an inadequate nature, totally at odds with the longevity Fred himself had enjoyed with Ryan Price in his riding years and which, as a trainer, he was later to achieve with Pitman, John Francome and Peter Scudamore.

The first official stable jockey was the Irishman Eddie Harty, who had literally telephoned Winter to offer his services. A fine horseman, skilful on the schooling grounds, Harty was later to return to Ireland and act for Fred, among others, in finding horses to buy. While he was based at Uplands, however, the partnership was not always amicable.

'When Eddie was riding for me, I think we got on each other's nerves a bit,' conceded Fred later, 'probably because we were both over-tense.' Then, early in the 1965–66 season, Harty broke his thigh and Fred had to disperse his favours elsewhere. Prominent among them was Anglo, a horse on whom Fred himself had won some long-distance hurdles for Ryan Price at the tail-end of his riding career. Since then he had been sent up from Findon to pursue a chasing career and, by great coincidence, he was destined to win the Grand

National for Fred, while Ryan Price, his licence reinstated and his great gift for training hurdlers unimpaired, became champion trainer again.

Anglo was a chestnut. Fred later decided that he did not care for chesnuts (or, more particularly, for their shared foibles of temperament) and would go out of his way to avoid having them in the yard. About Anglo, though, he had few complaints, only a feeling of surprise that he should win a prize of which Fred had believed him incapable. 'I never dreamed Anglo would win the National, although we had roughly planned his season with the race in mind,' explained Fred. 'On a park course he was nothing more than a moderate 3-mile chaser. All he needed was a distance of ground. Early in the season, though, I did say to his owners that he's not the best jumper in the world but with a bit more experience he might just make a National horse.'

A large part of Fred's surprise was due, perhaps, to a sense of humility at winning the National in each of his first two seasons of training. It was, he knew, an unthinkable achievement. 'It was almost embarrassing standing in the winners' enclosure again,' he explained, 'when you think of all the people who have been training horses for years and always had the luck go against them at Aintree.'

Such feelings did not affect Fred's planning for the race, however, which was as meticulous as it had been the previous year and followed roughly similar lines. The difference was that, this time, he was not having to instruct a jockey who was a complete stranger to British racing and a horse whose racing experience was over the posts and rails of the Maryland hunt country. The 1966 package was closer to ready-made than do-it-yourself.

With Harty injured, Fred gave the ride on Anglo to Tim Norman, very much a middle-of-the-road jockey for whom this was to be an isolated day of glory in an otherwise fairly humdrum career – the sort of unlikely hero, in fact, with which Grand National legend is fully subscribed. Norman, however, was the type with whom Fred liked to work – conscientious and receptive – and it was clear he had achieved an enviable understanding with Anglo during the season. He could also draw the correct weight – Anglo was out of the handicap proper and carried the minimum 10 stone in the National.

Looking back on the build-up, Fred said: 'Tim got on with the horse very well and they had great confidence in each other. From being a slightly chancy jumper, Anglo became very safe. In his last race before the National he ran quite well at Kempton which was not an ideal course for him, and finished fourth to Kapeno, who was one of the first half-dozen in the Aintree betting. Despite that run, I must say I thought Anglo was all of a 50–1 chance, which is the price he started at. With Tim it was just the same as it had been with Tommy Smith. We showed him all the old Grand National films. I told him where to go and what to do and it worked like a dream. He hunted round the inner, keeping out of trouble in the same way Tommy had done, and went to the front two from home.'

Anglo strode home by a staggering twenty lengths. Alone through-out Aintree's daunting run from the last, past the famous elbow and into the deafening clamour which tumbles down from the County Stand, he had made hacks of another forty-seven-strong field. Second, once again, was the mockingly named Freddie.

Unlike Jay Trump, Anglo did not have a triumphant lap of honour and a happy retirement. For him, as for Tim Norman, the National of 1966 provided unrepeatable glories. Anglo won one race the following season but, at Aintree, he tailed himself off and was pulled up on the first circuit. He never won another race and was labelled a lazy rogue. Only after he was put down was Anglo's reputation restored. He was found to have a ruptured heart; the surprise was that he had gone on racing at all.

Fred finished the 1965–66 season with thirty winners, an improvement of five on the previous year. The following season, he trained thirty-nine, yet the money brought in by that total was barely a third of the earnings the year before. The reason is simple – no Grand National. As he had won the race twice as a jockey and twice more as a trainer inside a ten-year period, people had begun to label Fred 'Mister Grand National' but, level-headed as ever, he knew he had no special right even to have a runner in the race, let alone the winner. The point was to be proved. In the next twenty-one years he had any number of further attempts at the elusive Aintree race, and a few near-misses. But Anglo, in 1966, was to be his last National winner. The fates were doing their balancing act.

Times moved on. The Winter stable, having split with Eddie Harty, appointed another Irishman as stable jockey. This time it was Bobby Beasley, whose riding skills nobody questioned and whose breeding for the job was impeccable. His grandfather had won a Grand National and ridden over fences, in Ireland, to the age of seventy-three; his great-uncle won no fewer than three Grand Nationals and was one of the most colourful sporting characters of his time.

In 1959, when Fred had been striving to win his first Cheltenham Gold Cup as a jockey, Bobby Beasley and Roddy Owen had condemned him to second spot again. Fred had a high opinion of Beasley's talent, and the new arrangement certainly produced some winners. But, as with Eddie Harty, it was destined not to last. Beasley, whose riding of Nicolaus Silver at Aintree Fred had so strongly commended to Tommy Smith, became an alcoholic and, in 1968, was forced to give up riding. 'He suddenly said to me just after the start of the season, at Fontwell in September, that he couldn't go on,' recalled Fred. 'That left me without a jockey.'

By then Fred was also without one of his hardest-earned records. The tally of 121 winners he had ridden in the 1952–53 season had remained untouched, indeed virtually unchallenged for fourteen years. Then, with Ryan Price topping the trainers' table for the second consecutive season in 1967, Josh Gifford, once the apprentice to Winter's sorcery, closed in on the record. Josh relates: 'I began the last day at Uttoxeter on 119, needing three for the record. Fred sent me a telegram to the course. It just said: "Two, not three. Good luck." It meant a lot to him, but he was still the gentleman he had always been.'

13

The class of the 1960s

Steeplechasing people seldom hesitate to tell a funny story, even when it is wholly against themselves. It is among their most endearing traits, this willingness to laugh at adversity, and it probably explains much about their attitude to danger. Josh Gifford personifies the breed.

In their years as trainers together, we shall see that Messrs Winter and Gifford, old boys of the hard school once marshalled by Captain Ryan Price, became very close friends. As the 1970s dawned, however, Winter was building on his early success at Uplands and seeking his first training championship; Gifford was nearing the end of a riding career in which he had been champion jockey four times.

Gifford recalls, somewhat ruefully, that he did not ride very often for his stable's former number one, much as he would like to have done. Two days from this era stand out in his memory. 'The first was at Lingfield in 1970. Fred was there to give a first run to Bula. Nobody knew how good he might be but he came there with a bit of a reputation, and when Paul Kelleway, who was down to ride him, got injured in an earlier race, I nearly knocked Fred over tying to get the ride. But, do you know, he walked straight by me three times and asked Stan Mellor to ride him instead. It hurt me a bit . . .

'The last winner of my career, later that season, was actually for Fred. It was a 2½-mile handicap hurdle and the horse's name was Pendil. He only carried about 10 stone 4 lb and got home by a head. Fred wasn't there and so I rang him up later to talk him through the race. I said: "He's not much good but he might find another little race somewhere." Three years later Pendil went off at odds-on in the Gold Cup and got beaten a short head!'

Gifford roars with laughter. A missed chance and a gross misjudgement, committed in a single season and linking the first two 'great' horses to come under Fred Winter's care: how can this be, some will ask, when he had already won two Grand Nationals, with Jay Trump and Anglo? Yes, fine staying handicappers, the both of them, brave jumpers who could gallop, and an enduring credit to their trainer. But not even Tommy Smith, not even Tim Norman, and certainly not Fred Winter, would soberly claim that either horse could match the sheer quality of Bula and Pendil.

Bula was at least to achieve some glory but Pendil was destined to be considered a bridesmaid at the highest level. These, though, were the pioneers of an extraordinary decade for Winter, in which the annual frustrations he had suffered as a jockey in the Cheltenham Gold Cup were uncannily to recur. Several times he felt he had a horse which deserved to win, but on each occasion he was denied. To make it very much worse, Lanzarote and Killiney, in Fred's view the best horses he ever trained, were killed in action. No one who loves horses as much as Fred, however businesslike his operation, can unflinchingly accept such losses and it is doubtful if anything else that occurred in his racing career, before or since, hurt him so much as these blows.

The 1970s had begun unpretentiously. F. T. Winter, after five years of training, was in the first division of the profession but not quite aspiring to the top of the table. In 1969–70 he had topped the half-century of winners for the first time but still fell some way short of Fred Rimell, champion trainer for the second successive year.

Rimell won the Grand National for the third time with Gay Trip. Winter had not won any of the elite races of the season but, at the Cheltenham Festival, he had given notice of a star in his yard. Bula won the Gloucestershire Hurdle, now known as the Supreme Novices Hurdle, by a contemptuous six lengths.

Bula's career had begun earlier that season, in the Lingfield race recalled by Josh Gifford. Bought in Ireland by Martin Molony, a riding contemporary of Fred's, he was described by his lad, Vincent Brooks, as being 'big, ugly and fat' on his arrival in the yard. He was also, according to Brooks, 'a stubborn so-and-so' and 'a lunatic'. As well as being unpopular with the lads, Bula did not immediately impress his trainer, who went to Lingfield with feelings of curiosity more than confidence. 'He had done nothing out of the ordinary at home,' said Fred, 'and I asked Stan to teach him a bit about jumping.'

A few minutes later, everyone was a little the wiser about this embryonic champion. He had set off mulishly, demolishing the first three hurdles, but as Mellor sat tight, he began to get a rare kind of 'feel' from the horse. Up on the stands of this once-beautiful course in the Surrey countryside, since massacred by conversion to all-weather racing, Fred had spotted the signs. 'At the top of the hill,' he recalls, 'I turned to the horse's owner and said: "Do you mind if he wins? Because I think he will." He flew in without being touched.'

In the course of that season, and the next, Bula was to set up a remarkable unbeaten run stretching over thirteen races, the twelfth of which was the 1971 Champion Hurdle. Gifford's judgement in 'almost knocking Fred over to get the ride' was, in this instance, fully vindicated for Bula consistently showed himself the possessor of a devastating burst of speed, brilliantly nursed by that tough, craggy yet so sensitive jockey, latterly a trainer in Newmarket, Paul Kelleway.

Having missed the ride at Lingfield, Kelleway still had something to learn about his new charge when he was reunited with him at Worcester a few weeks later, and he was to say: 'When I took him down [to post] he was very warm, and white at the gate. I thought: "This one's going to be a handful." So I let him switch off and he flew the last to win by five lengths.'

This race established a pattern which Kelleway was rightly determined to sustain. He reckoned that Bula's strength was his electrifying finish and he saved it ever more boldly, for use when a race, to other horses, would have been irretrievably lost. He won the Gloucestershire Hurdle the day before Persian War took the Champion Hurdle for the third successive year and secured his place among the hurdling immortals. A year later, taken away from his triple-winning trainer Colin Davies by his controversial owner Henry Alper, Persian War was to lose his crown to the young pretender from Upper Lambourn.

Fred may have been surprised quite how good Bula turned out to be – he had, after all, cost only 1,350 guineas at the Ballsbridge Sales – but the dissimilarity between his homework and his race displays was nothing new to him. He once observed: 'You must see a horse on the racecourse before you know. You can tell after two runs. It's no good thinking they can prove it at home; they can't. They can show if they can gallop. They can show that they can jump at home. But they've got to do both on the racecourse.'

Bula could do both and did so regularly to the surprise and delight of Vincent Brooks. Over the next few years he was to gain something of a name as 'the luckiest lad in racing'. Small wonder, because the second horse he 'did' was Pendil.

On arriving from the sales, Pendil made more of an immediate impression at Uplands than Bula even though, according to his lucky lad, 'he had a bit of a mad streak about him ... sometimes laid his ears back and ground his teeth.' Within a year Pendil had won six successive hurdle races.

The stable stars which Fred Winter needed in order to help make him champion had now arrived. In the 1970–71 season both Bula and Pendil were to become major names in the sport, and F. T. Winter was to finish top of the trainers' table, a position he was to make his own for the next five years. For one who had never wanted to train, Winter had mastered the art with staggering speed. It is neither fair nor accurate to say that he attracted wealthy owners who could send him good horses. Many of his winning horses were actually acquired relatively cheaply, either by Fred himself, with his eye and his instinct for horseflesh, or by one of his trusted 'scouts' in Ireland. He did have some rich and influential owners but he also had some, like the Oxfordshire lady for whom he found Soloning, who could just about afford a horse in training. It was important to Winter that he trained winners for people like this, because it deflected and deflated any claims that he had been put on a pedestal by the rich and famous. Throughout his racing life Fred had detested jealousy; as a jockey, he had barely been subjected to it, despite his phenomenal success, because he remained an honest, modest and unostentatious man. He was the same as a trainer but, in this sphere, anyone achieving an unusual success rate stands accused, by the envious and the malicious.

Unworthy jealousy never did cut much ice with Winter; success never changed him either. Far from putting on the social style to wallow in his own cleverness, Fred arguably retreated ever more into his chosen and private lifestyle, never lingering in racecourse bars, excusing himself from cocktail parties, ignoring the Lambourn pubs. 'Di prefers to eat at home,' he once said by way of explanation. 'Fred enjoyed staying in,' said Diana independently. The arrangement worked, no matter whose the initiative. The truth, perhaps, was that Fred Winter devoted all day, every day to horses, the riding of them, the watching of them and the talking about them. In the evenings he liked, so far as it was possible, to switch off, and it was pointless for any owner/jockey/journalist phoning him after the cocktail hour on a matter of less than utter urgency to look forward to a long and convivial chat.

Diana added, 'He never liked being late to bed during the season. At weekends he would sometimes have small dinner parties for friends and Freddy loved playing poker. He also played bridge, but was very bad at it. Uplands is a lovely house and we simply enjoyed being here.'

The domestic bliss was complemented, as is invariably the case in trainers' houses, by a variety of dogs. Fred's boxer, named Butch, lived to a grand old age and, in years to come, was joined by Mr Chips, Womble, and Mr Todd, not to mention a cat and a parrot.

And the girls, of course, were growing up. They had their ponies at first, and latterly Uplands housed some event horses in boxes and paddocks removed from the general run of the racing yard. All three girls inherited a love of horses and of riding over obstacles, but when they were old enough to think what they wanted to do in life, they had a father unrepentently against any plans to ride in jump races. 'He simply did not believe National Hunt was a woman's sport,' explained Diana, 'and I think he was right, although it sometimes annoyed the girls. They rode eventing when they were still quite young. Fred never came . . . he would just expect them to win!'

This, then, was the family life, a life in which Fred Winter was more quietly contented than his old roistering bachelor pals would have credited. With his burgeoning yard and his close-knit family he was a happy man and, as the 1970s began to bring in the bacon, a fulfilled one too.

Bula's path to the Champion Hurdle was unbeaten but far from undemanding. One of Winter's greatest training talents was in placing his horses where they had the best possible winning chance. There are trainers who do this by spending sleepless nights poring over the formbooks, or even by employing their own private handicapper to scrutinise the available options. Winter spent less time worrying about the opposition and more about the conditions which would be most suitable for his own horse – right-handed or left-handed course, still and undulating or flat and easy; plus, of course, the state of the going. This was typical Fred, concentrating on whether his horse was up to the job and allowing the others to do the worrying. It came out in his spectating habits too, for as Diana pointed out: 'He would never watch other people's horses – in fact he had no interest in

18. *Tempted back for a Veterans' race at Kempton Park . . . he won, of course.*

19. *The master of Uplands, and some of his loyal staff, with head lad Brian Delaney in the foreground.*

20. *Always sharp of eye, and invariably short of temper before breakfast!*

21. *Tommy Smith and Jay Trump. Fred educated them both to be Grand National winners in his first season as a trainer.*

22. *Harry Foster, the oldest and most recognisable stable lad in Lambourn.*

23. *Paul Kelleway jumps the last on Bula to win the Champion Hurdle.*

24. *But this one got away. Fred consoles Richard Pitman after defeat on Pendil in the Gold Cup.*

25. *Crisp, heroic runner-up in the Grand National.*

26–29. *Family and friends: brother John Winter; brother-in-law Doug Smith; Ryan Price and Josh Gifford; and the new man in charge at Uplands, Charlie Brooks.*

30 *and* **31.** *They were together 16 years, through triumphs and trials ... Fred and John Francome, who finally gave the stable a Gold Cup with Midnight Court.*

32. *With the Queen Mother after Plundering's Whitbread Gold Cup.*

33. *His favourite relaxation.*

seeing races at all unless he had a runner. Always he ran his horses when *he* wanted to, not in order to avoid others.'

Fred wanted to run Bula in Sandown's Benson and Hedges Hurdle, and did so despite the presence of some daunting opponents. Bula saw off his closest challengers by two short heads although, as Paul Kelleway explained: 'He tore a boot off at the last hurdle and almost stopped dead.' Then Fred wanted to go to Wincanton for a final run before the Champion, notwithstanding the presence in the field of Persian War. Bula romped home by ten lengths and was promptly made a short-priced favourite for Cheltenham. Despite soft ground and the taxing Cheltenham hill, neither of which was designed to suit Bula's style of running, the championship was won by a convincing four lengths, Kelleway hitting the front at the last hurdle and allowing Bula to sprint clear up the hill.

Pendil never got to Cheltenham in 1971. The route Winter had mapped out for him included a tilt at Newbury's Schweppes Hurdle, that annual February handicap so beloved of ante-post punters. He might have won some handsome bets, too, for he was going well behind the long-priced winner, an inmate of John Sutcliffe's canny stable, when he broke down. Disappointing, certainly, but not a disaster for a six-year-old whose future lay over fences. A split-tendon operation had him fit to run again by December, when he joined Bula in a triumphant procession of wins, Pendil in novice chases, Bula in some major hurdle races.

Although Bula's wins were frequently gained in mockingly emphatic fashion, he certainly had his problems this season. Beaten in his comeback race, albeit by an inferior horse receiving a massive 3-stone weight concession, Bula was then on the injury list for three months. Fred brought him back for the Kingwell Hurdle at Wincanton, which he won again, but an inspection on returning to Uplands revealed a bruised foot. From then on it was touch and go, Cheltenham being close and the peerless skill of the trainer fully tested.

At the festival, however, any doubts about the horse's well-being were swept aside as convincingly as the opposition. Bula was sent off at 8–11, making him the first odds-on winner since Sir Ken in 1954, and although there were traffic problems caused by fallers at the tricky downhill hurdle, the third last, Kelleway and Bula slipped past on the inner and stormed away to win by eight lengths, the biggest winning margin for forty years.

Kelleway and Bula were good for each other; Fred had recognised the happy marriage of their styles and encouraged it. But Kelleway, he felt, did not suit every horse, and he was now actively encouraging the advance of a jockey who had started race-riding relatively late and begun riding winners very much later. For Richard Pitman the road to the top had not been fast and smooth, even when he attached himself to F. T. Winter.

Pitman might have been obliged to follow his father's wishes and go reluctantly into engineering but for the mishap of failing all nine of his O-Levels. This, however, was what a jockey would call a soft fall. Academically catastrophic, it allowed the young Pitman to go into racing and pursue his private dreams. He was to be a very long time in catching them. He had his first ride at the age of seventeen; he was twenty-one before he rode a winner. Many would have given up long before but Pitman persevered, living on his wits. Finally they came to his rescue when he personally approached Fred Winter, then in his final year of race-riding, to ask if he could join him as a lad, with the hope of some rides, when he began training. Fred watched his applicant ride round Cheltenham that day and, although far from impressed, plainly saw enough to feel he would not be wasting space at Uplands.

Pitman was one of the originals in the primitive caravan there. Rough though it was, he never resented it, once saying: 'All that camping was part of the scene, part of growing up.' When he came to Uplands, Pitman had been engaged, and he married Jenny, later to become the leading lady trainer, in the autumn of 1965. This took him out of the caravan, which was something, but it did not immediately do much for his riding prospects. The odd winner came along, but Pitman was into his late twenties by the time his tide had irreversibly turned. The horse who did more than any other to establish his name was Pendil.

An extraordinary-looking horse, with what can only be described as two horns jutting from his forehead, Pendil never returned to hurdling after breaking down in the Schweppes. His season as a novice chaser was a sensation. He won five consecutive races including the Arkle at the Cheltenham Festival, for which he started odds-on, and the Welsh Champion Chase at Chepstow. 'He'll be better than Arkle himself,' crowed the Winter lads, supping their pints in the Maltshovel. The walls of the old bakehouse were impervious; they had heard it all before.

Pendil, however, began the following season as if proving himself to be the superior of the great Arkle were a mere formality. Bula set out to make it a hat-trick of Champion Hurdles, no serious judges willing to bet against him. And now Uplands was home to a brilliant young hurdler (Lanzarote), an exciting staying chaser (Killiney) and a live Grand National fancy (Crisp). The season of 1972–73 began with Richard Pitman's appointment, long-awaited and hard-earned, as retained stable jockey. With such a wealth of talent in the yard, this promised to be a spectacular season for Pitman and Winter. It did not, however, proceed according to plan.

Winter retained the trainers' championship and won more races (eighty-five) and more prize money (almost £80,000) than he had ever done before. And yet, come the end of the season, all those at Uplands would have needed prolonged persuasion that there was anything to feel happy about. The scale of disaster was, in their eyes, awesome. As the great climax of the season advanced, Winter horses were odds-on for the four main races at Cheltenham and clear favourite for the Grand National. Of these five races, only one was captured and the winner of it, Killiney, did not survive the season.

Winter's equanimity enabled him to cope with most things. Bula's demise in the Champion Hurdle, for instance, or Pendil's narrow failure in the Gold Cup. Bula, he acknowledged, had lost some of his spark and who, anyway, could ask a hurdler to win more than two Champions? As for Pendil, strongly fancied though he was, Fred would calmly have quoted the wise words of his much-respected father. 'He always told me that if a horse runs well, you should be happy. If you fancy a horse and he finishes in the first four, then you can't be far wrong.' But Killiney's death was different, souring the season as no ordinary defeat could have contrived to do.

No one knew quite how good Killeney was, or might subsequently be. No one was going to find out. The horse, known in the yard as the 'Gentle Giant', had won eight consecutive races for his owner, Mrs Enid Boucher, culminating in the race at Cheltenham now known as the Sun Alliance Chase, the 3-mile championship for novices. The following season, beyond doubt, he would be a leading fancy for the Gold Cup. There were those at Uplands who thought him the best horse ever to come into their yard and, for all Fred's outward lack of emotion, there are reasons to believe Killiney had won a privileged place in the heart of his trainer. 'He was wonderful,' Fred later told me. 'Gentle and kind, didn't have a vice in him. Such a pity we didn't have him for long. It goes deep to lose such horses and the only consolation is knowing that they had the best of everything beforehand.'

The fateful day was one week after the Grand National. The venue was Ascot, the event the Heinz Steeplechase. Killiney went off at 9–4 on, much as one would expect of a horse with his mighty reputation. At the second open ditch, perhaps distracted by a faller in front of him, he came to grief in a sickening somersault. The fall ended Pitman's season; it ended Killiney's life, the vet's bullet putting him out of his misery behind the screens once a badly broken shoulder had been discovered. There were those on the massive grandstand who cried and, if Fred Winter was not among them, this was one of the few times in his racing career when he came close.

For Pitman it was the climax of a nightmare which had begun at the very meeting where he had felt his dreams were about to come true. Seldom, if ever, can any jockey have begun the Cheltenham Festival with such an appetising selection of rides. Seldom can things have gone so badly awry.

Bula, of course, was not Pitman's ride. Kelleway and Winter were soon to go their separate ways but the team was unchanged for this year's Champion and so was the opinion of the bookmakers. Although Bula had been beaten by Pat Taaffe's Captain Christy in the Irish Sweeps Hurdle, a battle on 'home territory' at Prestbury Park was popularly thought to present an entirely different state of affairs. Bula went off at odds-on for the second consecutive year but, this time, never looked likely to repay such confidence, trailing in fifth behind Fred Rimell's new star, Comedy of Errors.

Pitman had been beaten into third place on Crisp, his intended National ride, in the Queen Mother Champion Chase, but had managed to win on Killiney despite the latter's clearly expressed preference for a right-handed course. And so to Pendil in the Gold Cup.

Pendil's season had been virtually uninterrupted glory. He had won good prizes at Ascot and Sandown before taking the Christmas feature, the King George VI Chase at Kempton, beating Fulke Walwyn's The Dikler by five lengths and prompting some festive ribaldry among the rival lads in the Lambourn locals. Pendil then showed he was plenty quick enough to win good races over 2 miles by going to Newbury and beating that spectacular jumper of fences, Tingle Creek, over the minimum trip. Speed, then, was not a problem; only stamina. For, as many other horses have proved since that time, the King George is not an accurate yardstick for the Gold Cup, Kempton's easy 3 miles bearing little resemblance to Cheltenham's draining 3¼. For Pitman it would be a matter of waiting, preserving his horse's energies. Even so, he was rightly confident. Pendil, after all, had won eleven consecutive races now.

Possibly comforting to the Pendil camp was the disruptive drama being enacted 'over the wall'. In The Dikler and Charlie Potheen, Fulke Walwyn possessed the two most obvious dangers to Pendil. The Dikler, though, was a far from easy ride and had already seen off a couple of senior jockeys before Walwyn united him with the Irishman Barry Brogan. The two got along famously and Brogan was content to ride The Dikler at Cheltenham even though Charlie Potheen, who would now be ridden by Terry Biddlecombe, was more the bookmakers' fancy.

Pitman had never been afraid to express his views to pressmen (as befits his later occupation as one of them) and after watching The Dikler win at Wincanton, some weeks prior to Cheltenham, had happily gone on record saying he had seen nothing to alarm him. Walwyn, when informed, retorted: 'He'll regret those words.' Soon, however, Walwyn's plans were in ruins as Brogan, whose life at the time consisted of regular visits to an Irish clinic in increasingly desperate attempts to 'dry out', at last succumbed to his chronic alcoholism.

Brogan's memoirs, some years later, told of the torment he suffered as he tried to come to terms with his condition and commit himself to riding at Cheltenham. 'Mr Walwyn rang the hospital every day to check on my progress . . . he made no attempt to influence me. The decision was mine and mine alone. It was a great temptation to accept but I knew, deep down inside, that it would be the wrong thing to do.' He also reveals something about the integrity of Walwyn who, having accepted Brogan's decision, 'stuck by me 100 per cent. Reporters kept pestering him about my whereabouts but he refused to divulge it and embarrass me.'

Ron Barry was engaged to ride The Dikler but there was time only for him to school the horse once before Cheltenham. Inevitably, confidence in Pendil increased still further.

As he did not bet, Fred had no strong views on the price of his horse. But he did respond, in his own way, to the undoubted pressure of training an animal apparently considered by all to be home and dry even before the Gold Cup tapes went up. His gruffness, invariably confined to that scratchy, pre-breakfast period, extended through the daylight hours. It reached a point where he refused to discuss Pendil, or his other great Cheltenham hopes, with anyone bar those most intimately concerned with them. Then, on the day before the meeting, Winter and Pitman drove to Prestbury Park and walked the course, plotting their detailed plans for each of the runners and Pendil, inevitably, in particular. It was, after all, the biggest race of the year and Fred was, hitherto, having as little luck in it as he had had as a jockey in the 1950s.

They agreed that Pendil must be held up, but not dropped right out – the ground was riding fast and Fred reasoned that he could give himself too much to do. After some debate it was also agreed that, if all went well, Richard should take Pendil to the front on the final turn, with one fence to jump. Their deliberations were so prolonged that there was nothing left to say in the paddock. They both knew what was wanted.

Biddlecombe and Charlie Potheen set off at a tremendous gallop, which suited both Pitman and Ron Barry. Pendil was held up in touch, as planned, and as the runners turned downhill for the last time, Pitman allowed him his head. Then, it all happened rather too fast. Pendil closed up so dramatically that he hit the front with a spectacular leap at the third last. Pitman knew he was there too soon but, now he was in front, he had to make the most of it. Three lengths clear at the second last, and Pendil's supporters were counting their money; at the last his lead was two lengths but he had still hardly come off the bridle. He had, however, been isolated in front longer than he wanted and until The Dikler came past him, half-way up the hill, he plainly felt there was no battle at hand. He fought back then, and tenaciously, but it was too late by a fraction. The Dikler held on by a head.

That this was an upset of monumental proportions was clear from the scene in the winners' enclosure, described by Mrs Cath Walwyn: 'It was extraordinary. Ron Barry had won the race for us and none of the press came near him. There were swarms of them around Fred and Pendil.'

Pitman refused to seek excuses. He blamed himself. 'If I'd waited a bit longer, he'd have won,' he said mournfully. The jockey, however, could in no sense be castigated for the equally agonising defeat of Crisp in that season's Grand National. He tried to make all the running, jumped impeccably and was caught only in the last strides.

Hindsight is easy, but it does seem that Crisp was attempting something pretty improbable in trying to give 25 lb to his conqueror, Red Rum.

Pitman and Pendil went back to Cheltenham for another crack at the Gold Cup the following March. Again they were odds-on favourites. Again the race dealt them only bad cards. At the second last fence, once more travelling like a winner and this time restrained behind the leaders, Pendil was brought down by the fall of High Ken.

He never ran in another Gold Cup. Ante-post favourite in 1975, he broke down at Kempton Park three weeks before the race. Lovingly nursed back to fitness, he had a season off and was once more the firm favourite for the 1977 race, but he slipped while doing some roadwork in Lambourn. It was the end. A great horse was retired without the fruits his talent deserved; Fred Winter was left wondering just what he had done to merit such misfortune in the Gold Cup. 'I've got a feeling about this race,' he said sadly, though not self-pityingly. Eventually, after thirteen years of training, his luck in the Gold Cup was to change, though this too was a story coloured with drama and intrigue.

14

Lanzarote and his lad

There is an institution at Uplands and his name is Harry Foster. Harry will not see his seventieth birthday again but he regards retirement as an imposter to be defeated at all costs. Harry, with his elfin frame and his sharp, urgent movements, has been in racing almost sixty years and at the Winter yard for twenty-five. Although long past pension age, 'he just keeps coming in', according to his long-time head lad, Brian Delaney. It would, he agrees, not seem the same without him.

Every established racing yard has its enduring character among the lads. Walwyns, 'over the wall', for years had a man known to all simply as Crottie, an Irishman whose speech could be unintelligible and whose timekeeping was legendary. Each new season there would be no sign of him reporting back to Saxon House until his long-suffering and singularly loyal 'guv'nor' sent the fare to his little village in southern Ireland. Once, it is said, Walwyn wearied of the game and sacked Crottie. It made no difference. He refused to leave, and stayed on for many more seasons, as much a landmark around Lambourn as Harry Foster himself.

Harry was once flyweight boxing champion of the Army, a talent he put to more dubious use in a celebrated scrap with another racing lad which led to a parting of the ways from one Lambourn trainer. This was one of many moves, for Harry was a wandering spirit until, in 1966, he arrived at Uplands as stable-lad. There he was to stay, contented in the way which he and his breed understand, and outsiders find a complete mystery. Life revolved around the yard, his two horses, the pubs and the betting shop. There was little variety and no craving for it. So long as his horses were winning and he could have a bet and a pint, Harry asked for nothing more from life.

In the mid-1970s one of Harry's horses made him a very happy man, proud in the way that parents become over their clever child, and relatively prosperous with winning bets. He will tell you of the times, his all-weather eyes misting over even now, as he recalls Lanzarote, the horse he still insists was the best to pass through Uplands. Theirs was a relationship destined to end in heartbreak, as so many do in the compulsive yet pitiless world of racing. Along the way, however, there were many uplifting moments, the moments which compensate a man such as Fred Winter for the harsh realities of his work. From Fred, Lanzarote received the ultimate testimony: 'He was,' he said, 'without doubt the best horse I trained.'

Now this was a horse with what racing folk would respectfully call a 'good owner' – an unusual one, too, as Lord Howard de Walden's distinctive apricot colours are seldom seen outside the higher ranks of flat racing. Lanzarote, though, was no better than moderate on the level and although his owner cheerfully confessed to being 'terribly ignorant about jumping', he knew enough about Fred Winter to take notice, and take action, when it was suggested he might send the horse to Uplands for a new career over hurdles. Fred's response to Lord Howard's personal request was, for him, skittishly enthusiastic. 'For you, sir, we'll build a box.'

So Lanzarote arrived at Lambourn as a three-year-old, late in 1971, and at first he did not impress his new trainer one bit. 'He looked like a herring,' was Fred's uncomplimentary assessment of the horse who was to be next in line after Bula and Pendil as the stable's household name. 'But he always had that charm, he wanted to do his best.' Harry Foster took charge of Lanzarote and doted on him. With his attention, and Winter's peerless skill for bringing the best out of horses, Lanzarote was launched on a path to stardom with victory in a juvenile hurdle at Kempton Park.

Despite the shattering of so many dreams at the climax of the 1972–73 season, these were heady years at Uplands. There was rarely a major meeting without a Winter winner, it seemed, or indeed a major race without a Winter runner featuring at the head of the betting. The yard was invariably full to its sixty-horse capacity, more boxes having been built to meet the growing demand from prospective owners. And as important as anything was the spirit within the place, a communal feeling which could only come from the top.

Successful yards are not always happy, and neither is the reverse inevitably the case, but for a great many years Winter ran his ship with a blend of discipline and compassion which most find so elusive. He might frighten new lads, with those withering eyes and that brusque voice, but they would learn soon enough that this was no tyrant.

Dave Dick knew the soft centre better than most and he explains: 'Fred and Fulke were very similar in many ways. They would grump and groan, sometimes scaring the lads, but it didn't mean anything. Fred's lads were always getting bollockings, but none got the sack and none walked out on him. That says a lot for the man and his organisation.'

Brian Delaney confirms the judgement: 'The guv'nor gave a lot of people rollockings over the years but we never had to sack anyone. The lads who did leave did so because they knew themselves that they were not matching up to the standard, or because they were bettering themselves. Over the years eight or nine have left us to go to other Lambourn trainers as head lad.'

If Delaney relays this last information with clear pride, it is justifiable. By being on the premises from day one to the very end, he could claim a substantial share of the credit for the atmosphere. At the peak of the yard's success Uplands employed thirty lads, and although in later years he was to bemoan deteriorating standards, Delaney would not have swapped his job for anything. 'There is never a morning when I don't want to get out of bed,' he declared, which is quite something coming from a man whose days habitually start at the unappealing hour of 5.30 am.

It has always been this way, from the time when Brian took over from Tommy Carey as head lad. Intolerable to some, no doubt, but Delaney would not want anything different. He values that first solitary hour of the day, an hour in which he will feed every horse in the yard, alone with his bucket, his bowl and horseflesh of a value that no one dares to calculate. His bungalow being on the fringes of the yard, he is feeding the first breakfasters by 5.45 am and he expects the operation to take him a full hour. 'It's a fearful hour,' he admits, 'because you go into each box worrying that the horse's legs will be OK. But is is very necessary, and definitely the best time to see horses.'

In those halcyon days of the 1970s the stable stars – Bula, Pendil and Lanzarote – were all stabled in the original row of boxes, facing the house. It came to be known as Millionaire's Row and it was here, every morning, that Brian began his feeding and his inspection of legs.

'By a quarter to seven,' he continues, 'the guv'nor would be up and creeping about in the house. He hardly ever slept longer. Normally I would find him in the kitchen, having his first cup of tea of the day and looking at the *Sporting Life*. This was the time to tell him of any problems with joints or coughs. With many trainers this could be difficult; but, whatever had happened, the guv'nor would take it in his stride. He always has been a man of few words, but a very expressive face!'

With this initial, important period of the day complete, the head lad's habit was to return briskly to his bungalow for a wash and a cup of tea. He would first, however, have woken all the lads who 'live in' – not, by the days of Lanzarote, in a caravan, but in the hostel, a long, wooden shack standing at the top of the yard (on the site of the notorious caravan in fact). Its accommodation is basic – a corridor of box-rooms, two bunks in each, and a small dining and lounge area; not much but enough for the needs and desires of most racing lads.

Harry Foster did not live in, even at the start of his association with Uplands. Separated from his wife, whose exasperation with him once extended to sending him to work with an unusual filling in his sandwiches – a rent book – Harry lived alone in a house in the centre of Lambourn, opposite the church but equally convenient, he will tell you, for the George, the Red Lion and Ladbrokes. His alarm clock has been set, throughout his time in Lambourn, for six o'clock and, unlike mechanically early risers like Brian Delaney, he has usually needed it. 'Sometimes I'm late,' he once admitted, 'and there have been times when I've been too drunk to get to work. But that hasn't happened very often really,' he added in self-mitigation.

By 7.15 am Harry Foster would have walked the half-mile to Uplands (hangover mornings excepted) and would be tending his horse – in this era Lanzarote. Delaney, ablutions and refreshments hastily attended to, would be back on duty, fielding a volley of questions from the lads with practised precision and ensuring that all was in order for the 'company commander' himself. 'We always pulled out, first lot, at 7.45 and the guv'nor would not expect to be even a minute late.'

The question of who rides what would generally have been sorted out the previous evening. This was another of Delaney's tasks, and he would pin up the day's arrangements on the work-board in the tack-room. Each day Fred himself would have his name against one of the racehorses, eschewing the tendency of many a trainer to view the gallops from a retired hack or, worse still, a Land-Rover.

'He would take on anything, too,' said Delaney with a look of grimacing admiration. 'Towards the end of his time, Mrs Winter asked me to make sure he didn't ride anything he shouldn't. I did my best, but if I suggested anything might be a bit fresh for him he would give me one of his looks. The truth was that, even at the end, he was so good he could ride anything.'

What Fred could not do, either then or later, was pretend to be bright and genial before breakfast. Ask anyone who has ever worked with him and the warning is always the same – 'Don't try to talk to him early in the morning.' Even Brian Delaney, whose proud claim is that he 'never had a cross word with the guv'nor in twenty-five years', knew it was wise for him to keep conversation down to the bare essentials at that hour.

'On the gallops he was always gruff,' explains Delaney. 'It was hard to understand him and, through the years, lads often went wrong because they had not taken in what he had said and were too scared to ask him to repeat it.'

Delaney also regularly witnessed an expression of the competitive instinct which has driven F. T. Winter through life. It came on work mornings, up on the downs, when Fred would elect to ride in the traditional two- or three-horse gallop. 'He would never admit it,' said Brian with a smile, 'but he would keep going until he got his horse's head in front, even if he had to keep riding while the other lads were pulling up. It was just something in him – what made him so good, I suppose.'

If Lanzarote was to do a piece of work, Harry Foster would partner him unless Winter decided that Richard Pitman should ride. This was the part of the job which Harry always enjoyed more than any other, the feeling of power and speed and the evocative memories of the days when he still believed he could rival Sir Gordon Richards in silks. Harry never aspired to the heights, in reality, but from the time when he began earning in Newmarket ('6d a week spending money,' he recalls sharply) he did ride eighteen winners, the last of them when just short of his fiftieth birthday. At first he resented the realisation that he was too old to go on race-riding, but he was a resilient, phlegmatic man and he adapted to his new consolations, which, with a horse such as Lanzarote to call his own, were considerable.

As in most jumping yards, 9.15 am was the time when the first lot came clip-clopping back to their boxes, where their lads would dress them over before heading to the hostel for their own breakfast. Brian Delaney would supervise, then peel off to his bungalow for tea and toast. Fred would go into the house for a meal punctuated by phone calls and explosions from the trainer as he opened the post or saw something irritating in the racing papers. It would also be attended by whatever guests happened to be on the premises that morning.

Breakfast is a ritual in jumping yards, and usually a good, fried ritual. Diana adhered to this convention, though confessed to being bewildered and irritated in turn: 'People in racing love to hear their own voices bellowing early in the morning, or so it seems to me,' she said one day. 'Fred was just the same. Then, at breakfast, there would often be an awful lot of people around the table, and most of the time I didn't quite know who they were. I sat at the other end and just got infuriated watching Fred playing with his breakfast and giving half of it to the dogs.'

For Fred the day would now continue with a session with Lawrence Eliot, going through entries and declarations, and a further attack of telephone calls, which Lawrence would field and screen for him. Those who were put through did not, as a rule, keep the phone engaged for more than a minute or two. Fred explained: 'It's up to a trainer to train his owners as well as their horses. I'm a very quiet sort of person and to have long conversations about an animal is a waste of time, so we keep it to a minimum. What they want to know, basically, is how their own pet is and when it's running next and how it will run.' Fred was careful to keep his owners within these boundaries, too. He did not approve of any owner inquiring about other horses in the yard and would be doubly short with anyone who transgressed.

Back outside, the second lot would pull out of the yard at 10 am. At noon Brian would supervise the lunchtime feed. At 12.30, more than five hours of the working day already done, the lads would break for their extended lunch hour. Some would go to the Malt-shovel; some, like Harry Foster, into the village for a pint of Guinness and a punt; others would lounge around the hostel. All of them had to be back on duty at 3.45 pm.

Delaney would check all the horses once again during the ensuing hour, looking particularly at the legs for any signs of heat or swelling resulting from the morning exercise. At precisely five o'clock he would report to the boss. Fred might very well have been racing during the afternoon but, when possible, would always seek to be back at Uplands in time for evening stables – not that he would always attend the ceremony. Delaney explains: 'I would report to him on the state of the horses and ask if he was going to go round them.'

There was no question of reluctance or laziness behind this doubt. Fred had other motives. 'This place runs like clockwork, always to the minute,' he once told me. 'When it fails, I want to know why. The lads know I will be with them every morning but they are not so sure of my movements later in the day. I go round the boxes at evening stables twice a week – but I never tell them when I am going. It keeps them on their toes, you see.'

'He never missed a trick,' nods Brian Delaney. 'And it was not just with the horses. He'd always find weeds in the yard when he came back from holiday in the summer. We thought we'd got everything spick and span but he would find one somewhere. Weeds bugged him, just like the sight of any straw where it shouldn't be. He has always had a neat and tidy mind, the guv'nor.'

Harry Foster, in line with all his twenty-nine colleagues at Uplands in the mid-1970s, worked twelve days on and then had a weekend off. Hard work and unsocial hours, it would seem to most, but to Harry it was more a lifestyle than a job. By six o'clock, having settled his two horses for the night, he would be hurrying home again with the urgent tread of one who values every minute of his day, no matter how ordered and routine it may appear to outsiders. He would cook himself a meal, a skill he had acquired through necessity, and then, in ceremonial order, visit the George and the Red Lion. A drink or two would be enjoyed in each – 'I'll drink anything really, beer, Scotch or brandy' – but if he had backed a winner that day or, more persuasively, if his own horse had won, old Harry might linger a little longer.

In the season of 1972–73, the one which was to end in such a sad and deflating way for all at Uplands, Harry enjoyed many a celebratory night in the Red Lion. Richard Pitman, he who once rode eighty-six consecutive losers, now rode a long succession of winners aboard Lanzarote, having inherited the ride from Paul Kelleway whose relations with the Winter stable were becoming more distant.

Lanzarote's finest hour that season came at Sandown Park, when, at 5–2, he won the William Hill Imperial Cup, always a competitive handicap, under a burden of 12 stone 4 lb. No horse since the war, before or after that season, has ever won the Imperial with such a weight. Pitman concluded: 'Lanzarote was much scopier than Pendil and very exciting right from the start. He had tremendous speed and, as an individual, he was very placid. In short, he was Mr Nice Guy with a lot of ability.'

Harry Foster would have echoed those sentiments and added more of his own. From the day the Imperial Cup was won, he was convinced – not without reason – that 'his' horse was the best hurdler in the country, and anguished that he was not entered for the Champion Hurdle. But Cheltenham followed hard on the heels of Sandown and, anyway, Fred Winter was not going to be rushed with Lanzarote.

With Bula now turning his attention to fences, the 1973–74 season was to see Lanzarote aim for, and reach, the very heights of hurdling success. To do so, he had to take on Comedy of Errors, the horse who had eclipsed Bula and others at the previous festival, the best hurdler Fred Rimell ever trained and rated something of a machine by all at his Worcestershire stables. There was, however, a line of form which gave the Winter camp every encouragement. In the 1973 Imperial Cup, Lanzarote had beaten Mon Plaisir by a length when conceding him 19 lb. In the Champion Hurdle Mon Plaisir was only fourth, but less than four lengths behind Comedy of Errors at level weights.

Despite this, and the compelling evidence of five pre-Cheltenham wins for Lanzarote by an aggregate of fifty-four lengths, Comedy of Errors would not be displaced as favourite for the Champion, having himself won two of the traditional Cheltenham trials before going to Ireland to take the Sweeps Hurdle.

Winter had a plan for the Cheltenham race and, as Richard Pitman later recalled, it was built on an admission 'that Lanzarote was not quite as good as Comedy' – heresy to Harry Foster, no doubt, but why should he care? He collected his winnings anyway, as the Uplands scheme was triumphant. Fred believed that the only way to beat Comedy of Errors was to stretch his stamina throughout the race, and further believed that Lanzarote, who stayed further than 2 miles, was the horse to do it. As extra insurance he ran another of his horses as a pacemaker. Once the race was under way, however, it was clear that the pacemaker was not capable of setting the required gallop. Pitman had to do his own donkey-work and did so consummately well, harrying the champion by going clear at the top of the hill. Comedy of Errors was not for nothing known as a true champion, and he rallied to draw level at the second last but, as Winter and Pitman had projected, had nothing left up the hill.

The Rimells and their connections maintained that their horse was not at his best that day for reasons which had nothing to do with any Uplands master-plan. Their view was possibly vindicated the following season when Lanzarote was beaten three times by his adversary, including a comprehensive defeat at Cheltenham, where the Winter horse was not even placed. But Fred now had three Champion Hurdles to go with his two Grand Nationals as a trainer. Only the Gold Cup, of the three great events in the jumps calendar, remained frustratingly unconquered. Would Lanzarote be the horse to break the hoodoo – and, in the process, become the first ever to add the Gold Cup to the Champion Hurdle?

Another two seasons were to pass before the answer became known. In 1975–76 Lanzarote, although now eight, was kept to hurdles. There are those who believe this to have been one of Fred's rare mistakes and that Lanzarote had become too entrenched as a hurdler when finally he was asked to tackle the larger obstacles. Winter, however, still had Bula to run in the 1976 Gold Cup. He went off the 6–4 favourite but ran unplaced. Fred had now trained five out of six favourites for the Gold Cup without managing to win it. 'I thought Bula was as well as I could get him,' he remarked, 'but somehow I felt on the journey here he wouldn't win.' Fred, perhaps, was just beginning to despair of the race. Lanzarote, brilliant novice though he was, did not put a stop to the misery when pitched into the deep end in the 1977 race.

It is unusual to find a first-season chaser taking part in the Gold cup; still more uncommon to find him so well supported that some will not hear of defeat. But then Lanzarote was no commonplace novice. He had won his three lead-up races to the Gold Cup in scintillating style, calming the nerves of his owner who, perhaps, had been influential in the delay over his horse's chasing debut. 'To be honest I was against him going chasing,' said Lord Howard later. 'I felt it would be terrible if he made one of his bloomers and broke his bloody neck at Taunton.'

But he didn't, and despite persistent problems with corns, through which he had to be nursed with all the skill and devotion that the Winter team could muster, he arrived at Cheltenham as second favourite. Four days before the race Brough Scott wrote, with ultimate confidence, in the *Sunday Times*: 'When (not if) Lanzarote's sweaty, white-starred face looks out from the tumult of the Cheltenham winners' enclosure on Thursday it will be easy to forget that along the way he has had enough problems to daunt even the toughest camel on the pumice-stone island from which he got his name.'

Harry Foster shared the confidence, declaring that his charge was 'better than he has ever been'. But the dream died, and the brilliant Lanzarote with it, in a fatal slip after the ninth fence. On the heaving Cheltenham stands, as the crowd 'ooohed' to the sight of the prone horse, Fred Winter slowly lowered his binoculars and wondered if the fates would ever relent.

15

Francome, faith and loyalty

The first thing which struck John Francome about the man who was to be his boss for sixteen years and his friend for life was that his fingernails were pristine clean. 'It might seem a funny thing to notice but it summed him up,' explains Francome. 'The guv'nor was a very smart guy when I first met him one summer evening in Lambourn and that was exactly the way he stayed.'

Francome was not at all interested in racing while at school and had never even heard of Fred Winter until dreadful exam results persuaded him that he might need to put his horseriding talents, already demonstrated in showjumping, to profitable effect. 'Then,' he recalls, 'it was all down to my Dad's logical thinking. Dad was a builder and had heard from a carpenter friend of his that Fred was a very nice man. Lambourn was only 12 miles from our home in Swindon and Dad knew that Fred had no sons, so reckoned that if I got a job there I would have a fair chance of getting some rides.'

Francome was granted an interview at Uplands on a Saturday in mid-September 1969. A little less than nine years later he was to ride Winter his first and only Gold Cup winner at a time when Francome's integrity as a jockey was being probed and doubted in a manner that was anathema to Fred. It was a dramatic, controversial time which neither man could have imagined possible during that first assessing meeting.

Fred, much later, was to call John the best jockey he had ever seen. He was also, occasionally, to call him some less complimentary things. By return Francome, in his rare serious moments, was to give thanks for 'the best man you could ever wish to work for' but, when feeling more flippant, was to indulge in some practical jokes of which his employer only sometimes saw the funny side.

At first, however, Uplands and its master presented a strange new world to the Wiltshire builder's son. 'It was an amazing yard to walk into,' recalls Francome, 'and the guv'nor was different from anyone I had ever met. The only work I had done up to then was six weeks in a car repair shop where you don't tend to meet the likes of Fred Winter. He was, and still is, the sort of man who commands respect as soon as you meet him – not quite of military bearing, but everything is correct and precise. He didn't frighten me as such but he was quite abrupt. I soon learned that this was his way with everyone. He never did waste words.'

Winter was dividing his rides, at the time, between Paul Kelleway and Richard Pitman and the appearance of this teenager of unruly appearance, already weighing as close to 11 stone as 10, can have done little to make him think he would soon need to alter his plans. But, having issued the warning that he felt Francome would become too heavy, he offered him the chance which, looking back, neither of them will regret at all, though it did not always look like turning out that way.

On his very first morning, Francome caused pandemonium in the yard. Having recovered from the unceremonious wake-up calls which were, and still are, Brian Delaney's 6.30 speciality, John went whistling into one of the boxes to muck out his horse and unthinkingly pulled his constant companion, a transistor radio, out of his anorak pocket. Loud pop music assaulted the calm of the yard and neither John's horse nor any of the others in the vicinity appreciated the change in routine. Some were merely agitated; Francome's own, closest to the cacophany, went beserk and might easily have finished off his new stable-lad in record time. Four horses broke their head collars and one got loose on to the Winters' carefully manicured and lovingly tended lawn which, as Francome says with wry understatement, 'didn't go down very well'. His first serious rollocking from the head lad was followed swiftly by a second, for an equally dangerous misdemeanour, and by eleven o'clock John was quietly convinced that his first day at Uplands would also be his last.

Francome and Delaney did not hit it off at first, quite possibly as a direct result of that unfortunate opening day. There were also times, usually early in the morning, when it seemed he was not Fred's favourite character. 'He was very grumpy early on,' says John. 'As soon as the work was over and we had finished any schooling he was OK, but he was a bad man to cross until then.' He had one particular morning in mind.

'I had been there a year or so and I didn't feel I was getting anywhere. I was doing my best to please the guv'nor too – I used to do all kinds of odd jobs for him, like mowing the lawn or picking his kids up from school. I would wash his car and even service it for him. It made no difference. I still didn't get any rides. Then one morning he told me to drive up to the schooling grounds and get on a horse that he intended to ride up there. I did as he said, or so I thought, but it was a foggy morning and I had got confused enough to drive to the wrong schooling grounds. After sitting in the car for a while, wondering why it was taking the others so long, I got out and walked to the brow of the hill, where I saw all the horses circling down below, waiting to school.

'This put me in a panic. I ran down the hill and stammered my apologies but the guv'nor went mad at me. He bellowed: "That's all right, son, it's not your fault – it's my fault. You're so bloody stupid I should have put up a blackboard and written your instructions on it." I felt pretty small by then but he had not quite finished. Doug Marks was up there watching and schooling and Fred turned to him and said: "This boy thinks he's going to be a jockey! He never will be . . . but he is a really good mechanic."'

Fred's derogatory view did not instantly change when Francome at last began to have the occasional ride. In December 1970 Richard Pitman recommended him to a Wiltshire trainer named Godfrey Burr, who put John up on his own horse, Multigrey, at Worcester. This, his first ride in public, produced the first of Francome's 1,128 winners. His second ride, and his first for Fred Winter, was a rapid cure for complacency. At Cheltenham, Francome was unseated from a novice chaser named King Street and broke his wrist. It was to become one of the paradoxes of his colourful career that although he partnered 575 winners for F. T. Winter in the succeeding fifteen years, his final ride for him, just like the first, ended in the most unwanted of formbook entries – 'unseated rider'.

'It was soon after I got back from that injury that the guv'nor put me up on one of his at Hereford. It was a televised meeting, which shows you how long ago it was, and as I was really struggling to do the correct weight I used what jockeys call 'pee-pills'. I took two of them, oblivious to the side-effects that they can bring, and as I was walking the course at Hereford I got cramping pains in my chest, so bad that I thought I was having a heart attack.

'It eased off after a time, but in the parade ring things got much worse: more chest pains – and an immobilising cramp in my hips and legs. I just about got on the horse but could barely move. He ran the race without any help from me at all and I think the guv'nor, who was watching on television at home, must have thought I was totally useless. It took me a long time after that to get going again to the point where they had any confidence in me.'

Francome, indeed, was having just the sort of weight problems that Fred had predicted at his interview. They were to be with him throughout his career but whereas, in his days as champion jockey, he could take the attitude that he would ride at a healthy minimum and no argument, it was altogether more difficult in his formative riding years. The more rides from which his weight eliminated him, the less likely he was to make a mark.

Following the Hereford incident, two months passed in which not a single ride came the way of J. Francome. His weight had risen above 11 stone for the first time and, utterly disillusioned, he decided to give up. The car repair business beckoned again – that way, he would at least be able to eat a square meal without feeling guilty. John went to the office to tell Fred but found it populated only by the yard's secretary, Lawrence Eliot; Fred, as was his wont whenever time permitted, was out playing golf with his now regular partner, Doug Marks. 'If he hadn't been, that would have been the end,' insists Francome, although perhaps in this he underestimates the judgement of his long-time employer. Making up his mind to hand in his notice after exercise the following morning, John did mention his decison to Brian Delaney. Brian made no comment, no effort to change John's mind, but he had already seen the talent in this wayward youngster and knew that his guv'nor had too. Without saying anything he put Francome's name down against a horse called Osbaldeston on the board for the next day's schooling.

'He was a bastard to ride,' relates Francome. 'More than just keen, he literally took off with you. But he had ability, being a half-brother to old Sonny Somers, and when he behaved well and jumped well for me on the downs that morning, the guv'nor came across and said I could ride him the following week at Worcester.'

Francome is unsure to this day whether there was any collusion between Delaney and Winter on this issue, but the upshot was contentment all round. Osbaldeston won at Worcester and John thought no more about giving up. Wild though he could be, Osbaldeston became one of Francome's most profitable servants. He won seventeen times on him in the next few seasons and he will tell you that he owes the horse his career.

John was gradually entrusted with more of the stable's fancied runners, riding as number two to Richard Pitman, from whom he says he learned a great deal about riding and as much about life. At the start of the 1975–76 season Francome became the stable's official first jockey, and immediately won the championship for the first of his seven times.

After six years he had grown close to Fred Winter; a mutual trust and respect had developed between them, which is just as well in light of what was to follow. Francome, ebullient and mischievous but perceptive with it, had also absorbed much about the secret behind the success of Uplands, a success that he was to share, and play a huge part in perpetuating, for another decade.

'The atmosphere was so good. That had a lot to do with it. Brian Delaney, despite our earlier differences, has for years been the best head lad anywhere in the country. He strikes the difficult balance between keeping the lads happy and making sure they do their work.

'Lawrence Eliot was just a lovely man to have around. He was a worrier about the entries, though, and he also loved to have a bet, which led to any number of wind-ups. If I rode a decent-priced winner for another trainer, Brian would go into the office and say to Lawrence: "Wasn't that a nice touch?" Lawrence would look blank and Brian would say: "Didn't Johnny tell you to back it? He told everyone else." Poor old Lawrence fell for it every time. Only one thing upset him more than missing a good bet and that was when he went fishing with Mrs Winter's mother and she caught more fish than he did.'

And what of the maestro himself?

'The guv'nor never changed in all the years I rode for him, and I shouldn't think we had three cross words all the time I was there. He never told me how to ride a horse and I never tried to tell him anything about training. We might disagree about the trip a certain horse wanted, that kind of thing, but I knew he would always do what he wanted. It was simple, really. Brian looked after them and I rode them. But Fred trained them and he always had the last word.

'He never gave me a bollocking after a race. It wasn't his way, and so far as I knew he has been the same with all his jockeys. I knew if I had ridden a bad race and I would come in and say so. Much better that way than trying to pull the wool over his eyes – that never worked. He was the only trainer I know who remembered what it was like to ride, and how things could so easily go wrong. You cannot account for people cutting across you or for horses falling in front of you. He understood that. As long as every horse you rode was at some stage of the race given a chance to win, he wouldn't complain.

'When you rode him a winner, he was no different. He would hardly ever say anything more than "Well done". If he was really pleased, he'd pat you on the back. He usually wore a pair of pigskin gloves and he'd have his hands behind his back as he grunted and nodded at you. And that was it. Even in the car on the way home, he would seldom say anything further about a race.

'Fred never was a talkative man. You could drive him racing, as I often did, and if he said three sentences each way, that was about your lot. A few of us jockeys who travelled together from Lambourn used to have a competition in the car to see who could guess how many words Fred would say on the way to Lingfield, or Fontwell. But we all got used to him after a while – that was just the way he was.

'Going racing together suited us both, too. I was quite happy driving, whereas he couldn't stand driving himself. And at the end of the meeting we would get in the car and go. We never went in the bar after racing and neither of us had any designs on going for dinner in London or anything like that. We couldn't wait to get home.

'One thing he didn't have was a sense of humour. He would never, ever tell you a joke. He could see the funny side of things sometimes, though, and in my last few years there he would actually chuckle if I took the mickey out of him. We had to go to Perth one day and we flew up. Someone at the course gave each of us a big, fresh salmon in a wicker basket which meant that, with saddles and riding gear, I was really weighed down. All the guv'nor had was his salmon in a bag. At the airport I slipped my salmon into his bag when he wasn't looking, leaving my travelling bag empty. He never noticed, and when we got home I kept a straight face and asked for it back. He didn't say anything, just smiled because he knew he'd been caught out.'

Not that the trainer was always so tolerant of his jockey's over-grown sense of the ridiculous. He might not have noticed Francome mimicking his style, to the merriment of all the lads, as he rode behind him on the schooling gallops one morning. But he certainly noticed when John deliberately pulled fellow jockey Vic Soane's foot out of the irons as they were riding work together. 'On the way back down to the yard,' Francome relates, 'he rode over to me and just said: "Racing isn't a game, son, it's a business."'

It was a business to Francome by 1975, and a very lucrative one too. His career was taking off and he was on the way to his first jockeys' title – but that did not stop him making what he still refers to as 'the most embarrassing error of my career' on a decent young chaser of Fred's called Floating Pound. Turning into the straight for the last time at Huntingdon, it had developed into a two-horse race between the two favourites – John on one, Andy Turnell on the other. It was only the second time John had ridden over fences on this East Anglian course and he had it in his head that there was only one fence left to jump. Accordingly, having cleared what he thought to be the last, in good style and in front, he headed for home – only to be dimly and then devastatingly aware of Turnell jumping another fence and laughing. The crowd was not laughing, at least that section of it which had seen their likely winnings thrown away, and the reception was evil. Just at that moment, Francome recalls, he would have given a lot to jump off the horse and run straight to his car to avoid having to face his livid trainer. But Fred was not livid. 'All he did was put his hand on my shoulder and say: "Bad luck, son." I couldn't believe it, and I have never forgotten it.

'For a man with this great competitive streak, this will to win, the guv'nor was the best loser in the world. He always seemed to be in a worse mood if we had had three or four winners, almost as if he thought it wasn't quite fair. If we'd had three odds-on shots turned over and another horse break down, he'd be chattier than usual on the way home.

'If someone else was having a lot of winners and we were going through a lean spell, he never showed any jealousy at all. That is why people had so much time for him. He was also incredibly honest. He never stopped one of his horses in my sixteen years and I don't suppose he did it with any other jockey. They always ran on their merits. He has always been a man of great integrity, too. If he said he would do something, he did it. And there was never any question of fiddling the owners – if a horse had a leg, he would ring up and tell the owners straight. Neither did he encourage owners who were looking to lay out a horse for a gamble in a particular race. More often than not he would tell them to take their horse somewhere else.'

All of this is pertinent to the time in question, because gambling, and perceived integrity, were at the heart of the investigation into John Francome and the bookmaker John Banks early in 1978 which led to a suspension for Francome and a total racecourse ban of three years for Banks. It was a high-profile case which Francome still maintains received disproportionate attention and punishments, but it tested the bond between Winter and his jockey to the full, and might easily have sabotaged his latest attempt on the elusive Gold Cup.

Francome was no stranger to the vicissitudes of this race. He had ridden Bula in 1975 and 1976 and Lanzarote in 1977. But both horses, he felt, had suffered from spending so long as hurdlers: 'As a consequence, they never jumped the larger obstacles as fluently as they should have.'

Midnight Court was different. Dave Dick had persuaded Fred to pay £15,000 for this horse in Ireland and he was a chaser through and through. This did not stop him winning two hurdle races in his first season at Uplands but then, put to fences, he quickly fulfilled his true potential. Although he was only a novice, Fred favoured taking him to the Gold Cup and, as Francome reflects, that was that. 'He was very decisive about what a horse would do. They always came first, and he always gave them plenty of time, but if he made up his mind to run somewhere it didn't make a blind bit of difference what Brian or I might say. And the fact is that Midnight Court was unbeaten that season, and was an exceptional horse.'

When the festival arrived, Francome, and thereby the Winter yard, was in the grip of a bad trot. Nothing was going right and, on the Wednesday afternoon, twenty-four hours before Midnight Court was due to run the tenth steeplechase of his young life in the country's elite jump race, John looked out of the weighing-room at the teeming rain and thought that things could hardly get any worse. He was spectacularly wrong, as he discovered when summoned by the chief of racecourse security, former flying squad officer Bob Anderson, to an interview room. Inside sat two security chiefs, a female stenographer and Fred Winter. The subject under discussion was Francome's relationship with John Banks, allegations that information had been passed to him concerning certain horses, and the underlying inference that some of those horses might have been stopped.

The interview, described by Francome as 'a police-type interrogation', did not spare the jockey's feelings, nor was it intended to. 'I began to feel like a criminal, and I don't mind admitting that for a few moments in there I was frightened,' he said. Unsatisfied with

John's insistence that he had never told Banks, a genuine friend, anything he would not have said to either Winter or the owners, the security service pronounced that the matter would be referred to the Jockey Club and a formal disciplinary hearing.

This was not designed to give a jockey the most restful night's sleep before one of the greatest riding opportunities of his career and Francome was openly relieved when the morning brought snow and Gold Cup day was abandoned. It was rescheduled for Cheltenham's April meeting, four weeks later, and this had various ancillary benefits for the Winter yard. Midnight Court preferred firmer ground, and was to get it in April, by which time a number of the original dangers to him had fallen by the wayside.

There remained, however, the John Banks affair, hanging over Francome everywhere he went. He recalls expecting to be sacked by Winter immediately after that first interview at Cheltenham. 'I didn't quite know what to say to him as we came out of that room. Finally, I said: "Look, despite what has gone on in there, I want you to know I have never stopped a horse in my life." He said: "Son, if I thought for a moment that you had, you wouldn't be standing there – you would be lying down." He never mentioned it again, never bothered me about it, but of course I knew he could not entirely ignore it and for a while it seemed I would lose the ride on Midnight Court. Graham Thorner won on him at Chepstow, soon after Cheltenham, but luckily he didn't jump for him and I was back on board for the Gold Cup.'

Winter's unbending support for his jockey through this difficult, divisive time has never been forgotten by Francome. He repaid the debt in the best way possible, by breaking the Gold Cup hoodoo. In a slow-run race, which suited Midnight Court's unproven stamina, Francome sat quietly and confidently behind the leaders as they descended the hill for the final time. On the last bend, the gap he wanted appeared on the inside rail. Francome, a master at the manoeuvre, was through in a trice and the race was as good as over. Francome was relieved enough for himself to aim a V-sign at the press box as he passed the post. But to this day he says he was even more delighted for his faithful, supportive 'guv'nor'. This was a day when he received the full treatment in the winners' enclosure – the grunted 'Well done' and the pat on the back!

16

Second in command

The bigger and more successful a racing yard becomes, the greater the need for skilful delegation. The time comes when even a trainer and his head lad cannot cope with the relentless demands of boxes filled to capacity and owners clamouring for news and, for Fred, that time arrived in the mid-1970s when, after ten years as a trainer, he took on a paid assistant.

Three men held that post at Uplands in the years before Winter's enforced retirement and all are now successful Lambourn trainers in their own right. Nick Henderson, the first assistant from 1975 until 1978, was subsequently twice champion jumps trainer from his base at Windsor House in the heart of Lambourn itself. Oliver Sherwood, recommended by Henderson as his successor, stayed six years with Winter during which time he married one of Fred's daughters, Denise. He now trains one of the country's most powerful teams of National Hunt horses. Finally Charlie Brooks, who would by instinct have been a professional footballer and by inheritance a stockbroker, took over in 1984. Three years later he found himself obliged to take greater authority, at first on a temporary basis but eventually as the new master of Uplands.

Henderson, Sherwood and Brooks have more than a job in common. They are all from tolerably wealthy families, all were educated at public school, rode in races only as amateurs and had the option of different, more conventional careers. All, in fact, were markedly unlike Fred Winter in almost every conceivable way, but the trainer's judgement of character had not let him down, as the trio's later records demonstrate. These were the men to whom he was to grow closer than anyone in their time at Uplands, and there was not a side of F. T. Winter, public or private, that they would not witness, such are the proximities of the job.

The background of affluence actually dates back still further in the Winter story, for although Nick Henderson was the first full-time assistant to be employed, a series of amateur pupil-assistants preceded him. These included Anthony Mildmay-White, Anthony Stroud (now racing manager to Sheikh Mohammed) and, unforgettably, the son of Lord Harrington, the Honourable Steven Stanhope, who gave up a hell-raising existence in his native County Limerick for the more reserved lifestyle of racing in the south of England. By all accounts, it did not noticeably cramp him; stories of D.C., a family nickname which emanated from his young sister's inability to pronounce his Christian name, are legion. An Old Etonian, like Winter's last assistant Charlie Brooks, Steven Stanhope had a sense of adventure which extended beyond the simple pleasures of riding his own horses over fences. John Francome, who was making his way up the ladder of professional jockeys at the time, remembers receiving a painful injury to his legs and shoulders in a fall at Market Rasen where he had been driven by Stanhope in an old mini-van. He recalls how the journey home was sickeningly uncomfortable but that the gallant Stanhope, ignoring his own sharp hunger, refused to stop for food until he had his shaken passenger safely back in Lambourn. On the way the mini-van had a puncture in Oxford. 'It was then,' explains Francome, 'we discovered we didn't have a spare tyre.' Unabashed, and quite unwilling to wait several hours for the AA rescue service, Stanhope then drove the remaining 28 miles on three good tyres, 'wrestling with the steeing wheel as the van maintained its newly balanced direction towards the verge'.

Aristocrat or not, Stanhope later admitted to being 'frightened' by his initial encounter with Fred Winter, another thing he shares with Messrs Henderson, Sherwood and Brooks. Stanhope came to Winter, as so many do, on third-party recommendations. 'I knew nothing about him but my father wanted me to go to someone who was honest and who could train and from whom I would learn. Virtually everyone said Fred Winter.' He was lucky in that his elder brother, Lord Petersham, counted Dave Dick among his greatest friends. A word was dropped in the right ear and, on a Sunday afternoon, the introductions were made at Uplands.

The Hon. Steven later recalled of this first meeting with Fred: 'He was quite frightening. One was very careful what one said. He told me: "You're welcome to come. I'd like to have your horses but I don't need them and I'm not going to pay you."'

With the ground rules thus laid in his singularly blunt manner, Winter evidently got along fine with his titled Irish amateur. Stanhope moved into a rented cottage in Lambourn and began, after a respectable time, to pick up regular rides. He also picked up something of a reputation, for although he freely conceded that things were not quite as they are in Ireland, where 'it's often a drunken, waste-of-time life', he did know how to enjoy himself and he was, after all, a bachelor and an amateur.

Stanhope was eventually to go back to his native Ireland and marry. He never did become the high-profile trainer of his ambitions. One who did, however, was the man who shared Stanhope's years at Uplands and then stayed on. Nick Henderson spent six years as an amateur jockey and counted the prestigious Foxhunters' Chase at Liverpool among his conquests. His horses were stabled with Winter and, a couple of mornings each week, he would report early to Uplands, ride out first lot and then drive back to London where, for a time he considered mercifully brief, he worked in the city.

Henderson was born close to Lambourn but racing had certainly not been force-fed. Quite the opposite, in fact, for although his father, John, was a social racegoer who had even ventured into horse ownership on the flat, it was assumed within the family that Nick would enter the stockbroking profession. This was an idea from which he cringed ever more and when, in 1975, Stanhope left and Winter decided to take on a full-time assistant, Henderson gratefully accepted the offer.

The subsequent three seasons were nothing if not eventful. For two of them F. T. Winter was champion trainer and in the third, after all the rich promise and shattered hopes with Pendil, Bula, Killiney and Lanzarote, the yard finally won the Gold Cup with Midnight Court, ridden by John Francome. In years to follow Francome and Henderson were to become close friends; Francome would partner many of the winners which established Henderson as a training force and, in the ironical way of things in racing, a major rival to his old boss, to whom he publicly credits his ability to make good tea (a testimony of which Fred might be disproportionately proud) but to whom, privately, he acknowledges an enormous debt and a wide-ranging influence.

Like those who were to follow him as Fred's assistants, Nick found that a few seasons at Uplands were an education that he would neither resent nor reject. Since taking out training licences themselves, Henderson, Oliver Sherwood and Charlie Brooks have all followed the dictates of their old master. They have sought and bought similar types of horses and prepared them in similar, patient styles. They have run their yards the same way, down to employing head lads from the Uplands academy (prop. B. Delaney) and, at least in the case of Sherwood, developing an obsession about weeds!

Henderson decided in 1978 that it was time he started out on his own as a trainer and stopped being on his own as a man. So in June he married Diana, daughter of that great racing Corinthian John Thorne, and in July he acquired a licence to train from Windsor House. The question of the vacancy at Uplands had already been resolved – indirectly more by Diana than her husband.

Oliver Sherwood takes up the story: 'It all came about through my knowing Diana when we were kids at Pony Club. It was odd the ways things happened – I'd known his wife much longer than he had and, through being with Fred, Nick had known Denise years before I did. Anyway, the Hendersons knew that I was seeking a job in racing and Nick was good enough to recommend me.'

The Sherwood family owns a considerable portion of the prime farming land of Essex and it had always been assumed (much as Nick Henderson's family had him marked down for the city) that one of the sons would return home to take on the running of the farms. It has not worked out as planned, for both Oliver and his younger brother Simon, of Desert Orchid fame, are now training in Berkshire. Both began as amateur riders and Oliver continued that way, combining his duties as Fred's paid assistant with the pursuit of the amateur championship.

Sherwood came to Uplands with his father, Nat, and it was apparently a close-run thing which of them was more intimidated by the interview. 'With me, it was a case of being terrified by simply meeting Fred Winter, who was a god to me,' says Oliver. 'Having said that, he certainly does cut a daunting figure. It's the sharp eyes that do it, I think. Even my father was quite frightened as we stood in the drawing-room and he tried to make conversation.'

The discourse between Nat Sherwood, wealthy landowner and aspiring owner of very decent racehorses, and Fred Winter, taciturn trainer, went something like this:

Sherwood: 'It is very good of you to take my son on.'

Winter: 'Yes, he's a lucky man.'

Sherwood: 'Er, we have this horse in Ireland we're keen on, and we would very much like to bring him over here for you to train at Uplands.'

Winter: 'If he's good enough, I'll have him.'

Oliver Sherwood later became convinced that this economy of speech, seen by some as aggressive and by others as bordering on plain rude, was 'just Fred's basic shyness coming out'. But on that first afternoon in the drawing-room he was not aware of that possibility, and nor was his father. They could have been affronted but, like so many others before and since when confronted by the bluntness of Winter, they were not. The horse mentioned by Mr Sherwood was duly brought across from Ireland and received the seal of approval from the trainer. The horse's name was Venture to Cognac and, four seasons later, he was thought good enough to run in the Cheltenham Gold Cup. Ridden by Oliver, he was sent off the 6–1 third favourite but finished unplaced behind Michael Dickinson's Silver Buck.

In the six years that Oliver spent with Fred he learned much about the great man's predilections and came quickly to terms with the fact that punctuality rated high among them. 'I was not a bad timekeeper, but nothing like as sharp as I am now. When I married Denise I found that, although she was late for everything else, she was always on time to go racing. She had got used to this by knowing that her father would leave her behind if she was not ready. It has rubbed off on me as a trainer, too – I can't stand being kept waiting by anybody.'

There was a morning, however, when Sherwood's sense of timing let him down and his 'guv'nor' reacted inimitably. 'I was living in a house in Eastbury, a couple of miles down the road from Lambourn, and for some reason I overslept,' he recalls. 'The first thing I heard was a carhorn outside my window. I blearily looked at my clock and it was 8.45. I was ninety minutes late for work. That panicked me, but not half as much as the sight of Fred behind the wheel of the car that had woken me!

'There was snow on the ground, which was a relief in a way, as it meant that I had probably not missed anything important, but I still knew better than to expect a genial welcome when I rushed out in a half-dressed and unkempt state. All Fred actually said was: "I don't want this to happen again – it's unprofessional," and then, to all intents and purposes, it was forgotten. This was his way. He would not spare you if you were in the wrong, but once he had bollocked you, that was the end of it.'

Sherwood was once not spared the full venom of Fred's tongue after riding a bad race but, as he ruefully concedes, the cause was more his attempts to camouflage the crime than the crime itself. 'It was the only time when he seriously tore me off over riding, but it was one of the most humiliating experiences of my life.'

It happened just before Christmas 1979. The brief festive recession was looming and, as usual, Winter had some fancied runners for the Boxing Day meeting at Kempton Park. These plans, however, were thrown into confusion when John Francome was injured. He was riding Chumson, favourite for the Welsh Grand National, that annual slog through the perennial mud of Chepstow. Chumson was brought down and Francome dislocated his shoulder. He called it the most painful injury he ever suffered, curtailing his riding for six weeks and costing him the jockeys' championship for the only time in seven seasons. Winter had been at Chepstow to watch Chumson run and was understandably concerned by the outcome. His mood was not improved by watching his assistant trainer, and stable amateur, partner another of his horses, Esparto, in a hurdle race at Towcester.

'It was very rare for Towcester to be on television and that was my downfall,' admits Sherwood. 'Esparto was a useful horse, there were only seven runners and on form it looked a two-horse race between mine and Badsworth Boy from the Dickinson stable. Tommy Carmody, who rode that one, obviously thought so too, and we played cat and mouse for so much of the race that we had no chance of catching one of Toby Balding's that had made all the running.

'As Fred wasn't there, I told the lad in charge that Esparto didn't like the sticky ground, which I knew to be nonsense. He had already won on the soft and would do so again. I was just looking for an excuse.

'When I got back to Lambourn I went breezing into the drawing-room to see the guv'nor. Fred was there, in his usual chair. Di and two of the girls were there too, including Denise, whom I was taking out at the time. Stupidly I tried the same excuse on Fred, telling him that my horse had run a cracking race but just hated the ground. Well, he laid into me, in front of the family, and I have never felt so small in my life. It was the Saturday before Christmas and I'd been looking forward to a good night out with Denise, but I left that room feeling so awful I just went home.

'The next day I did not know quite what to expect, but Fred just came across and said, quite calmly: "Next time you make a mistake, I want to be told the truth about it." He was quite right, of course, and I was aware that he thought much worse of me for being dishonest about it than for making a balls of the race. I've never forgotten that, and when I started training I told my jockeys I always wanted the truth, without any bullshit.'

Life in a training yard is never quiet, partly as a result of the syndrome, described by Diana Winter, in which 'racing people love to hear their own voices bellowing'. But it is a precise science, not only in the preparation of a particular horse for a particular race but also in the unseen minutiae, such as entries, declarations, booking of jockeys and, in a few cases, the confirmation that a horse will wear blinkers. Mention this to Oliver Sherwood and it brings forth another story of error, though without the subsequent explosion.

In the 1980–81 season Derring Rose was one of the best staying hurdlers in the country. He was also one of the most temperamental. He won Ascot's Long Walk Hurdle but John Francome, who rode him that day and thereafter, had to nurse and kid the horse until asking him to come with a decisive late effort. The previous year he had won at Kempton, Liverpool and Ascot when trained by Alan Jarvis and ridden by the stylish Andy Turnell. Now, in his first season at Uplands, he was becoming more wilful and more enigmatic with age and Fred had decided that he was a natural candidate for blinkers.

Derring Rose's target for the season was the Waterford Crystal Stayers Hurdle, over 3 miles and 1 furlong, on the opening day of the Cheltenham Festival meeting. He had been a good third in the race for the previous season and plainly had an outstanding chance now, if he consented to do his best. Fred considered that the blinkers were essential to this aim. Oliver, whose job it was to confirm all the runners with Weatherbys each day, forgot to declare them.

'When I told Fred what I'd done, he just grunted "Hell!" and stomped off. I was convinced that my mistake had cost us any chance, and as we didn't have too many other fancied runners at Cheltenham that year, I felt terrible about it. I didn't sleep a wink on the night before the race but then Johnny, who had just won the Champion Hurdle on Sea Pigeon, went out and won on Derring Rose by all of thirty lengths. As we walked into the winners' enclosure, Fred put his arm around me and said: "Well done. Do that more often."'

Two other things which lingered in Sherwood's mind about Winter were his approach to work mornings and his tactics with owners. Work mornings were, of course, conducted under the legendary restrictions of Fred's pre-breakfast temper, but it was something else which impressed itself on his son-in-law.

'There was no pre-planning about which horse would do what with whom,' he explains. 'I always have to do this sort of thing the previous night and get it written down, but Fred would sort it out in his head up on the gallops. He would trot up and down on his horse and then give his instructions. The trouble with this was that he would mutter at the lads so that some of them did not understand what they were being asked to do, but no one dared to ask the guv'nor to repeat anything. This was a failing of his – he simply wasn't very good at explaining things, and I think it came down to shyness again.

'Another weakness, to my mind, was that he very seldom spoke to the lads on the way back from exercise to ask them how their horses had gone. Brian would always be on at him to talk to the boys and get some feedback but perhaps he had just got fed up with twenty years of bullshit. And then, of course, he was always so bad-tempered at that time of day that he may have frightened them into silence anyway.'

One lad most certainly frightened by Winter was Neil Fearn, who featured in a celebrated incident repeated endlessly around Lambourn in succeeding years and doubtless embellished scandalously. It was during the 1983–84 season and Winter had taken to using a short-cut to the downs through the Rhonehurst yard previously manned by Richard Head and subsequently to be used by Sherwood himself. The Heads, responsible for such quality chasers as Border Incident and Uncle Bing, had recently retired from training and were happy for the Winter string to come through their yard each day. On the morning in question Fred was impatient to be on the gallops early to be sure of the best ground and was not pleased when he found that the gate which led out of Rhonehurst on to the downs was, unusually, shut.

'Fred told Neil to get off his horse and open the gate,' relates Sherwood. 'He began wrestling with the bolt and soon saw it was a hopeless task. "It's locked, guv'nor," he said, but Fred took no notice at all, swore and told him to hurry up because we didn't have all morning. Neil made another despairing effort to twist the steel and then repeated that it was locked, whereupon Fred lost his temper, jumped down from his horse and growled: "Do I have to do every bloody thing myself?"

'It didn't take him long to ascertain that the bolt was indeed immovable, but that did not calm him. Instead he turned to Neil and shouted: "You stupid boy, it's locked!" Mrs Head had been roused by the fuss and she now came out to apologise for the fact that she had locked the gate but for some reason didn't have the key. Fred proceeded to shout at her, too, telling her she had ruined an entire morning's work. Later that day he sent her a huge bunch of flowers.'

Here was the enigma of the man, the quick spark and then the long, slow glow. 'He would sometimes freak, and then it would be forgotten,' says Sherwood. 'Not every day, but maybe once a fortnight. And the strange thing was, he was much better when the horses were running badly. It was as if he had no trouble laughing off the lows but worried like hell when things were going too well.'

Things did not go euphorically well at Uplands during Oliver Sherwood's time. There was a steady supply of winners, and Fifty Dollars More did win the Mackeson Gold Cup and Brown Chamberlin the Hennessy. But the trainers' title, in the late 1970s and early 1980s, was annexed by the north, the years of Peter Easterby being followed by the years of Michael Dickinson.

Sherwood's final year, however, was personally memorable. Winter was second in the trainers' table, sending out the most winners but earning slightly less stake money than Dickinson. Sheikh Ali Abu Khamsin, one of the yard's major patrons, was champion owner and John Francome who, controversially, rode none of the Sheikh's horses, was once more champion jockey with his own personal tally of 131 winners. A Sherwood was champion amateur too, Simon emulating his elder brother by dint of three winners in the season's final twenty-four hours. As for Oliver, his riding career came to an appropriate climax when Venture to Cognac, the family horse Fred had said he would take 'if he's good enough', proved that beyond question by winning the season's major amateur event, the Foxhunters at Cheltenham.

Only a fortnight separated Cheltenham and Aintree that year, and the Sherwoods did not go to the well too often with their horse. Oliver was there on the day of the Liverpool Foxhunters, though, and he would have paid special attention to the rider of a horse named Gay Tab who, to quote the official formbook was 'behind when refused seventh'. This inauspicious effort was piloted by Mr C. Brooks who had just been informed that he was soon to become the new assistant trainer to his long-time hero.

Charlie Brooks had already been at Uplands for two years when the call came and did not contemplate being there very much longer. It was not that he had not enjoyed his time, or thought it not worthwhile, simply that he could see no way of progressing. Strange how things happen; six years on, he is a successful and ambitious trainer in his own right.

Charlie's introduction to Fred Winter came about by a typically eccentric route. He had spent six months working for the Lambourn yard of Nick Gaselee after leaving school and, at that time, his sister had come to know Fred's daughters and gone on holiday with them. It was while he himself was on holiday, in Corfu, that he made the luckiest chance encounter of his life. 'I was walking down a beach when I met Jo Winter,' he recalls. 'I had met her a few times in Lambourn and I said rather coyly to her that I was thinking of writing to her father for a job. I wasn't, but I now had the idea in my head.

'I had found out that Fred's pupil-assistant, who also rode as an amateur, had left, and I was given an interview for the job. Someone told me I should put on a suit and tie, which amazed me, as I hardly acknowledged their existence at the time, but I did as instructed and went along, telling myself that at least I could say I had walked into Fred Winter's house.

'He turned me down pretty quickly. Said I was too inexperienced and too heavy which, of course, was quite right. On the way out I spontaneously asked him if he was looking for any stable-lads. I surprised myself more than him by this question, but I had suddenly decided that there was only one man in the world I wanted to work for, and this was him. I think I would have been prepared to ask him if he wanted a cook for the lads' hostel next.

'Fred tried to find Brian Delaney, who does the hiring and firing, and thank God he didn't. I don't think an eighteen-year-old Old Etonian would have appealed to him. So Fred came back, found me still there and told me to start on the following Monday. I was vaguely aware that this interview had passed in a bit of a mist and that everything had somehow gone wrong. I also knew that I would have forgotten all about racing if the guv'nor had turned me down.'

Two years on, he was heartily wishing that he had been turned down. 'It was a Monday, I shall always remember, and I was mucking out, which I never did get to enjoy. I'd done two years as a lad and I thought I'd had enough. The first year was exciting because it was different. I mean – I actually got to do things like play tennis with John Francome! But in the second year it all went thin on me. My rucksack felt heavier by the day and, although I was pleased to have tried the life, my riding hopes were not going well and I just wasn't enjoying it any more. I had pretty much committed myself to going into the city and taking a stockbroking job, where at least I would get a cup of coffee in the morning.'

What Charlie did not know was that Fred had decided it was time his son-in-law, as Oliver had by now become, moved out from under his wing and ran his own yard. Oliver was nervous at the prospect. 'Fred pushed me into it,' he admits. 'He told me I had been with him too long. I was still frightened to take the plunge but he came up one day and said he had decided to ask Charlie to take over from me. I gulped, but knew he was doing it for my benefit.'

Having informed Oliver of his plans to further his career, whether he liked it or not, Fred now had to impart to Charlie the information that he was about to be promoted. Diana and Jo both apparently believed that the maturing Old Etonian, now pushing twenty-one, would make an ideal assistant, and although unimpressed by the boy's riding, Fred felt there was that certain something about young Brooks. But, in the classically shy manner which manifested itself in different ways throughout his life, he did not immediately make himself clear.

'The guv'nor came up to me in the yard that day and asked me what my plans were,' recalls Brooks. 'He had previously advised me that it might do me good to go and work for an overseas trainer for a year or two. I told him my thoughts about going into stockbroking and he just looked at me, grunted, and wandered off again.

'The next afternoon I was mowing the lawn when he came stomping across, looking, I thought, pretty grumpy. Very particular about lawns, he is. Likes the lines to be straight. So I braced myself for a bollocking when he ordered me to stop the mower. Then he said that Oliver was going to leave at the end of the season and I had two days to consider whether I would like to take over.

'I replied that, if he didn't mind, I would like to accept straight away. After all, so far as I was concerned, this was rather like the chairman of ICI asking me if I would care to be his assistant. It didn't require any further agonising. At first, maybe, I still thought it might only be a temporary thing which would look good on my CV when I went into the city, because I never did think I would be a trainer. But when I discussed the job with Oliver, a few days later, he said quietly but firmly that it was not something I could just do for a year and then abandon. Tradition and continuity and all that!'

Charlie may ostensibly have been only a lad until now but he had already experienced revelation, embarrassment and utter terror in the job, all in the space of a few minutes at Sandown Park in January of 1984.

One of the consequences of Brooks joining the Winter stable, even in a relatively menial capacity, had been that his mother had sent more than one horse to be trained at Uplands, with the express intention that her son should do the race-riding where possible. Through witnessing this particular owner–trainer relationship, Charlie learned a little more about his new boss.

'He could be very abrupt with the owners, even though he liked a lot of them. But he loved the lady owners and was always better with them. His voice would change when he was speaking to a woman and, with my mother, he was absolutely charming – gentle and kind, even when telling her about my riding.

'At that time we had a horse called Fionnadoir, who had some ability but was a complete headbanger. I couldn't ride one side of him but, despite that, he'd won a hurdle by thirty lengths at Devon and so we took him to Sandown for a novice handicap. The trouble started in the parade ring when my sister arrived in a black leather jacket, ripped-up jeans and dark glasses. I thought: "I can't believe this, the guv'nor will go mad," but instead he absolutely loved her. I reckon if it had been my brother dressed like that he would probably have thrown him out of the paddock. No sooner was I on the horse and out of the parade ring than things grew worse. The horse got loose, pinned his lad against that wall by the walkway to the course and then threw his head back so that the reins were down between his legs. With that, he set off with me, and we were doing a good, swinging canter towards the plate-glass door of the members' bar. Somehow we avoided that disaster and got down to the start, but the horse was still unruly so John Francome, who was riding for another trainer, grabbed hold of him and led me meekly round like a child on a leading rein.'

There were other humiliations to come, other lessons to be learned – the usual one about punctuality, for instance. 'I was once two minutes late to go racing. The guv'nor left me behind. I was actually driving into the yard as he was driving out but he didn't stop, didn't even look at me. He was the same with everyone, though, including the owners. There were no exceptions. If he had a duke coming for second lot and he was ten minutes late, he'd swear about him and then go without him.'

Like Sherwood, Brooks also made one blunder with entries and quaked at the reaction it would bring. 'The golden rule in my job at Uplands was to walk out of breakfast to the telephone and deal with all the runners for the following day, as the Weatherbys deadline is ten o'clock. One day something happened in the yard at breakfast time and I stupidly allowed myself to be distracted. By the time I had dealt with it I looked at my watch and it was 10.01. I felt the blood rush to my head, because I had left two horses in at Ascot which the guv'nor had no intention of running.

I had my head in my hands when Fred came into the office. I was straight with him about what I'd done, admitted that it was a big error and promised that it wouldn't happen again. He was a good man to make a ricket for. He never raised his voice, just told me that I would have to go to the races and explain the position to the stewards. He would forgive you making almost any mistake once, but I knew if I had done it a second time, it would have been different.'

Charlie Brooks was the end of a dynasty, the last of the men who were drawn into racing, when family ties pointed elsewhere, purely because they could work for Fred Winter. And, as the last, and the man now in charge at Uplands, perhaps he sums up what they all feel when he says: 'Where would we be without Fred Winter? I know I would be nothing. I couldn't even ride . . . I wouldn't be in racing.'

17
Winding down

In the summer of 1980 Fred Winter suffered a stroke. It was mild, to the point that he was slightly surprised to be told he had had one, but it was a preliminary warning that, in his mid-fifties, he was not as indestructibly robust as once he had been.

He began to feel ill at the end of a gourmet weekend in France. On the ferry his condition deteriorated but it was only through a specialist examination, back in England, that a stroke was diagnosed. The first effect of this news was that Fred gave up cigarettes. He had smoked from the age of seven, a habitual, anxiety smoker, of around thirty cigarettes a day. But, as with most things in his life, one he had decided it must be given up, there was not a problem and soon he was sharply recommending any of his acquaintances who were still inclined to light up that it was time they mended their ways too.

A second effect was that Fred took stock of himself and eased back on life's throttle. The changes were not dramatic, indeed they were scarcely discernible to an outsider. But Fred had paid his warning the compliment of a respectful nod. He began to delegate more duties to his assistant, Oliver Sherwood, who would often represent him at the races, and although he remained very much a hands-on trainer, riding out every morning as usual and scrutinising the yard with all the old thoroughness, he was a shade more careful, a shade more phlegmatic.

'I lead a quiet life these days,' he told me, a couple of years after his stroke. 'I will go to any local meeting, within an hour and a half or so, and there are certain tracks I like to attend, such as Fontwell. But the thought of sitting in a car for four or five hours doesn't appeal these days. Often I am more use at home. Anyway, I take the view that nothing can happen now which hasn't already.' Then, having expressed this untypically sanguine outlook on life, Fred thought for a second before asking: 'Does that sound boastful? I do hope not.'

If some of the incentives had diminished, however, the professionalism which Winter unceasingly demanded of everyone at Uplands continued unimpaired. The fifty-nine boxes were invariably full and, if the quality of horse inside them could not match that of the heady days of the early 1970s, well, what yard's could? Fred's principles remained the same as ever, in the purchasing and preparation of his horses and, in his singular way, the training of his owners.

In this aspect, he would never change. Brevity and economy of contact might have been Fred's catch-phrase for dealing with his owners. It was not, in most cases, that he did not like them, simply that if he was to work productively for them, it was not best achieved by wasting time in idle conversation and desultory socialising. Fred summarised his attitude by referring to an owner who had sent him a horse some years earlier. 'I used to ride for this man ages ago, and he wanted to talk about his one horse till the cows came home. He started telling me exactly what it ate, and all the work it did, so I quickly cut him short. I told him that *I* would now be training the horse and that I would feed it and give it whatever work I thought it needed. He got the message and our later conversations were scaled down to simply how the horse was and where it was going to run. Which is all that any owner needs to know, apart from some indication of how his horse might run when he does go to the races.'

Many trainers, and many owners for that matter, will cringe at this bald assessment of the requirements of a successful relationship. Most trainers, especially those of a younger vintage, expect to give their owners rather less cursory treatment, while some are positively sycophantic, and have owners who appreciate it. None of this ever impressed Fred, no matter how much of it he witnessed. He had his ways, and if the owners did not like it, they could go somewhere else.

'Dealing with owners was something in which the guv'nor was lacking,' admits Brian Delaney, the head lad. 'When we started up, he was OK, because the owners he attracted were horsy people who understood the job and its demands. But in later years the type of owners changed. They want more contact with the trainer now, they want to come to the yard with their friends and they expect to be entertained. The guv'nor didn't want to know about that side of it. But I'll say one thing – all the owners respected his decisions. No one argued.'

Other trainers would secretly have admired Fred for achieving such subservience through such blunt means. But what those around him respected more than anything was the recurring theme of integrity. Fulke Walwyn's wife Cath, who now holds the licence at Saxon House with her husband in ill health, says: 'There always was a lot of rivalry between our yards as next-door neighbours, but that came more from the lads than from Fred and Fulke, who remained very good friends. Things can sometimes get difficult with trainers living on top of each other, but we never had any fall-outs with Fred. Many trainers will try to pinch your owners, but Fred would never do that.'

There were times when it seemed Winter would far sooner have his horses without the encumbrance of owners, as Oliver Sherwood recalls. 'Most trainers are stuck with a few owners that they can't stand. Fred eventually wouldn't take them. He didn't think it was worth the aggravation just for an extra horse. When I was about to start out on my own, he was always telling me to begin as I meant to go on. He told me never to have owners in for breakfast and, if they wanted to come to the yard in the mornings, to put them off to second lot, when you could go up in the car with them to watch their horse school.

'One of the pleasures of training,' added Oliver, 'seems to me to be giving pleasure to nice people who have horses with you. Because of that I find it very hard to give my owners bad news. Easily the worst part of the job is coming back from morning exercise knowing that a horse has broken down and you must phone the owner and tell him. I don't suppose Fred found it easy, but he would always do it immediately and he never coated the bad news with any flannel.'

Diana Winter's breakfast table was the scene for many such mournful episodes but she says: 'Fred would deliberately avoid saying that a horse had broken down. He simply wouldn't talk about such things at breakfast – in fact he didn't talk about much at all. In a way it was him trying not to worry me with his problems. It was also an expression of what he always believed, that women had no place in racing. I accepted that. I saw it as his job and felt I should leave it to him.'

Fred was also notably honest with owners on the subject of gambling, which he could not stop but would do nothing to encourage. For a man who worked so marvellously well, for so many years, with one of the most open and ebullient of gambling trainers, Ryan Price, Fred was correct to the point of puritanism. He did not bet himself, either on his horses or anyone else's, and he steadfastly refused to 'lay a horse out' simply so the owners could have a big punt at false odds. Diana explains: 'He never liked this practice when he was riding, and it reached the stage where Ryan would never tell Fred if they were having a punt. Then, when he started training, he made a point of telling all the owners that his would not be a gambling yard. No one took their horses away through it.'

The Winter view was that horses should always run on their merits, although this did not mean that they should be knocked about before they were ready for it. As John Francome recalled, all that was asked of Fred's jockeys was to put every horse into the race with a chance at some stage. If they were too weak, no need to knock them about. If they were not good enough, come back and say so. Francome usually did and this, combined with the evidence of his own eyes, would be passed pitilessly on to the doting owners.

Fred believed that there was little point in kidding an owner along if he had a horse which was next to useless. The owner was wasting his money and Fred was, to some extent, wasting space. He would receive the same basic fees from an owner of a poor selling plater as he would from the owner of a Gold Cup winner, but the selling plater would not be bringing any win percentages into the yard. Clear him out and there was a chance to fill the box with something of more ability.

'A lot of owners don't like being told that their horse is no good,' points out Oliver Sherwood. 'They prefer to hear excuses for the fact that he has finished tailed-off again, no matter how improbable. They like to hear their trainer say that things will be different if we run him over a new trip, or make the running with him, or try him in blinkers. Fred would never do that. He would always tell them if he felt their horse had no prospect of winning a race. Eventually, of course, he was in a position to do so, but it was his policy from the start and it has to be right. Once the owner has got over the dent to his ego, he will be saving money that would otherwise just be poured away.'

This is essentially just another example of a familiar Winter ethos – that the training of racehorses is down to common sense, and that the same should apply to the owners. His rigid rules about honesty with owners whenever it affected their pockets were, however, slightly relaxed in later years when it came down to what he considered more trivial matters, such as his presence at the races. Many owners like to have their trainer alongside them on the stand when their horse runs.

It is easy to understand why: ownership, to the majority, is not a business but a bit of sport which can transcend into fantasy and have its roots in pride and ego. If I had a horse with Fred Winter, I expect I would like him next to me on the steps at Fontwell or Towcester (my sights are sensibly low), his binoculars raised to his sharp eyes and the growling voice emitting the occasional mutter of comment or encouragement. Fred's view was that, more often than not, he was wasting his time. 'I can chat to the owners, of course,' he once explained, 'but I certainly can't do any more to make the horse win.'

And so, just occasionally, he told one or other of his owners a white lie. Brian Delaney was in on the ruse and explains: 'Towards the end Fred really didn't like travelling far at all, especially to certain courses, and if we had one runner at Plumpton and another at Taunton he would tell each of the owners that he had to go to the other meeting, when actually he would go off and play golf.'

On the occasions when he did go racing, Fred would sometimes drive to the course, but he would hardly ever drive home. That job fell to Oliver, or to John Francome or, in the closing years of his career, to Charlie Brooks. Once at the races, Fred's first mission would not be to seek out his owners (he would have a drink with them after their race, if at all) but to find his close friend and former riding colleague at Findon, Josh Gifford.

In the interim since they both moved on to training, their old 'guv'nor' Ryan Price had enjoyed some twilight triumphs. Concentrating on the flat, he won the 1972 Oaks with Charles St George's filly, Ginevra. One of the first congratulatory telegrams he received was from Fred. The Captain remained effervescent to the end, which came late in 1982. At the funeral Dorothy Price spoke as Ryan would have wanted his widow to speak. She asked both Fred and Josh to buy her a horse. 'I told them that I wanted them to dead-heat in the Schweppes,' she recalled, faithful to the great handicap which had brought her husband so much success but so much anguish and controversy too. It did not quite work out that way, of course, but seven years later Admiral's All, whom Fred had purchased for her, won a novice chase at Newbury on Schweppes day. Mrs Price enjoyed that.

There always had been a bond between Winter and Gifford, even though Josh is fifteen years the younger and came into racing viewing Fred as an untouchable idol. A little of that idolatory has endured everything but, as trainers together, on equal terms, the generation gap meant nothing and they became firm friends.

Charlie Brooks relates: 'If I went racing with the guv'nor we would always get there three-quarters of an hour before the first and he would go straight off to find Josh in the owners and trainers' bar, where they would probably have a couple of large gin and tonics. They were very close.'

Gifford remembers the days fondly, but somewhat differently. 'We both had arrangements with our jockeys,' he says. 'We'd take our own cars so long as they drove back. But Fred would often take his flask of coffee and his sandwiches and he would usually be sitting in the car, eating, when I arrived. I was always heading for the bar and this was often the cue for a pompous lecture. "Why do you drink so much, Josh?" he would say. "You don't need to." But he enjoyed his gin and tonic too.'

It was one such assignation over the Gordon's which led to firm evidence that Fred was, indeed, taking life at a steadier canter. They agreed, not without some trepidation, to take a mid-season holiday together, something that the Fred Winter of old would possibly have regarded as an untimely luxury if not a dereliction of duty. But now it was to become a regular habit.

'This all started one January day at Lingfield,' confirms Gifford. 'We were both having a bad run at the time and it had been in my mind that a holiday might do me good. I suggested it to Fred in the bar and his immediate reaction was: "Do we dare?" By the time we had drunk another gin, our minds were made up, and we went away, with our wives, at about the same time for the next four years.'

The Canary Islands, Lanzarote and Antigua all enjoyed the business of the refugees from an English National Hunt season and both trainers agreed that they should have done it years earlier. Wherever they went, however, the men's routine centred on the golf course.

'We usually agreed to meet in the hotel lobby at eight in the morning,' recalls Josh. 'I was often five or ten minutes late, and every time, without fail, I would find Fred stomping around indignantly, pointing at his watch. Even on holiday, punctuality was all-important to him.'

Although relaxing away from the anxieties of Lambourn and Findon, the trainers could not entirely cut themselves off from the realities of their life, and periodical phone calls would be made back to their respective assistants. 'Fred would usually come off the phone gloating, because he'd had three or four winners and I hadn't had any!'

Fred's competitive instincts would come out at golf, of course, but also when the two couples played whist after dinner. 'Fred would take it very seriously,' said Josh, 'and when I made my regular silly mistakes, he would sometimes show a real flash of temper. "Getting a boy to do a man's job" was his favourite saying when I played a hand badly.

'Fred has always had it in him to be a very pompous man, you know,' Gifford continues. 'He even showed himself to be a bit of a wine-snob on holiday, and that had some unfortunate side-effects for me. We'd take it in turns to choose the wine at dinner and I would never be very fussy. One night I ordered a bottle of something and Fred sent it back. Said it tasted like Tizer. I was embarrassed by this so Fred told me to taste the new bottle. I had a sip and told the waiter it was fine. Fred then tasted it and said: "That's even worse!" I got a bit fed up with this and told him he could order what he wanted but I would drink what we'd got. Fred ordered something different but after a few glasses of my bottle I was doubled up with stomach pains and had to go to bed. Fred thought it was absolutely hilarious!'

As the 1981–82 season neared its climax, the Winter yard confronted a crisis of the unseen, insidious sort. The country's leading owner at the time was the only Arab to make serious incursions into jump racing, Sheikh Ali Abu Khamsin. Athough he spread his favours among a variety of trainers, Uplands housed some of his very best horses, including Fifty Dollars More and Half Free who, between them, were destined to win three of the next four runnings of the Mackeson Gold Cup, the handicap chase at Cheltenham which is traditionally seen as the first major event of each National Hunt season. On each occasion, the horses were ridden not by Fred's stable jockey but by Richard Linley, whom the Sheikh had chosen to retain.

This had been expedited during the course of the season, Francome having previously ridden the Sheikh's Uplands horses with considerable success. The Sheikh stated that he had jettisoned Francome because he was 'insulted' that he had decided not to ride his Fifty Dollars More in the Arkle Chase at the Cheltenham Festival. Francome had, indeed, chosen to ride the other Winter runner, Sea Image, for the owners of Midnight Court, George and Olive Jackson, but he privately believed that there were murkier reasons for a decision which hurt and soured him. He had been beaten into fourth place, behind the redoubtable Wayward Lad no less, at Ascot on Fifty Dollars More earlier that season and he suspected that the Sheikh believed he had stopped his horse. In fact Fifty Dollars More ran that day with sore shins, which prevented him jumping with any confidence, and Francome gave him a particularly tender ride for that reason.

Francome's natural pique at being jocked off some very decent horses is perhaps secondary, within this episode, to the role of Fred Winter. Hitherto he had always maintained that the horses in his yard would be ridden by whoever he nominated, and that the owners could either accept this proviso or go elsewhere. Now here he was acceding to the demands of an owner that all, not just one, of his horses should be henceforth be ridden by a jockey who had no connection with the stable at all.

There are, perhaps, not very many things in his career that Winter would do differently, given the chance, but Brian Delaney believes this would be one of them. 'If Fred could have his time again, he would not have allowed that to happen. Apart from anything else, it opened the way for other owners to do the same thing.'

Although resentful, Francome later reasoned a case in defence of his invariably loyal boss. 'I can see it must have been very difficult for him. If he had said he wanted me to ride the horses come what may, he would probably have lost them. How far do you take a principle? But at the time I was a bit upset by it.'

Despite the loss of some high-quality rides, a persistent chest virus and the attentions of a new riding star in Peter Scudamore, Francome finished the 1981–82 season as joint champion. Scudamore, twenty winners ahead, broke his arm in a fall at Southwell with five weeks of the season remaining, whereupon Francome roused his dampened spirits and set off in a headlong pursuit which covered well over 3,000 miles and brought him into contact with some highly dubious animals. Four days from the end of the season he drew level with Scudamore and promptly, as promised, declared his season over. It had been a punishing, sometimes reckless few weeks, but at the end of it came a gesture of which Fred Winter himself would surely have approved.

While Francome was criss-crossing the country in his search for winners, Winter was parked in his favourite armchair at Uplands, telling me his exalted opinion of him. 'I would say it is a toss-up between three, Bryan Marshall, Martin Molony and Johnny, as to who is the best jockey of my time,' he said. 'Johnny has been a marvellous stable jockey. At times he is absolutely brilliant, probably the best of the lot. He has got everything. But there have been occasions when he has upset me. He will go right round the outside, come in fifth or sixth and them jump off and say he's pleased. I have to bite my tongue then, because he is a sensitive bloke. But the silence on those days is worth it for the winners he has ridden which no one else would have come close on. Everyone has bad days. Jockeys are no different.'

It was a fulsome testimony, notwithstanding the rider about Francome's 'away days', and it was doubtless repeated just as genuinely three years later when the association of sixteen seasons came to its natural end with Francome's retirement. The fact remains, however, that despite all the mutual loyalty down the years, during their last two years together they did not co-exist quite as contentedly as before.

Francome, of course, was involved in more sinister deeds when his home telephone was tapped and the tapes sent to a national newspaper. Fred was not visibly concerned by this development but then, as Francome reflected: 'He didn't even like talking about anything unpleasant that was happening at the time, whether it be about stewards, phone tapping or whatever.'

Just how much had permeated into Fred's consciousness may now never be fully explained but Francome came, latterly, to the conclusion that he was not trusted quite as he had been before.

'Until then, the only time we had fallen out at all was around the time of the John Banks affair. Although he was very supportive, he still thought I hadn't tried as hard as I should on some of the horses. For my part, I was convinced that there was something wrong with them, but Fred would not hear of that until I rode one at Lingfield which cruised up to win the race and then found absolutely nothing. I never picked up my stick, just let the horse coast in, but he came back totally exhausted. Fred realised then that something was amiss and everything was OK between us again.

'It was during that season that we were riding back from the downs together, shortly after Cheltenham, when he suddenly said that someone had told him I was offered £5,000 to stop Rodman in the Triumph Hurdle. I thought he was going to add that the "someone" had been from the Security Services and that it was a serious matter, but it turned out to have been somebody's dentist! I told him not to be so silly and he never mentioned it again.'

The syndrome repeated itself in the 1984–85 season, Francome's last. This was to be the year when, with Michael Dickinson having gone in search of new conquests across the Atlantic, Fred Winter returned to head the trainers' list for the eighth and last time. It was not, however, a season of uninterrupted glory, as Francome remembers: 'The horses were wrong for a time but, once again, the guv'nor felt I wasn't trying hard enough. He never quite said as much, and we were still perfectly friendly but, underneath, things had become strained between us.'

It was brought to a head by a horse called Sailor's Dance and a young jockey called Jimmy Duggan, who had joined the Uplands staff on the recommendation of Francome. Duggan won a conditional jockeys' race on Sailor's Dance at Devon and then kept the ride when the horse next ran at Worcester. He duly bolted in again; he was a very useful hurdler, one of the best novices of his year. Cheltenham was coming and Sailor's Dance was inked in for the Supreme Novices Hurdle, the opening event on day one. Winter decided that Duggan should ride, and phoned Francome to tell him so. The stable jockey did not take this well and drove directly down to Uplands to debate the matter. There he was told by Winter that if it meant so much to him, he could ride the horse. Francome accepted but still felt slighted that, as a champion with sixteen years' service behind him, he should have to fight to secure a ride ahead of a boy. 'I nearly told him where to stick his job there and then,' he said later.

Sailor's Dance ran well below par at Cheltenham and Duggan regained the ride two weeks later at Liverool, where the horse won impressively. This time Francome had not even demurred. 'By then I had just resigned myself to the fact that the guv'nor actually didn't want me to ride for him as much as he used to. I had already decided to get out before the end of the season and I think he honestly couldn't wait for it! We still had plenty of winners, though, and when he only had half as many the following season I think he realised I might have had a point.'

The last Cheltenham of Francome's career was probably an event he would like expunged from the memory, though with his facility to worry about little he probably did so years ago. It began with Sailor's Dance and continued with The Reject, an aptly named horse who fell at the second fence in the Arkle Chase. Francome's left foot caught in its iron and he was literally hung upside down as the horse got up and trotted away. Francome later admitted to being terrified and when, the following month at Chepstow, the very same horse fell again, he got up, walked gratefully back to the weighing-room and announced that he had ridden his final race.

The Reject was neither the best nor the worst horse that Francome rode for Fred Winter; it was simply a coincidence that he hastened his retirement. And, despite the mutual doubts which surfaced in that final season, Francome retired as champion jockey and left Winter as champion trainer. Both were as delighted for each other as they were for themselves. If it had not always been a smooth partnership, then the most successful teams seldom are. It had undeniably been a great one.

Now, for what transpired to be the closing chapter of his training career, Fred was obliged to seek a new stable jockey. He might have appointed Ben De Haan, a faithful number two for two years; instead he nominated the next champion jockey in appointing Peter Scudamore.

18

The cruellest fall

The August evening of 1987 when Fred Winter tumbled down the stairs of his beloved home at Uplands signalled the end of his racing career. It had been a glorious and enduring career, almost half a century in all, and at first nobody was prepared to believe it was over. Fred, everyone seemed to assume, would go on forever.

Only gradually did it dawn upon the racing world that, even when he recovered from the physical damage inflicted by the fall, Fred might never again be fit enough to resume command of his domain. A second stroke, far more severe than his first, had accompanied the accident, and its cruel legacy was to limit its victim's mobility and render him virtually incapable of speech or writing. He would never work again.

Fred had long been proud of a particular picture, hung above the fireplace in his comfortable lounge. It was an impression of a steeple-chase in progress, the horses all properly saddled but jumping the course without jockeys. In a sense, this is what now occurred at Uplands. The horses would go on running, as Fred undoubtedly wished, but the 'company commander', as he once called himself, would no longer be in sharp-eyed, dapperly-dressed control.

Fred had continued to enjoy the routine he knew so well right up to the time of his accident, although the pace of the yard was perhaps not what it had been and the trainer, justifiably, was spending rather more time on the golf course and tending his roses than he might once have done. Still, the winners kept coming. Perhaps the 1985–86 total of forty-one was strikingly low for Winter, but the trainers' title was won with forty-six – by his former assistant, Nicky Henderson. The following season Winter increased his winners to fifty-one but

Henderson was equal to the challenge and retained his title. It was becoming an interesting duel between the master and his ex-pupil, one which Fred, though past his sixtieth birthday, was not resigned to losing. There were, too, some major prizes brought back to Uplands in these mid-1980s seasons. The Mackeson Gold Cup had become something of a fixture at the place, and Half Free made it three times in four years for the trainer–jockey team of Winter and Linley. A horse called Glyde Court won the Kim Muir Chase at the Cheltenham Festival two years in succession and, as we shall see, there were other Festival winners for the yard.

One feature of the 1985–86 season, however, was an uncertainty over the riding plans at Uplands, something of which Winter could not be accused since his very early days of training, when he personally considered that the size of his yard neither merited nor attracted the retention of a leading jockey. John Francome's retirement was, in one sense, a spontaneous act as, in picking himself up and counting his blessings after The Reject had trampled all over him at Chepstow, he made the straightforward decision that he did not intend to risk such treatment for even one more day. But it had always been planned, between Francome and Winter, that this would be the jockey's final season and it surprised some in the sport that Fred did not act positively to acquire a big-name replacement. The job of first jockey at Uplands, after all, remained something that no one with an ounce of ambition in him would turn down.

Instead, possibly out of an unusual indecision but more probably through a loyal regard for the riders already resident at Uplands, Fred tackled an entire season without an officially retained jockey. Linley, of course, continued to ride all the horses owned by Sheikh Ali Abu Khamsin, and certain horses were ridden by Fred's assistant, Charlie Brooks. But the majority of day-to-day mounts were divided between Jimmy Duggan, of whom Fred plainly had high hopes, and Ben De Haan, one of Uplands' most faithful unsung servants.

Ben has one of those curious, complicated stories behind his entry into racing. His mother was housekeeper to Charlie Smith, a trainer and the brother of Fred Winter's brother-in-law Doug Smith, the former champion flat jockey who tragically killed himself. It was Charlie Smith who recommended his housekeeper's boy to Fred, and Ben started at Uplands shortly before his sixteenth birthday, in the summer of 1975. His starting salary was £2 a week.

He came with high ambitions, as so many do, and might well have been terminally disillusioned before he ever got to weigh out for the first time. 'I had been here four years before I had my first ride. There were many occasions during that time when I thought I was in the wrong job.' He had not known what to make of his 'guv'nor' from the start – 'he hardly spoke to me at the interview' – but, being an essentially private person himself, he did not much mind that. Then, just when he was at last receiving some encouragement in his riding hopes, he had one of those unfortunate early-morning altercations on the downs which, it sometimes seems, have been suffered by everyone in Winter's employment.

An abiding character in the Winter yard at the time was a resilient staying chaser called Rough and Tumble. He was placed in the Grand Nationals of 1979 and 1980, the closest Fred was to come in the race after Crisp's gallant failure in 1973, but this was certainly not an easy ride. Ben 'did' the horse at home and was told one morning he would be riding him in a piece of work.

'Rough and Tumble ran away with me on the gallops,' he explains simply. 'The guv'nor went berserk. He shouted at me: "You want to be a jockey and you can't even keep hold of a horse!" I felt pretty small but, two mornings later, he got on Rough and Tumble himself and it ran away with him too!'

In four years at the Uplands hostel, prior to buying his own house down in the village, Ben saw the caring side of Fred Winter too. 'I had a car accident,' he recalls. 'It was a hit and run, and it shook me up a fair bit. I had no idea what to do but the guv'nor fixed me up with a solicitor and sorted the whole thing out.

'I have always got on well with him, really, and I think it is because we are very similar types. Neither of us says very much. Fred would never offer advice unless you went to ask for it, and it needed guts to go and see him. If you did, he would always try to help, no matter what the problem was.'

It was a horse called Stopped who kick-started Ben's career, having contributed to souring John Francome's two years earlier. Stopped had gone off favourite for the 1978 Imperial Cup handicap hurdle at Sandown and came from a long way off the pace, via some traffic problems, to finish third. There was suspicion, both official and on the grandstand, that Francome had done to the horse what its name dictates, and although he escaped being referred immediately to the Jockey Club (his explanation was not 'accepted' but 'recorded'), the race became an integral part of the subsequent inquiry into Francome's association with the bookmaker John Banks.

Perhaps it was not surprising that Francome should take against the horse after this experience, and when he graduated to fences, De Haan soon became his partner. In March of 1980 De Haan had his first Cheltenham Festival ride and won the Grand Annual Chase on Stopped, to his own memorably wide-eyed amazement and Fred's quiet satisfaction.

De Haan, looking back on the day, remembered how he had expected a lengthy issue of instructions from Winter but had received none. 'He told me I knew how to ride Stopped better than he did.' He remembered how he talked to the horse all the way around Cheltenham's demanding 2-mile chase course, 'calling him names, mainly', and how he was aware of the enormous grin spreading across his boyish face as they crossed the line. 'It's funny,' he said, 'I used to hate that horse because he was always scraping up his bed and was generally a bloody nuisance to look after. But I wasn't complaining that day.'

Two days later, aiming to cash in while the horse was well and the pickings were rich, Winter ran Stopped again, in the Cathcart Chase. A short-priced favourite for an unusual festival double, De Haan and his mount were cruising in the lead when they came down at the uphill fence. It was a long walk back across the track for one deflated jockey and he received no sympathy when he reached the weighing-room. 'The guv'nor was waiting for me, and all he said was: "Why did you fall off it?"'

De Haan never did make the big time in terms of challenging for the jockeys' title – indeed, he has never yet ridden thirty winners in a season – but in 1983 he briefly became a household name as he rode Corbiere to victory in the Grand National, following the inside course which Fred Winter had always preached to his Aintree jockeys. Corbiere, however, was not trained at Uplands, but down the Upper Lambourn lane at Weathercock House, once the 'solitary confinement' for Jay Trump during the anxious days of his Aintree preparation but now a spruce and spreading training centre for Jenny Pitman.

Ben's loyalty to his only racing employer was now put to its most serious test, for he was offered a retainer to join the Pitman yard as first jockey. Jenny was fast becoming a formidable force in training and it was a job which would have tempted anyone with an eye on the future, but Ben declined to sever connections with Uplands. 'I could have gone to Jenny,' he said thoughtfully, 'and she did go on giving me some rides. But the guv'nor is such a genuine man to ride for that I really didn't want to leave.'

Some years on Charlie Brooks held up the relationship between Ben and Fred as an example of all that has been good about the yard. 'Ben has been through the Winter treadmill and he knows no bullshit,' he said. 'He has respect, he is educated and he is loyal. A lot of jockeys have come and gone in his time, and he has never commanded the number one job, but he has seen it through. As for Fred, I think he was messed about by Ben and Jenny Pitman for a while but he was so pleased Ben was doing well that he let him go on riding for her even when it was inconvenient.'

It nearly happened for Ben De Haan in 1985. Out of the bold, imposing shadow of Francome for the first time in his ten years at the yard, he cannot have helped nurturing the hope that he would now assume the mantle of senior stable jockey and ride the pick of the horses. For a time, he did, although Duggan was also accorded a generous share of work. But as that season drew to a close Fred had recorded his poorest tally of winners for many a year and some of his owners were becoming noticeably fidgety. The stable had two Cheltenham winners that year – Glyde Court, ridden by the Irish amateur John Queally and Half Free who, in the absence of the injured Linley, was ridden by Oliver Sherwood's brother Simon. When, at Aintree, Simon Sherwood also won on Fifty Dollars More, there was understandable speculation that the stable jockey's job might be offered to him, but Winter had made up his mind to approach the new champion-elect, Scudamore.

The son of Fred's riding contemporary Michael Scudamore, Peter was in the process of winning the jockeys' championship outright for the first time and, if his percentage of winners to rides was the lowest of any champion for more than a decade, this said something about his obsessive self-motivation and self-denial. Fred would have admired this in much the same way that he admired Lester Piggott. When, at the end of his own riding days, he was asked to nominate the sportsman he most admired, he said of Piggott: 'Perhaps he is an odd cove in some respects, but that man works terribly hard and suffers physical and mental hardship to succeed. I love a trier, and can't stand people who don't try.'

Scudamore, like Piggott, has never been naturally light. Like Piggott, whom he too regarded with some awe, Scudamore sometimes existed on coffee, a cigar and the sauna bath in order to draw the correct weight and broaden his scope of possible rides. Unlike Piggott, and certainly unlike Francome, he was not a natural, but worked incessantly to improve all aspects of his riding. Fred could recall his attacking the job in a very similar way, and thoroughly approved.

The problem was that Scudamore had a retainer to ride for David Nicholson, who trained a cricket-ball throw from the jockey's home at Condicote, just the other side of Stow-on-the-Wold from Fred's home during his own riding days. Scudamore and Nicholson had been a team since Peter started out as an amateur, eight years earlier, and Nicholson was justly proud that he had helped his jockey to the championship. Winter, as usual, went about the matter in a correct and dignified fashion but there can be no pretending that Nicholson was not distinctly unhappy.

Scudamore saw it simply as the one job he could not refuse. 'I had grown up on stories about Fred Winter from my father,' he said. 'Even if his horses had not been going well that season, it was still to my mind the top job in jump racing, and although I was very grateful to David for all his support over the years, it did not occur to me to turn it down.'

In a matter of months Scudamore found he had tapped into a goldmine, for not only did the Uplands horses begin to run better the following season, but he also obtained a secondary agreement to ride for the fast-rising star of training, Martin Pipe. The two jobs together were to ensure that he could not be supplanted as champion jockey, barring serious injury, in the forseeable future. Sadly, however, what might so easily have been a fascinating association with a man whose riding career he had, perhaps unwittingly, imitated to huge effect had only a year of real communication to run.

The lead-up to Cheltenham that season was not fluent for the Winter yard. All manner of things seemed to go against them, and the meeting could not have got off to a stickier start as Celtic Shot, much fancied for the Supreme Novices Hurdle, fell at the first flight. Scudamore, whose personal festival spirits were raised by winning the Queen Mother Champion Chase on Pearlyman for John Edwards, began the final day anxious to ride a winner for his new 'guv'nor' and believing that his best chance lay with I'Haventalight in the Ritz Club Chase which traditionally follows the Gold Cup.

'He was a good chaser but I rode a very bad race on him,' recalled Scudamore later. 'Mr Winter did not mince his words and it was a well-merited rollocking.' The harsh words were still ringing in Scudamore's ears when he went out for his final ride in near-darkness, the card have been delayed by a snowstorm just before the Gold Cup. It was a chance ride in the Cathcart on Half Free, poor Linley having been injured again on the first day of the meeting, and Scudamore did not waste the opportunity to, as he put it, 'salvage some of my reputaton with the guv'nor'.

This was to be the last Cheltenham Fred attended as a trainer and, Half Free's win aside, there was an appropriate result to the Fox-hunters Steeplechase for amateur riders. Observe, looked after at home by Harry Foster and once a real fancy for the Gold Cup, took the race piloted by Charlie Brooks, for whom life was about to change.

It is difficult to quantify the shock factor involved when Fred had his fall. So many people were affected. The drama, concern and uncertainty within his immediate family, during his lengthy spell in hospital, was reflected around his yard, which employed upwards of thirty people, and among his legion of friends. Some, who had been close to the man for many years, visited him in hospital and came away choked with emotion, believing he could not possibly pull through the ordeal.

That he survived, with his mind intact, was the greatest possible relief to all who knew him. But what of Uplands, his pride and joy for twenty-three years? As Ben De Haan expressively recalled: 'What stunned all of us was the fear that the yard could come to a standstill without him.'

Brian Delaney expands on the feeling: 'I felt numbed with shock at first, and then for all of us there was this period of uncertainty, of not quite knowing what we should be doing and what might become of the place. What upset me more than anything was that I'd had it in mind that Fred would only go on another twelve months anyway, just long enough to prepare the ground in his own way for Charlie to take over. I would love him to have retired quietly to his garden and his golf, still coming round to see the horses whenever he chose. Then this had to happen.'

Delaney, for all his understandable despondency, was a tower of strength. In conference with Diana, her daughter Jo and Charlie Brooks, it was decided that operations must continue as normally as was possible while Fred recuperated.

Scudamore, too, played a more prominent role. Brooks leant on his experience of both horses and courses in mapping out the season for the Uplands inmates. Scudamore relished the responsibility, even if he hated the circumstances. Brooks, at first overcome by the burden being thrust upon his young shoulders, also began to flourish. He admits he grew up during that first season without Fred, drawing on everything he had learned from him and, increasingly, employing his own engaging personality in dealing with the owners. Most, if not quite all, stayed faithful during this difficult time and the staunch efforts of all concerned were triumphantly vindicated on a sparkling March afternoon at Cheltenham when Celtic Shot won the Champion Hurdle.

David Horton, owner of Celtic Shot and a great supporter of the yard, was convinced from some way off that his horse would win the Champion. Scudamore was not so confident. He recalls having Sunday lunch with Mr Horton at the beginning of January and being struck by the owner's belief. 'I did not discourage him. I had no shortage of faith in the horse's ability, it was just that I had been there before.' Scudamore, indeed, had been second three times in the race, on Broadsword, Cima and Gaye Brief, and could have been excused for suspecting that it was to inflict the same jinx upon him that the Gold Cup did, twice, on Fred.

When Celtic Shot was well beaten at Sandown by Celtic Chief, in his last run before the Champion, it seemed Scudamore's fears might be accurate. But, by his own admission, he had not ridden a good race that day. 'Mr Winter did not need to say anything to me when I saw him,' he recalled. 'He just looked at me and I knew how he felt.'

At Cheltenham, Scudamore altered his tactics and changed his luck. Making more use of Celtic Shot than at Sandown, he took control of the race at the second last and, although the Irish horse Classical Charm threw down a serious challenge at the last, Celtic Shot stayed on gallantly, uphill and into a wind, to make a fairy tale come true.

Back at Uplands, Brian Delaney, glowing with quiet pride, got up from his chair and turned away from his television. He had watched the race alone at home. 'I used to like going to Cheltenham but we had such bad luck in the Gold Cup that I stopped.' Now he went out of the front door of his bungalow and walked up to the main house.

'The guv'nor had never shown much emotion in the past over our big winners,' said Delaney. 'That day, when I walked into the room where he was watching television, the pleasure on his face was a treat to see. Although he couldn't say as much, I was always sure he was pleased we had kept the yard going without him and now he was delighted that we had brought home a big race.'

Charlie Brooks took over the licence, in his own name, for the following season. The era of Fred Winter was over, but Fred himself had not lost the instincts which had made him great, as two of his longest-serving colleagues and friends would frequently observe.

'He is supposed to do certain exercises,' says John Francome, who visits him each week. 'Sometimes he might get lazy about it, but if I told him he couldn't do something, he would make sure he did it. It's the will to win. He never lost it.'

'Fred had an SIS dish installed so that he could always watch the racing on his TV,' says Brian Delaney. 'One day I went up to sit with him. A greyhound race came on and, just for fun, we each picked a dog. He chose number six, which ran wide and just got beaten. Fred was almost purple with anger. We had no idea who the dogs were and we had no money on it. It was just his old competitive streak coming out.'

Index

Anglo, 83, 96, 114–16
Archibald, George, 10
Army commission, 6–7
assistant trainers, 149–61

bachelorhood, 12–13, 24–5, 26, 27
Barry, Ron, 127, 128
Bartholomew, Percy, 3, 5, 8, 43
Beasley, Bobby, 103, 116–17
Beaver II, 56–7, 60, 64
Biddlecombe, Terry, 127
Brogan, Barry, 127
Brooks, Charlie, 149, 150, 152, 157–61, 174, 179–80
Brookshaw, Tim, 47
Bula, 118, 119–21, 123, 125, 126, 137, 138, 147
buying horses, 110, 121

Carmody, Tommy, 154
Carton, 8, 9, 11
Catholic faith, 23, 31
CBE, 67, 68
Champion, Bob, 109
Champion Hurdle victories
  as jockey, 29, 48, 49, 50
  as trainer, 123, 137, 180
Ciechanowski, John, 106
Clair Soleil, 18, 22, 29–30, 38, 48
Comedy of Errors, 126, 137
competitive instincts, 31, 41, 65, 68, 76, 134, 168, 181

Crisp, 125, 126, 128–9

Dale, Syd, 76
Davis, Snowy, 22, 24, 25, 29–30, 58, 72
De Haan, Ben, 174–5, 176–7
Delaney, Brian, 84–5, 86, 99, 112, 113–14, 132–3, 134, 135–6, 143, 144, 179, 180
Derring Rose, 155
Devon Loch, 33
Dick, Dave, 4, 8, 9, 12–13, 14, 15, 16, 17, 27, 28, 33, 39, 41, 57
Dickinson, Michael, 157, 170–1
Duggan, Jimmy, 171, 174, 177

Easterby, Peter, 157
Eliot, Lawrence, 84, 85–6, 135, 144
equine flu, 99–100, 104

falls and injuries, 2, 10, 11, 13, 24, 25–6, 35, 47, 54, 70–1
family life, preference for, 43–4, 121–2
Fare Time, 48
Fearn, Neil, 156–7
Fifty Dollars More, 168, 169, 177
first winner as trainer, 98
Flame Gun, 48, 83
flat-race jockey, 5–6, 58–9
Foster, Harry, 130–1, 133, 134, 136, 137
Francis, Dick, 33, 53
Francome, John, 109, 140–2, 143, 144–

Francome, John – *contd.*
  5, 147–8, 150, 154, 169–70, 172,
  174, 175

Galway Gestival, 66–7
gambling, 164–5
Gifford, Josh, 19–20, 21, 41, 56, 69, 74,
  117, 118–19, 166–8
Gilbert, Johnny, 41
Gold Cup victories
  as jockey, 50–1, 55–6
  as trainer, 148
Gold Cup/Champion Hurdle double,
  49
Grand National victories
  as jockey, 38–9, 58
  as trainer, 107–8, 115–16
Grand Steeplechase de Paris, 60, 61–4,
  111–12

Halloween, 17–18, 29, 45
Harty, Eddie, 114,
Henderson, Nick, 149, 150, 151–2,
  173–4
Herbert, Ivor, 48

integrity, 22–3, 83, 146, 164

Jay Trump, 87, 88, 92–5, 97, 98, 99,
  100, 101–3, 104–5, 106, 108, 111–
  13
Jelliss, Henry, 5
jockeys' status, 36, 40
John Banks affair, 147–8, 170, 175
jumping debut, 8

Kelleway, Paul, 120, 123–4, 136, 141
Killiney, 119, 125–6
Kilmore, 57–8, 70, 75–6
King, Jeff, 76
King George VI Chase victories
  as jockey, 17, 29, 50
  as trainer, 126
Kitsbury Orchard, 34

Lanzarote, 119, 125, 131, 134, 136–7,
  138–9, 147
Lehane, Johnny, 70–1

Linley, Richard, 168, 174, 179

maiden century of winners, 18–19
Manderin, 52–3, 54, 55–6, 61, 62–3
Marks, Doug, 80–1, 142, 143
Marshall, Bryan, 16–17, 103
media attention, 12, 14, 32
Mellor, Stan, 49, 64, 118, 120
Midnight Court, 147, 148
Mildmay-White, Anthony, 150
Moloney, Jack, 107
Moloney, Tim, 12, 29, 33
moods, early-morning, 134, 141, 156

National Hunt starter, rejection as, 71–2
nerves, dealing with, 10, 11, 26, 68,
  97, 107
Nicholson, David, 178
non-triers, dislike of, 22–23, 146, 165
Norman, Tim, 115–16

Oaksey, John, 46, 51
O'Brien, Vincent, 18
O'Neill, Jonjo, 109
orderly nature, 44–5, 114, 136
Osbaldeston, 143–4
owners, Fred's handling of, 110, 135,
  160, 163, 164, 165–6

Paget, Dorothy, 15, 16–17
Pas Seul, 48, 50, 55
Pendil, 118, 119, 121, 123, 124–5, 126,
  127–8, 129
perfectionist nature, 1–2, 37, 42
Piggott, Keith, 103
Piggott, Lester, 177
Pipe, Martin, 13, 22, 178
Pitman, Jenny, 16, 124, 176
Pitman, Richard, 86, 114, 124, 126, 127,
  128, 129, 136, 137, 141, 144
placing horses, talent for, 122
Plumpton, dislike of, 13–14
Price, Dorothy, 20, 21, 166
Price, Ryan, 11, 19–20, 21–2, 25, 30,
  38, 56–7, 69, 73–4, 75, 79, 115,
  166
prize money, 17, 75, 110, 125

punctuality, 114, 153, 160–1

racing debut, 4
riding style, 14
riding and training, differences be-
    tween, 78
Rimell, Fred, 69, 119, 137
Rimell, Mercy, 16

Saffron Tartan, 49–50, 55
schooling horses, ineptitude at, 20–1,
    73, 81
Scudamore, Michael, 34, 44
Scudamore, Peter, 169, 172, 177–9, 180
season record, 16
Sheikh Ali Abu Khamsin, 157, 168
Sherwood, Denise (F.W.'s daughter),
    43, 149
Sherwood, Oliver, 149, 152–6, 157,
    159, 160, 162
Sherwood, Simon, 152, 157, 177
Smith, Doug, 10, 33, 174
Smith, Harry Worcester, 88–90
Smith, Pat (F.W.'s sister), 10, 33
Smith, Tommy, 87, 88, 90–2, 93, 94–9,
    100–8, 111, 112–13
Sobell, Michael, 83
Stanhope, Steven, 150–1
Stephenson, Mary, 91, 93, 94, 105, 106
Stroud, Anthony, 150
Sundew, 36–7, 38–9

Taaffe, Pat, 55, 56
The Dikler, 126, 127, 128
Thorner, Graham, 148
training, ambivalence towards, 53, 72,
    84

Tucker, Bill, 26, 71

United States, racing in, 67
Uplands
    breakfasts at, 135, 164
    daily routine, 132–6
    purchase, 80–1

Valentine, Mrs Miles, 67

Walden, Lord Howard de, 131, 138
Walwyn, Cath, 46
Walwyn, Fulke, 46, 52, 53, 54, 64, 80,
    81, 127, 130
weight, 6, 13, 44, 59
Winter Snr, Fred (F.W.'s father), 3, 4,
    5, 8, 23, 26
Winter, Diana (F.W.'s wife), 27–9, 30–
    1, 35, 43, 62, 72
Winter, Fred
    champion jockey, 18, 33, 34, 45, 46
    champion trainer, 111, 125, 151
    childhood, 3–4
    children, 43, 122
    jumping debut, 8
    marriage, 32, 33–4
    racing debut, 4
    retirement from racing, 65–6, 68, 72,
        76, 78
    suffers strokes, 162, 173, 179
Winter, Joanna (F.W.'s daughter), 43,
    158
Winter, John (F.W.'s brother), 42–3,
    110–11
women in racing, disapproval of, 43,
    122, 164